Michael Wardle

K £11.50

26

# THE NEW CAMBRIDGE HISTORY OF INDIA

## Indian society and the making of the British Empire

# THE NEW CAMBRIDGE HISTORY OF INDIA

*General editor* GORDON JOHNSON

Director, Centre of South Asian Studies, University of
Cambridge, and Fellow of Selwyn College

*Associate editors* C. A. BAYLY

Smuts Reader in Commonwealth Studies, University of
Cambridge, and Fellow of St Catharine's College

*and* JOHN F. RICHARDS

Professor of History, Duke University

Although the original *Cambridge History of India*, published between 1922
and 1937, did much to formulate a chronology for Indian history and describe the administrative structures of government in India, it has inevitably
been overtaken by the mass of new research published over the last fifty
years.

Designed to take full account of recent scholarship and changing conceptions of South Asia's historical development, *The New Cambridge History
of India* will be published as a series of short, self-contained volumes, each
dealing with a separate theme and written by a single person. Within an
overall four-part structure, thirty complementary volumes in uniform format
will be published during the next five years. As before, each will conclude
with a substantial bibliographical essay designed to lead non-specialists
further into the literature.

The four parts planned are as follows:

## I The Mughals and their Contemporaries.

## II Indian States and the Transition to Colonialism.

## III The Indian Empire and the Beginnings of Modern Society.

## IV The Evolution of Contemporary South Asia.

A list of individual titles in preparation will be found at the end of the volume.

# THE NEW
# CAMBRIDGE
# HISTORY OF
# INDIA

## II · 1

*Indian society and the making of
the British Empire*

### C. A. BAYLY

SMUTS READER IN COMMONWEALTH STUDIES,
UNIVERSITY OF CAMBRIDGE

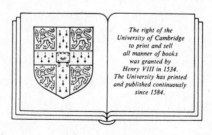

The right of the
University of Cambridge
to print and sell
all manner of books
was granted by
Henry VIII in 1534.
The University has printed
and published continuously
since 1584.

CAMBRIDGE UNIVERSITY PRESS

CAMBRIDGE

NEW YORK    NEW ROCHELLE

MELBOURNE    SYDNEY

Published by the Press Syndicate of the University of Cambridge
The Pitt Building, Trumpington Street, Cambridge CB2 1RP
32 East 57th Street, New York, NY 10022, USA
10 Stamford Road, Oakleigh, Melbourne 3166, Australia

© Cambridge University Press 1988

First published 1988

Printed in Great Britain by
Redwood Burn Limited, Trowbridge, Wiltshire

*British Library cataloguing in publication data*

Bayly, C. A.
Indian society and the making of
the British Empire. –
(The New Cambridge History of India)
1. India – History – 18th century
2. India – History – 19th century
I. Title
954.03    DS463

*Library of Congress cataloguing in publication data*

Bayly, C. A. (Christopher Alan)
Indian society and the making of
the British Empire.
(The New Cambridge History of India)
Bibliography.
Includes Index.
1. India – History – 18th century.
2. India – History – 19th century.
I. Title.   II. Series.
DS463.B34 1987   954.03   87–704

ISBN 0 521 25092 7

*Frontispiece*: 'John Mowbray' by Thomas Hickey, c1790.
India Office Library and Records, London.

# CONTENTS

v

# MAPS

# GENERAL EDITOR'S PREFACE

*The New Cambridge History of India* covers the period from the beginning of the sixteenth century. In some respects it marks a radical change in the style of Cambridge Histories, but in others the editors feel that they are working firmly within an established academic tradition.

During the summer of 1896, F. W. Maitland and Lord Acton between them evolved the idea for a comprehensive modern history. By the end of the year the Syndics of the University Press had committed themselves to the *Cambridge Modern History*, and Lord Acton had been put in charge of it. It was hoped that publication would begin in 1899 and be completed by 1904, but the first volume in fact came out in 1902 and the last in 1910, with additional volumes of tables and maps in 1911 and 1912.

The *History* was a great success, and it was followed by a whole series of distinctive Cambridge Histories covering English Literature, the Ancient World, India, British Foreign Policy, Economic History, Medieval History, the British Empire, Africa, China and Latin America; and even now other new series are being prepared. Indeed, the various Histories have given the Press notable strength in the publication of general reference books in the arts and social sciences.

What has made the Cambridge Histories so distinctive is that they have never been simply dictionaries or encyclopedias. The Histories have, in H. A. L. Fisher's words, always been 'written by an army of specialists concentrating the latest results of special study'. Yet as Acton agreed with the Syndics in 1896, they have not been mere compilations of existing material but original works. Undoubtedly many of the Histories are uneven in quality, some have become out of date very rapidly, but their virtue has been that they have consistently done more than simply record an existing state of knowledge: they have tended to focus interest on research and they have provided a massive stimulus to further work. This has made their publication doubly worthwhile and has distinguished them intellectually from other sorts of reference book. The editors of the *New Cambridge History of India* have acknowledged this in their work.

The original *Cambridge History of India* was published between 1922 and 1937. It was planned in six volumes, but of these, volume 2 dealing with the period between the first century A.D. and the Muslim invasion of India never appeared. Some of the material is still of value, but in many respects it is now out of date. The last fifty years have seen a great deal of new research on India, and a striking feature of recent work has been to cast doubt on the validity of the quite arbitrary chronological and categorical way in which Indian history has been conventionally divided.

The editors decided that it would not be academically desirable to prepare a new *History of India* using the traditional format. The selective nature of research on Indian history over the past half-century would doom such a project from the start and the whole of Indian history could not be covered in an even or comprehensive manner. They concluded that the best scheme would be to have a *History* divided into four overlapping chronological volumes, each containing about eight short books on individual themes or subjects. Although in extent the work will therefore be equivalent to a dozen massive tomes of the traditional sort, in form the *New Cambridge History of India* will appear as a shelf full of separate but complementary parts. Accordingly, the main divisions are between I. *The Mughals and their Contemporaries*, II. *Indian States and the Transition to Colonialism*, III. *The Indian Empire and the Beginnings of Modern Society*, and IV. *The Evolution of Contemporary South Asia.*

Just as the books within these volumes are complementary so too do they intersect with each other, both thematically and chronologically. As the books appear they are intended to give a view of the subject as it now stands and to act as a stimulus to further research. We do not expect the *New Cambridge History of India* to be the last word on the subject but an essential voice in the continuing discourse about it.

# PREFACE

The aim of this work is rather different from that of earlier Cambridge *Histories*, including the old *Cambridge History of India*, iv (1929) and the more recent *Cambridge Economic History of India*, 2 vols (1982 and 1983). All these works attempted to one degree or another to be 'authoritative', 'definitive' or at the very least, to provide a good deal of basic factual material. This volume cannot hope to do that in view of its length and the complexity of the subject. Besides, the notion of a Western history seeking to be authoritative, in some sense to master India, has become a little dubious. Rather, this should be seen as an attempt to provide a single author's synthesis of some of the more important work and themes which have appeared in historical studies of India, written in the subcontinent and outside, over the last twenty years. As such the book is partial, argumentative and thematic, rather than exhaustive, balanced and chronological.

The book deliberately deals with some episodes and types of history which were the staple of the older volumes, notably the conquests in India under Lord Wellesley and the Rebellion of 1857. This is because history cannot be written without the history of events, and because however subtly refracting are the mirrors through which area specialists now see India, these events remain critical to non-specialist understanding of the subcontinent, and indeed of world history. At the same time some current specialist themes, ecological change and the nature of resistance, for instance, have received attention because they demand some treatment at an all-India level. Other subjects, the history of the poor, of changes in the micro-economy of the districts, of specific policies implemented by provincial colonial governments: these are better tackled by the regional and thematic volumes which will appear in this series.

Much of the historical writing on India since 1960 has been a persuasive attempt to argue the importance of regionalism: political, economic and cultural. This volume notes regional differences as far as possible, but attempts to draw themes together at an all-India level. This is not because the powerful case for different regional histories has been ignored, simply that most regional and local studies assume the existence of processes working at a broader level, and if only for heuristic reasons these should be considered in their own right.

For the same reason I have not hesitated to use terms such as 'capitalist', 'class', 'class formation', 'bureaucracy', 'aristocracy' and 'gentry' in my analysis. This is because I consider, firstly, that there were indigenous concepts and understandings of the social order which very closely approximated to these Western terms, though of course, one must always bear in mind the uniqueness of Indian cultural and social forms. There are dangers in glib comparison, but on the other side excessive Orientalist purism has done little except make India seem peculiar to the outside world. These terms are also employed because general changes in India's and the world's economy and governance during the period considered here were, in fact, bringing into being social groups and relationships which were similar to those of contemporary western Europe. These groups and relationships never lost their specifically Indian character but they are nevertheless amenable to comparison at an international level.

I have used the less 'corrupt' Anglo-Indian forms of Indian place-names and personal names used by the early twentieth-century literature. Poona is English for Pune, and Ganges for Ganga, as surely as Munich is for München and Florence for Firenze. On the other hand, I have not suppressed Indian names and terms simply to make things easy for a Western audience since audiences who read English are no longer overwhelmingly Western. In the old days the British used to like India without Indians and Indian words as they liked France without the French and French words. Those days are gone.

My colleagues will know where in this book their work has been drawn upon, even if they are not directly referred to. I hope that it has not been distorted too much in the process. But some more specific debts must be acknowledged. Among many institutions in India the staff of the Connemara Library, Madras and Professor Mehboob Pasha and the staff of the Muhammadan Public Library, Madras, provided invaluable assistance. I must also acknowledge the help of Sri V.A. Sundaram, I.A.S. Among those who have provided useful criticism are Susan Bayly, Sugata Bose, Raj Chandavarkar, Sunil Chander, Hiram Morgan, David Washbrook and above all Peter Marshall who patiently corrected far too many errors. They are warmly thanked.

Finally, Neil McKendrick, David Fieldhouse and Graeme Rennie helped this project to completion in an indirect, but no less important manner. I am very grateful to them.

C. A. BAYLY

# INTRODUCTION

When H. H. Dodwell published his fifth volume of the *Cambridge History of India* in 1929, this book also became the fourth volume of the *Cambridge History of the British Empire*. The aim of the work was to chronicle the conquest of India by British arms and its transformation by British institutions. This must have seemed a very appropriate theme in the years just preceding the Statute of Westminster of 1931, which laid new foundations for the British Empire and Commonwealth. But since that date there has been a considerable change of perspective. Historians working after 1929 have, if anything, emphasised the importance of India to Britain's world rôle in the nineteenth century even more strongly. However, the nature and extent of India's transformation has been vigorously debated from perspectives that would have seemed alien, even offensive to the interwar authors.

The importance of India for Britain's imperial system lay in both the military and economic fields. Seizure of the cash land revenues of India between 1757 and 1818 made it possible for Britain to build up one of the largest European-style standing armies in the world, thus critically augmenting British land forces which were small and logistically backward except for a few years during the final struggle with Napoleon. This Indian army was used in large measure to hold down the subcontinent itself, but after 1790 it was increasingly employed to forward British interests in southern and eastern Asia and the Middle East. More symbolically, the Indian army opened up a second front, as it were, against the other great Eurasian land powers, Russia, the Ottomans, France and Austria. This reinforced the significance of the dominance of the Royal Navy at sea. From its Indian base Britain had already begun to construct informal empires of influence and trade in the Middle East, on the China coast and in East Africa during the first two decades of the nineteenth century. The campaign against the French in Egypt in 1799 and the seizure of the Cape of Good Hope in 1795 and 1806 anticipated at key points the global strategy of Victorian England.

Scarcely less significant was the Indian contribution to Britain's growing economic power. Though it is unlikely that East Indian fortunes made a critical contribution to the British industrial revolution, Indian raw material exports, notably cotton and opium shipped to Europe and Asia, helped balance Britain's whole Asian trade, while India's revenues were a significant indirect subsidy to the exchequer. True, Asian trade still only represented about 16 per cent of Britain's global trade in 1820. But India was already becoming a fair field for the exports of the key sector of Britain's industrial economy, the textile industry, and a market whose importance was to be greatly increased after the improvement in communications in the 1850s. India also provided cheap raw materials and indentured labour which had begun to open up valuable plantation economies in Sri Lanka, the Caribbean and Mauritius before mid-century.

However, this perspective from the history of the British Empire has come to seem rather restricted since 1929. For the East India Company's conquest and patchy exploitation of India can also be seen more broadly as one of the first and most striking examples of the forging of dependent economic relations between the north European world economy and non-European societies, a process which later engulfed much of the rest of Asia, Africa, Latin America and the Far East. Though its per-capita income was certainly much lower than western Europe's, Asia still remained in 1700 the world's major centre of artisan production and accounted for a huge slice of world trade, consonant with its 70 per cent share of the world's population. Europeans were already important to Asian economies in that they provided much of the silver imports which helped Asia's great kingdoms to expand and develop. But their rôle in internal trade and even in inter-Asian trade remained relatively small. That situation was significantly altered by 1800, and transformed by 1860. By this time Europeans controlled the largest and most valuable parts of inter-Asian trade and Asia's international trade, while also commanding the most valuable parts of her internal economy. The epochal growth of differentials in income between Asians and Europeans that followed the shift of Asian economies from being producers and exporters of artisan products to mere exporters of agricultural raw materials is only now being reversed in parts of East Asia.

All these arguments would have been understood by the authors of 1929, even though they would have given much more weight to the political rather than economic aspects of European dominion in Asia.

Where they would have differed much more from recent historians was in their estimation of the causes of the East India Company's rise to power and the depth and the nature of Britain's transformation of India. The *Cambridge History* starts from the assumption that the centralised Mughal empire was in purely degenerative decline, along with the Indian economy and society. Consequently, the English East India Company was forced to intervene in order to protect its own trade and the political stability of its clients. Now, however, the Mughal empire seems a much less substantial hegemony, its decline a much more complex and ambiguous process, and the society of eighteenth-century India more varied than the stereotype of decline and anarchy which is the unwritten emblem of the authors of 1929.

The crisis of eighteenth-century India now appears to have three distinct aspects. First, there were cumulative indigenous changes reflecting commercialisation, the formation of social groups and political transformation within the subcontinent itself. Secondly, there was the level of the wider crisis of west and south Asia which was signalled by the decline of the great Islamic empires, the Mughals and their contemporaries the Ottomans and the Safavids. Thirdly, there was the massive expansion of European production and trade during the eighteenth century and the development of more aggressive national states in Europe which were indirectly echoed in the more assertive policies of the European companies in India from the 1730s, and notably of the English Company after 1757.

The first and second chapters of this book deal with the Indian aspect of the crisis and concentrate on commercialisation and political change within India itself. One of the interesting revisions which has arisen out of recent studies of the late-Mughal period and the early eighteenth century is the view that the decline of the Mughals resulted in a sense from the very success of their earlier expansion. Local gentry, Hindu and Muslim, prospered in Mughal service or flourished under their loose régime and began to separate themselves off as a more stable landlord element throughout much of northern India. It was not so much impoverished peasants but substantial yeomen and prosperous farmers already drawn into the Mughals' cash and service nexus, who revolted against Delhi in the late seventeenth and early eighteenth century. Hindu and Jain moneylenders and merchants, who were the oil which worked the expansion of commodity production and the Mughals' taxation systems, easily provided the economic basis for the local kingdoms and provincial magnates that ultimately supplanted the power of Delhi, or emerged to prominence in areas where the Mughal writ had never run. Commercial growth which had succoured the power of Delhi ultimately eroded it. Commercial men, scribal families and local gentry consolidated their power at the expense of the centre. Many of these elements later provided capital, knowledge and support for the East India Company, thus becoming its uneasy collaborators in the creation of colonial India.

However, these processes of economic change, and the emergence of regional kingdoms in eighteenth-century India were fraught with conflict. Wars between the Mughals and their recalcitrant subalterns damaged trade and production in many areas even if commercialisation and the creation of kingdoms fostered it in others. India's crisis, then, reflected the conflict between many types of military, merchant and political entrepreneur wishing to capitalise on the buoyant trade and production of the Mughal realm. In the early eighteenth century this conflict was supercharged with a wider regional conflict reflecting commercialisation and a crisis of empire throughout the whole central and eastern Islamic world. In 1739 a Persian army invaded India and conquered Delhi. In the 1750s and 1760s Afghans invaded north India, following their harrying of Iran. The military and tribal leaders of these regions had also been drawn into the wider mercantile and political world of the great Islamic empires. Now they too demanded their patrimony in silver, booty and land-control as those older supremacies dissolved.

Yet the third, and widest, level of conflict was associated with the growing power of the Europeans who had for long operated on the fringes of Asian trade and politics. Asia still remained marginal to European trade and world power; until 1820 the Caribbean and the Americas were vastly more important. Yet the increase of European, and especially British trading activity and commercial power had already transferred much of the most valuable areas of inter-Asian trade into British ships before 1750. Burgeoning private trade and the ruthless creation of monopolies in tropical produce by the East India Companies had bitten deep into the wealth of coastal India by the 1780s. To begin with, as the second chapter of this book shows, Europeans working in India were dependent on the support of Indian commercial groups which had augmented their own wealth and influence during the transformation and commercialisation of the late Mughal

4

empire. In a sense Indian capital and expertise was drawn inexorably into a partnership with the alien invader. But in time the English East India Company began to create its own state using the territorial revenues of Bengal. This fusion of military and commercial power revealed the Europeans achieving on a larger and more ominous scale what Indian local rulers had been doing for the last century. The demands for tribute, the sale of military power for protection and the growth of European inland trade all conspired to erode the foundations of regional and local kingdoms in the subcontinent's interior.

This expansion was a slow, piecemeal penetration using lines of power and flows of commodities and silver which already existed. But two developments transformed the crisis and speeded it up after 1780. These new forces are dealt with in Chapter Three. First, was the change in the ideology and grasp of the state in Europe which accompanied the French revolutionary and Napoleonic wars. The French threat to Britain and its overseas possessions was well understood by Dodwell and his generation. But the matter went deeper. War galvanised the whole taxation and political base of British society. The reaction of gentry and merchant was distantly reflected in the governor-generalship of Wellesley (1798–1805) when the Company went on a general offensive against oriental government in India which was now legitimated by a true imperialist ideology.

Secondly, the stakes in India had been raised by the emergence of more powerful and determined kingdoms in the shape of Mysore in the south and the Marathas in the west. These realms also sought to harness and canalise the buoyant trade and production which had been given play during the expansion of the seventeenth century. Yet, unable to deploy power at sea and restricted to less productive inland tracts of India, these powers withered and were defeated. Nevertheless, their resistance and response forced the British to construct yet more powerful armies and also significantly changed the social and economic face of large parts of inland India. Indians remained, therefore, active agents and not simply passive bystanders and victims in the creation of colonial India.

There were thus many threads of continuity between pre-colonial India and the India of the Company. One thread was commercialisation and the marketing of political power. This had created many of the conditions for the decline of Mughal hegemony and had provided the Europeans with the tools to unlock the wealth of inland India. As the British sought to tax the subcontinent and also to extract commodities for international trade from her, Indian commercial people continued to underpin the growth of imperium. On the fringes of the colonial state Indian capital, peasant colonists and inferior administrators played a vital part in the subordination of tribal and nomadic peoples and culture to the discipline of production for the market. Indian gentry, now transformed into landlords, and scribal people also supported a political framework within which the conflicts which arose from these social changes could be accommodated. India was made tributary to the capitalist world system, but the dynamism of its deeper social changes and the endemic resistance of its rural leadership helped determine the nature and extent of the subcontinent's tribute. The first chapter therefore begins by considering some general social and political changes which seem to emerge from the complex historical record of late pre-colonial India.

CHAPTER 1

# INDIA IN THE EIGHTEENTH CENTURY: THE FORMATION OF STATES AND SOCIAL GROUPS

India in 1700 had a population of some 180 million people, a figure which represented about 20 per cent of the population of the entire world. Over much of this huge land mass from Kashmir in the north to the upland plateau of the Deccan in the south, the Mughal dynasty at Delhi fought to maintain an hegemony which had been consolidated in the second half of the sixteenth century by the Emperor Akbar. In the farther south of the peninsula Hindu warrior chieftains vied for control of villages, many claiming parcels of the authority of the Hindu Vijayanagar kingdom which had faded from the scene in the later sixteenth century.

Under the Emperor Aurangzeb (1658–1707) the Muslim power at Delhi still shook the world. The Emperor remained capable of commanding a remarkable concentration of soldiers and treasure, if only in certain places and during some months of the year. In the 1680s the Mughals had destroyed the last independent Muslim kingdoms of the Deccan. In the following generation they continued to expand. Their lieutenants pushed down to the south-eastern coast and began to demand tribute from the Hindu warrior chiefs of all but the most remote parts of the former Vijayanagar domain. In 1689 they had beaten off the threat from the Hindu Maratha warriors of the western Deccan and had savagely executed their war-leader, Shambaji. In 1700 the Maratha capital, Satara, was taken by the Emperor's siege trains. Even in the north Mughal power was still strong. In 1716 they had suppressed a revolt of Sikh landholders and farmers in the Punjab. By the time of Aurangzeb's death imperial finances were already in disarray, strained to breaking point by the need to maintain constant campaigns throughout the whole subcontinent. After 1712, the imperial centre was immobilised by factional conflicts which culminated in the murder of the Emperor Furrukhsiyar in 1718. Despite this, however, Indian notables and Europeans trading from the ports of the coast still regarded the Mughal emperor as one of the great kings of the world.

The decline of Mughal power over the next century was dramatic. Though historians in the last two generations have begun to ask questions about the nature of the Mughal empire, particularly about the degree to which it ever was a centralised state, there can be no doubt that politics in the subcontinent underwent a significant change. The main problem for the Mughals, even at their height, was the restiveness of the Hindu warriors and peasant farmers, buoyed up with new wealth from trade and military service and harassed by the demands of the Mughal tax-gatherers. Hindu landholders of the warrior Rajput and Jat castes flew into rebellion whenever they sensed the central power was weak. The Marathas, and, later, the Sikhs, recovered from their defeats in the opening years of the eighteenth century. By the 1730s the rich lands of Malwa to the south of Delhi had become subject to the Maratha warriors of the Deccan. Delhi's treasury already suffering shrinking inflows from the Punjab and Awadh was further depleted. So the emperor faced the invasion of the Persian monarch Nadir Shah in 1739 unsure of the loyalty of his own great commanders but certain that the Hindu landholders would 'raise their heads in revolt' as soon as the Shah's armies set foot in Hindustan.

Hereafter the decline of imperial power speeded up. Provincial governors in Awadh, Bengal and the Deccan surreptitiously consolidated their own regional bases of power in the aftermath of the Persian, and later the Afghan, invasions (1759–61). In 1757 the English East India Company seized control of the rich province of Bengal, and in 1759 it rolled up the last vestiges of Mughal influence at Surat on the west coast. After a brief rearguard action in defence of the core area of Delhi the Mughal emperor submitted in 1784 to the 'protection' of the greatest of the Maratha war chiefs, Mahadji Scindia. With the defeat of the Marathas by the British armies of Lord Lake in 1803, Delhi was occupied by the Company, and the Mughal was reduced in European eyes to the status of a pathetic 'tinsel sovereign', surrounded by the emaciated ladies of his harem and chamberlains who maintained the shadow of his authority through the reiteration of court rituals.

The suddenness of the collapse of Mughal power and magnificence astonished European contemporaries and appalled the Muslim poets and learned men for whom the Delhi throne had been an ancient and venerated source of patronage. For many historians of the recent past the twilight of the Mughals and the eighteenth-century 'anarchy' con-

8

tinued to be the only important set of events in the history of eighteenth-century India. Yet this perspective, concentrating as it does on Delhi, on the politics of the court and the decline of the Mughal grand army, seems now, for all its drama, not so much wrong as manifestly inadequate as a theme with which to encompass the changes overtaking the subcontinent.

## IMPERIAL DECLINE AND
## THE CONSOLIDATION OF SOCIAL GROUPS

One new perspective has already emerged, though research is still at a very basic stage. The eighteenth century saw not so much the decline of the Mughal ruling élite, but its transformation and the ascent of inferior social groups to overt political power. The great households of the Mughal nobility (called *umara*; generally persons with an official rank: *mansab*) were not a class as such, but they evidently did have considerable influence on the nature of social organisation in Mughal India. Merchant groups, free cavalry soldiers and Hindu administrators all worked within their ambit. Noble households had considerable economic influence; in Bengal they participated in external trade. Elsewhere they sold grain and probably lent money to the non-Muslim commercial communities. In the eighteenth century such households broke up and dispersed alongside their exemplar, the Mughal court, or they were radically transformed. In the early eighteenth century the system of assignments of revenue on which the noble households had subsisted began to break down. Too many new nobles were absorbed into the system as Aurangzeb made his conquests in the south and tried to placate its indigenous nobility. Local revolts cut into the rents and customs dues on which the nobles lived, while the imperial treasury became less and less able to pay cash salaries.

However, other social groups which had long been forming, though politically dwarfed by the Mughal nobility, began to emerge more clearly into the limelight. First, there were the Hindu and Muslim entrepreneurs in revenue – the so-called revenue farmers. These men, often relations of the old nobility, sometimes local princes or simply adventurers, combined military power with expertise in managing cash and local trade. Their households were organised on principles similar to that of the older nobility, but their relationship to the regional rulers was largely mercenary and contractual. They took a 'farm' of the revenue of a given territory in return for a cash payment to the ruler, and hoped to benefit from the difference between what they had paid and what they could collect. They were not bound by loyalty or by the military ethos which had sustained the mansabdars. Such men attracted condemnation from the more traditional commentators of the period. Yet they were an indication of the fact that the commercial economy survived and even expanded in the eighteenth century, as the scramble for cash revenues and control over production and labour intensified.

Secondly, Indian merchants who were largely Hindus of the 'traditional' commercial castes or Jains appear to have become politically more important in the eighteenth century. The commercial interest had always been crucial in the organisation of the great Mughals' revenue and the trade in agricultural products and artisan goods which sustained it, but had never achieved much political visibility. With the decline of the nobility this situation began to change. Rather than receiving capital from the nobles, big merchant houses now lent money to rulers and nobles. As the Mughal treasury collapsed they became more important in India's capital markets, moving money from one part of the country to another with their credit notes. In this capacity they came into contact with foreign merchants, supplied them with resources, and at the same time benefited from the Europeans' own growing political significance. By the middle of the eighteenth century the indigenous merchant people were a powerful interest in all the major states which had emerged from the decline of the Delhi power. Even in the far south where the Mughals had never had much control, combinations of revenue farmers and local merchants wielded much influence in the politics of the small military kingdoms.

Thirdly, many of the features of the nineteenth-century landed class were consolidated in the eighteenth century. The weakening of Mughal power enabled local gentry to seize privileges which they had once been denied. Zamindars (landholders) began to tax markets and trade and to seize prebendal lands which the Mughal élites had once tried to keep out of their hands. Families of servants of the Mughals and relatives of the old nobility bought up proprietorial rights over land or quietly converted non-hereditary into hereditary rights. To some extent the Mughals were forced to acquiesce in this 'rise of the gentry' since they needed local support in their battles against the Marathas or Sikhs. But often these insurgent warrior groups themselves attained the rôle of a gentry in their localities, controlling labour and production and carving out effective proprietary rights in land. Strong kinship links at the sub-district (*pargana*) level facilitated their survival in the face of state demands.

In the midst of military conflict and disruption, therefore, the eighteenth century witnessed a significant stage in the formation of the social order of modern India. These developments were themselves the culmination of the slow commercialisation of India under the loose but dynamic Mughal hegemony. Commercialisation meant much more than the slow increase in the use of money in the economy. It meant the use of objective monetary values to express social relationships. Royal 'shares' in produce were expanded creating a need for new markets and financial institutions. Such shares and privileges were increasingly sold on the market. Rents, houses, the proprietary rights of landholders and headmen were more regularly exchanged by sale and mortgage. Statuses and offices were leased and sub-leased. Developments of this sort were also speeded by the growing contacts between India and the European international economy which facilitated commercialisation through imports of bullion and demand for artisan products. The receding tide of Mughal rule, as it were, revealed these slowly consolidating interests in Indian society. Yet at the same time Mughal decline was itself a result of the creation of new wealth and social power in the provinces where it could not easily be controlled by the distant monarch in Delhi. It was, after all, many of the areas and groups which had been most successful in the seventeenth century who revolted against or surreptitiously withdrew from under the Mughal umbrella in the eighteenth. The same areas and groups – Bengal, the commercial communities, the new gentry – in turn became the foundation of the British colonial régime.

How far can these social groups which became more politically powerful in the eighteenth century be considered 'classes', even in the looser sense in which the word is applied to pre-capitalist interests? Certainly, some of the more rigid orientalist interpretations which emphasised the unique and incomparable features of the Indian social scene appear less convincing now. Caste, for instance, was not an immutable 'given' of Indian society. Castes were constantly in the process of formation and change, notably in periods such as the eighteenth century when political authority was very fluid. Again, Indians of the pre-colonial period certainly possessed categories of social distinction which reflected differences of economic power. In addition to words such as zamindar or *raiyat* (agrarian dependent) which reflected legal statuses on the land, there were words such as *bhadralog*, *bhallalog* and *ashraf* in common use in north India and Bengal which implied 'gentry' and comprised notions of landed economic power as well as status. These were terms which at this time were applied to members of different castes and religious communities. In the same way the term *mahajan* (lit. 'great man') was often applied to merchant people across the lines of caste in the same way as *bakkal* ('grocer') could be a derogatory equivalent. There were also a variety of words which designated a managerial class (*mutsaddi*, *amlah*) and also inferior agrarian interests (for instance, *malik* or agrarian boss).

In addition contemporary writers, amidst their bitter complaints about political decline, seem to be aware of social changes. The Persian chroniclers savage the growing pretensions of *bhumias* or 'little rural potentates'; the rise of low men devoid of proper training in accounts and 'grocers' into positions of trust is denounced. Doubtless there were some such cries of woe in earlier periods of Indo-Islamic history, but perhaps they can be seen to have much greater meaning in a period when the commercial economy and a literate political culture capable of recording rights and power had penetrated so much deeper.

To this extent the interests which come into sharper relief during the 'decline of the Mughals' might be regarded as 'classes' in a loose sense, and the collisions between different groups might be seen as 'class conflict'. Moreover, the form of the post-Mughal state itself across India was very widely determined by the growing power of landlords, literate administrative people and Indian capitalists. As we shall see in Chapter 2 merchant people restricted the authority of the rulers of Bengal and Benares after the second decade of the eighteenth century.

However, contemporaries do not seem to have thought of these shifts primarily in terms of regional or all-India 'classes'. Agrarian magnates sought to establish Jat or Sikh or Maratha kingdoms of righteousness, not landlord power, even if the occasion for their conflicts with the Mughals was often conflicts over revenues or the destination of the agrarian surplus. Merchants and revenue farmers became more influential in the post-Mughal states; kingship became more commercialised. But the rhetoric and aims of politics remained very much what they had been under the Mughals. These were not Indian varieties of mercantile states. A balance must be struck therefore between emphasising the particular features of Indian tradition, worship and patronage which went into the making of the late Mughal order and the unintended consequences of political and economic changes which were tending to consolidate new types of power across the subcontinent. 'Class formation' would at best be a shorthand, and an inadequate shorthand at that.

## VARIETIES OF POWER IN EIGHTEENTH-CENTURY INDIA

Commercialisation and group formation provide themes which run through the whole period covered by this book. Another such theme, then, is the differentiated and hierarchical nature of power in India which means that localities could sometimes be shielded from changes at a wider level. This theme creates ambiguity and contradictions in historical analysis. But it is important to stress that 'empire' and 'state' always remained limited political entities in India. This was not because India was a society dominated by caste in which the state could not take root, as many orientalists have asserted, but because there were many sharers in the dignity and power of kingship with overlapping rights and obligations.

The Mughals claimed universal dominion; sometimes they achieved political dominance in India. But for the majority of their Hindu subjects power and authority in India had always been more like a complicated hierarchy than a scheme of 'administration' or 'government'. The Mughal emperor was *Shah-an-Shah*, 'king of kings', rather than king of India. He was the highest manifestation of sovereignty, the court of final appeal, for Muslims an earthly successor to aspects of the authority of the Prophet Muhammad. But many of the attributes of what we would call the state pertained not to the emperor or his lieutenants, but to the Hindu kings of the localities, the rajas or to the notables who controlled resources and authority in the villages. The emperor's power and wealth could be great, but only if he was skilled in extracting money, soldiers and devotion from other kings. He was a marshal of kings, an entrepreneur in power. His tools were at once the siege-train and the royal honours given out at the great assemblies (*darbars*).

Even the rajas, for all their importance as guardians of the caste order and sacrificers-in-chief of the Hindu religion were dependent in turn on the warrior farmers who controlled the villages. These village magnates also participated in the mystique of kingship. Ultimately they were the real lords of men and resources in India. It was the build-up in the Punjab and western India, and the Ganges valley, of dissident coalitions of such magnates, determined to fight off demands for taxes and assert their status as warrior kings or gentry in their own right which spelled the end of the all-India hegemony of the Mughals.

Some historians have described this political system in terms of 'levels of power'. This is useful provided one remembers that there was constant interaction, alliance making and alliance breaking between powers at these different levels. Even under strong emperors, the hierarchy was always shifting and realigning. Village farmer-warriors could overrun their neighbours, collect revenue from the villages and become recognised as rajas by the imperial court. Equally, servants of the court, Muslims from outside India as much as Muslims and Hindus from within India, could use their authority to build up landholdings around the small towns and become local magnates.

This chapter starts by examining the changes in the imperial hegemony during the eighteenth century, then moves to the petty kingdoms and finally to the magnates of the villages who controlled production. There follows a discussion of the Indian economy and society in the eighteenth century. Yet these divisions only constitute a device for organising themes. Developments at all these levels and in all these domains were linked.

## THE PERSISTENCE OF MUGHAL CULTURE

One reason that the 'fall of the Mughal empire' now appears a rather limited theme around which to organise the record of the eighteenth century is that the emperor continued to be a fount of authority throughout India long after his military power had atrophied. If anything the sacred mystique of the imperial person increased after 1707. The emperor Muhammad Shah (1719–48) once again asserted the imperial right to adjudicate between different Muslim schools of law which had been foresworn by the purist Aurangzeb. He also resumed use of the title 'Heir of Ali' (son-in-law of the Prophet) and reinstituted the office of imperial chronicler, emphasising again the emperor's role as the shadow of God on earth.[1] During the wars which occurred after 1759 between factions of Mughal notables, the Marathas and the British, possession of the imperial person and imperial proclamations became an important resource for aspiring kingmakers. The value of the royal charisma grew in importance even as the royal purse emptied.

All powers seeking to establish their rule in eighteenth-century India needed to acquire imperial titles and rights. The Sikhs and the Marathas, for instance, represented traditions which might seem to refute the right of a Muslim state to rule them. The Sikhs derived authority from their holy book, the Guru Granth Sahib, while the Marathas developed and extended the ideal of Hindu kingship expressed in the protection of brahmins, holy cattle and holy places. Yet the rulers of both these warrior polities sought to become agents of Mughal sovereignty. The Maratha king Shahu had walked barefoot and made obeisance at the tomb of the Emperor Aurangzeb at Khuldabad in 1714; Mahadji Scindia, the greatest Maratha warlord towards the end of the century, received the title of Regent Plenipotentiary of the empire when he became dominant at Delhi in 1784. The Sikhs, unbending as they seemed to be in hostility to the monarchs who had slain several of their great religious teachers, made ceremonial offerings to the throne in 1783, as they sought to strengthen their political position in the environs of the capital.

Even when regional viceroys had begun to found dynasties and engross imperial offices and perquisites, the emperor's ultimate authority, as opposed to his power, was rarely challenged. The rulers of Bengal, Hyderabad, Awadh and the Carnatic held off from seeking the title of emperor or invading his quasi-religious functions. Certainly, the Nawab of the Carnatic (Arcot) delighted in the appellation of 'Sultan of India' conferred on him by the citizens of the holy city of Mecca in return for charitable offerings.[2] The rulers of Awadh at the beginning of the nineteenth century – encouraged by British officials – attempted to assert their equality with Delhi as 'universal kings' of the

[1] Muzaffar Alam, 'Mughal imperial decline and the province', unpub. Ph.D. diss. Jawaharlal Nehru University, 1981, p. 8.
[2] M. H. Nainar (ed.), 'Tuzak-i-Wallajahi', *Sources of the History of the Nawwabs of the Carnatic, Madras Islamic Series*, 4 (Madras, 1956), 244ff.

Shia branch of Islam.[3] But these developments had little wider significance. Only Tipu Sultan of Mysore, uneasy as a newcomer with the traditions of the Indo-Persian nobility and contemptuous of the flaccidity of Mughal power, took up the title of emperor. Even Tipu maintained a respectful communication with the imperial court. So it is not surprising that the British too maintained the form of imperial grants and participated in the rites of Mughal authority – at least down to 1848. Richard Wellesley, Governor-General 1798–1805, warned his aides to show respect to the Emperor as 'almost every class of people ... continue to acknowledge his nominal authority'[4] during the most expansive period of empire-building, and it is arguable that British success was facilitated by this scrupulous regard for Mughal authority.

A second reason why the fall of the Mughal empire seems an inadequate general theme is that the spirit of Mughal administration went marching on even when Delhi's military power lay mouldering in the grave. In the south the frontier of Muslim rule continued to expand with the fall of the Hindu Nayaks of Trichinopoly to the Carnatic rulers in 1732 and the later expansions by their successors into the lands of the chieftains of the far south. The rule of the Nawabs of the Carnatic was often no more than a loose hegemony, but the Hindu warlords were invested with the titles of Mughal dignity while Mughal-style jurisconsuls (*kazis*), urban executives (*kotwals*), authorities in law (*muftis*) and revenue agents were appointed. Even where non-Muslim kings came to power the forms of the old system were usually maintained. The Muslim officers continued to play an important part in the politics of holy Benares even after a Hindu raja engrossed power in 1738. In the early nineteenth century the new Sikh ruler of all-Punjab appointed Muslims as judicial officers in the city of Lahore. Very often the new rulers (and this included the English East India Company) issued their coinage from Mughal-style mints with the Mughal emperor's name prominently displayed. Prayers for the emperor were still said in mosques throughout India.

The agents who maintained and spread this administrative culture were drawn from the petty Muslim gentry of north and central India, from central Asian or Persian immigrants, and in the Deccan and the

---

[3] M. Fisher, 'The imperial court and the province: a social and administrative history of pre-British Awadh', unpub. Ph.D. diss., University of Chicago, 1978.
[4] M. Martin (ed.), *The Despatches, Minutes and Correspondence of the Marquess Wellesley, K.G.* (London, 1837), iv, 153.

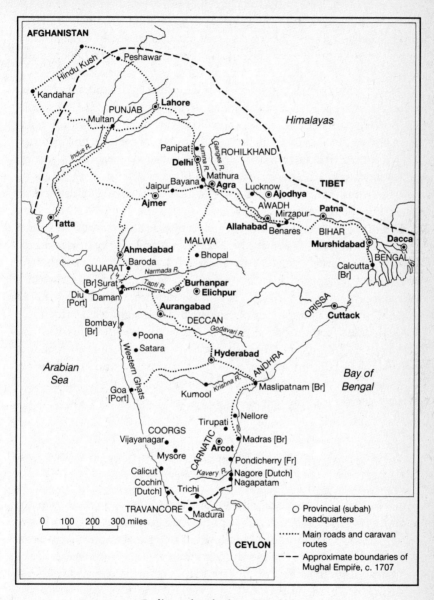

AFGHANISTAN
Hindu Kush
Kandahar
Peshawar
PUNJAB
Multan
Lahore
Indus R.
Himalayas
Panipat
Delhi
Jumna R.
Ganges R.
ROHILKHAND
Jaipur
Bayana
Mathura
Agra
Lucknow
Ajodhya
TIBET
Ajmer
AWADH
Mirzapur
Patna
Tatta
Allahabad
Benares
BIHAR
Murshidabad
Dacca
MALWA
Bhopal
BENGAL
Ahmedabad
Calcutta
[Br]
Baroda
GUJARAT
Narmada R.
[Br] Surat
Tapti R.
Burhanpar
Elichpur
ORISSA
Diu
[Port]
Daman
Cuttack
Aurangabad
Bombay
[Br]
DECCAN
Godavari R.
Poona
Satara
Arabian
Sea
Hyderabad
ANDHRA
Bay of
Bengal
Western Ghats
Goa
[Port]
Kumool
Krishna R.
Maslipatnam [Br]
Tirupati
Nellore
COORGS
Vijayanagar
CARNATIC
Arcot
Madras [Br]
Mysore
Pondicherry [Fr]
Calicut
Kavery R.
Nagore [Dutch]
Cochin
[Dutch]
Trichi
Nagapatam
TRAVANCORE
Madurai
0   100   200   300 miles
CEYLON

○ Provincial (subah)
   headquarters
⋯⋯⋯ Main roads and caravan
       routes
╴ ╴ ╴ Approximate boundaries of
       Mughal Empire, c. 1707

1  India under the later Mughals

south, from Hindus of the writer castes who had taken to Persian learning. They were all influenced by the classical tradition of administrative practice summed up in the Emperor Akbar's great Domesday book of India the *Ain-i-Akbari* (*circa* 1590) and later manuals on land-revenue management. This notable expansion of the Mughal style of government drew learned men of the Muslim gentry into new regions. Citizens of Delhi and Agra went east to Bengal, just as Hindu Bengalis were to follow British administration west into upper India in the next century. One of the most ancient and prestigious of the Muslim service clans of the west coast, the Navaiyit lineage, found office in the frontier state of Arcot and in the kingdom of Mysore which only fell to a Muslim ruler, Haider Ali, in 1761. Learned men and soldier-administrators of the northern Indian Muslim religious schools took service in the new realm of Bhopal which only stabilised in the first decade of the nineteenth century.

Even if in matters of authority and administrative culture there was much continuity between the highpoint of Mughal hegemony and the eighteenth century, surely the mechanics of political power were drastically modified? Here too the record seems less clear-cut than it did sixty years ago. Certainly political authorities based on India's ancient ecological and cultural regions became significant after 1707. Yet this 'decentralisation' of politics was itself anticipated by the very successes of Mughal expansion. It was on the basis of the expanding commercial economy of the seventeenth century and the slow accumulation of wealth by literate Muslim gentry, Hindu landholders and merchants that the quasi-kingdoms of the eighteenth century were built.

## THE TRANSFORMATION OF THE MUGHAL PROVINCES

The most striking political change of the eighteenth century was the long metamorphosis of Mughal provincial government which led to the creation of autonomous kingdoms in Bengal, Awadh and Hyderabad. Alongside them the Hindu Marathas and Sikhs created political systems within the ambit of the imperial domains which also made use of many of the administrative methods of the Mughals. Ironically, these new political formations derived in part from attempts by the Mughals to strengthen the foundations of their rule. Murshid Kuli

Khan, the Mughal governor who stands as lineal predecessor of the independent Nawabs of Bengal, was sent by the emperor to rationalise the finances of this rich province in 1704. He consolidated and brought to obedience the great Hindu and Muslim zamindars (landholders) of Bengal. In the process the offices of revenue manager (*diwan*) and governor (*subahdar*) which previous emperors had tried to keep separate were gradually amalgamated. Murshid Kuli Khan and his successors, notably the Nawab Alivardi Khan (1740–56), also began to fill local offices and confer revenue grants on their own dependants, and slowly slipped out of control of Delhi. Until 1739, and Nadir Shah's invasion of the capital, the large Bengal revenue was religiously sent to Delhi, but thereafter remittances became less regular. The emperor was often in the hands of enemies of the Bengal régime; the commercial links which alone made the remittance of silver possible withered as Delhi consumed less of Bengal's fine cotton goods; and Bengal itself was financially hard-pressed in the aftermath of Maratha invasions in 1742 and 1744.

Factional conflict at Delhi and the impotence of the emperor after 1712 strengthened these tendencies towards provincial autonomy. A long struggle in the 1720s between leaders of the Indian-born faction at court and notables of Iranian or Central Asian origin encouraged Asaf Jah (Nizam-ul-Mulk), Aurangzeb's former commander, to build up a power base in the high plains of the Deccan which by the time of his death in 1748 had become a recognisable political entity (though not a centralised realm) and precursor of the later princely state of Hyderabad. The Persian-born war leader Saadat Khan (Burhun-ul-Mulk), who became vazir or viceroy of the Empire, similarly moved his political base from Delhi to the rich but turbulent province of Awadh in the 1720s and 30s when his enemies triumphed at the court. As in Bengal these potentates amalgamated offices which the Mughals had tried to keep separate, though their bases of power were the offices of governor (subahdar) rather than revenue manager (diwan) as in Bengal. Early on Asaf Jah and Saadat Khan began again to ensure that their descendants inherited these newly amalgamated offices in what was a clear break with Mughal tradition. All these grandees were in a position to enhance their independence when Delhi fell to Iranian and Afghan invaders in 1739 and 1759–61, though they continued to supply and aid the imperial court until the end of the century.

The spirit and forms of Mughal provincial government changed only slowly. Asaf Jah's testament to his successors, recorded in 1748, urges them to respect the emperor as overlord and not to threaten the hierarchy of rulers. Since the Deccan had once been made up of six different Muslim kingdoms, 'it is right that the ancient families of the realm should be properly looked after', though none should be allowed to accumulate offices. The ruler of Hyderabad should seek accord with the Maratha zamindars, 'but he should maintain preeminent the dignity and prestige of Islam and never allow them to overstep the bounds'.[5] This old policy of enticement and suasion of local élites would best be pursued if the ruler moved around the country in tents, but he should allow the soldiers regular leave in order for them to father children. The tactics and goals of the eighteenth-century potentates were not greatly different from those of previous Mughal governors, only their tenure was more permanent and the ability of Delhi to discipline them much reduced.

The regional power-holders also inherited the problems of previous Mughal governors. In Bengal, where the Hindu landholders were more pacific and the money economy and trade was more developed, the nawabs and later the British had some hope of regular revenues and a degree of control. In Awadh the picture was mixed; Saadat Khan chastised the fiercely independent Rajput landholders of the central and southern territories, but warrior domains and revenue peculators quickly asserted themselves if the centre was momentarily deflected. In the Deccan and the Carnatic the neo-Mughal régimes flourished only fitfully, dependent on many cross-cutting alliances with local Telugu and Maratha chieftains. Yet, to an extent, Hyderabad was able to utilise the memory of the authority of the old, independent Deccani sultanates, and the Nawabs of the Carnatic, that of Vijayanagar.

All these modified provincial authorities gave Mughal élites the chance to deepen their hold on power in the regions, if they were clever and persistent. In the Deccan as in other parts of the empire Mughal military officers had once lived on assignments of revenue which were constantly changed to prevent them being transformed into heritable rental holdings. In the later eighteenth century in some parts of Hyderabad such grants did, however, tend to become hereditary. This created a more settled landholding class which negotiated its revenues and military commitments through agents settled in Hydera-

---

[5] Nizam-ul Mulk's Testament, 1164 Hegira, Yusuf Husain Khan, *Nizamu'l Mulk Asaf Jah I* (Bangalore, 1936), pp. 284–90.

bad city. In Awadh and Bengal clients and family members of the new ruling houses were also able to amass large bundles of proprietary rights and rights to farm revenue from the state which in course of time became hereditary estates (zamindaris in Bengal; *talukdaris* in Awadh and Hyderabad). Seeking allies in local society the regional rulers allowed locally resident Muslim families to build up areas of revenue-free land acquired during the later Mughal period and convert them into fuller proprietary rights. In this way they hoped to contain the power of the indigenous (largely Hindu) clans more effectively. It is an apparent paradox that during the 'fall of the Mughal empire' many families of former Mughal servants were able to establish a much closer control over the resources of the countryside and become local power-holders. Once again, it was the very success of processes of change set moving during Mughal expansion which helped undermine the fabric of their empire.

In the same way the transformed Mughal provinces provided a context in which entrepreneurs in revenue and trade could function, as the next chapter will demonstrate. In the early eighteenth century the rulers of Hyderabad, Awadh, Bengal and even the hard-pressed administration in Delhi tried to continue Mughal military practice and Mughal military salaries. In the second half of the century European weapons, methods and military advisers became more common. All this needed money and Hindu trader bankers or Muslim revenue farmers who could provide capital became increasingly influential. The Jagat Seths (Hindu bankers) became the key force in Bengal politics; Agarwal bankers 'commanded the state' as far as revenue matters were concerned in Benares. Even in the Maratha states banking firms became overt actors in local politics.

## WARRIOR STATES AND MUGHAL PRACTICE

The great non-Muslim warrior states – Marathas Sikhs and Jats – represented, of course, something more than simple devolutions of Mughal power to the provinces. The elements of continuity and change are quite difficult to distinguish, however. The rise of these warriors did reflect popular movements of peasant insurgency directed in part against the Indo-Muslim aristocracy. The Marathas drew their strength from the ordinary peasant and pastoralist castes of western India, now under arms and aspiring to the life-style of the ancient

Hindu kings. Maratha victories fostered a sense of community identity expressed through the Marathi language and Hindu devotional religion. The Brahmin administrators who increased their power in the first half of the eighteenth century pictured the Maratha state as a classic 'Brahmin' kingdom, protecting the holy places and sacred cattle. The Sikh leaders who dominated the Punjab after the Afghan invasion of north India during 1759–61 were often of humble origins – the descendants of Jat peasants, village servants and pastoralists from the dry west of the Punjab. Their sense of identity too, nurtured through the military brotherhood of the Khalsa (founded 1699), was sharpened by both political and religious conflict with the Mughals. To emphasise their Hindu and Sikh beliefs the leaders of all these movements tried hard to ban the slaughter of sacred cattle in the lands they conquered.

Yet the relation between Hindu and Sikh and the Muslim empire was ambiguous and became more so as the century moved on. Rebellion and schism had been the essential force behind Mughal expansion, indeed behind the expansion of Islam throughout west and south Asia. Rebellion did not imply a total severance of political relations or the creation of sharply defined territorial entities. The treaties made between the Mughal and the Marathas at the beginning of the century and in the 1780s, therefore, continued to recognise the position of the emperor as pinnacle of the hierarchy of kings. Even the new Sikh rulers patronised Muslim holy men; they established police officers and jurisconsuls modelled on the Mughal officers and used Mughal methods of revenue collection. The trend was most strikingly illustrated in the case of the Jat state of Bharatpur near Delhi. Here the ruler Suraj Mal began to expel his own clansmen and caste fellows from positions of power during the 1750s and imported the whole panoply of Mughal revenue collection in their stead. Even on the fringes of the Maratha domains where the Marathas had once taken their feared 'portion' of the revenue (or *chauth*) from farmers, their plundering incursions had given way to an efficient form of the Mughal revenue system by the 1760s. As Maratha power moved north during the 1770s and 1780s with the emergence of the great war lord Mahadji Scindia from beneath the hegemony of Poona the Mughal elements in their régime became more marked. Mahadji's army in the late 1780s had as many Muslim as Hindu soldiers (drilled often by Europeans) and the basis of his revenue collection was in the environs of the old Mughal capital of Agra. Those movements which began as plebeian reactions against Mughal domination came to prosecute the aims of Mughal rule with its own methods.

## THE EVOLUTION OF LOCAL KINGDOMS

The Mughal model was influential throughout India. But on the fringes of these semi-autonomous regional states or operating within their domain existed a host of smaller kingdoms which owed them only nominal allegiance. Muslim chroniclers often viewed this lowest rung in the hierarchy of kings in India as little more than a rabble of bucolic landholders or recalcitrant chiefs. However, they often represented the remnants of constellations of Hindu polities, built on the power and expressing the values of the dominant landholding communities which had once ruled the country without much intervention from above. They were important because they provided the context within which economic and cultural change occurred and also because it was by the suborning of these smaller entities as much as by the penetration of the regional powers that the British came to dominate the subcontinent.

These kingdoms had different origins and related in different ways to the organisation of power and production in the countryside. One great swathe of such kingdoms running from Gujarat in the west to Awadh in the east had been created by the expansion and migration of the Rajputs ('sons of princes'). The Rajputs were the archetypal Hindu warrior order. It appears to have been a much looser category in the pre-colonial period than it became in the nineteenth century when stricter endogamy and aspirations to purity in life-style became common among the princes protected by the British. Many Rajputs in the eighteenth century belonged to shifting bands of professional soldiers who attracted followers by marrying women from lower caste Hindu or even Muslim families. This Rajput world was topped out, particularly in Rajasthan, by a constellation of kingdoms which had survived for generations sometimes in conflict with the Mughals, sometimes as their servants. These were not, of course, centralised or territorial states. Rival rulers often held assignments of revenue in each others' domains. Moreover the possibilities for the aggrandisement of any one state had been limited both by the power of Muslim armies and by the fact that the most exalted families had to marry with families removed by many degrees of relationship from their own clans. This tended to fragment and diffuse power among the Rajput kings.

In the Deccan and the south the rôle of the Rajputs was filled by Telugu-speaking warriors who had also spread into the rich river valleys of the Tamil country over many generations. Untouched until the seventeenth century by the levelling tendencies of the great Mughal revenue systems, these potentates supported the great temples such as Tirupati and Madurai, and venerated Vaishnavite sectarian leaders who became their gurus or religious teachers. In this way they were assimilated into the ancient culture of the south. The Hindu dominion of Vijayanagar which had exercised a loose authority over much of the south until the late sixteenth century had established a style of kingship, worship and religious art which continued to be represented by potentates such as the rulers of Madurai and Mysore. But power was highly diffuse with war-band leaders from yet less Hinduised groups on the fringes of settled agriculture (the so-called poligars or *palaiyakarars* of the warrior tribal Kallars and Maravas) exercising the functions of protection and tribute taking in the villages on behalf of their nominal overlords.

Alongside the transformed remnants of the older systems of Hindu states stood a number of kingdoms more recently established by warriors or clever entrepreneurs in the management of land revenues, usually rising from the flotsam and jetsam of the Muslim conquest states of the north and the Deccan. Afghan warrior mercenaries had established compact sultanates around several armed base-camps throughout India. Some had preceded Mughal rule in the 1680s; others had arisen as its servants, still others as a result of the emperors' attempts to retain their power after 1707. Notable examples of Afghan sultanates were the Rohilla kingdoms near Delhi; the principalities of Bhopal and Mandu in central India; and the southern Afghans of Ginjee, Nellore and the far south. To create such kingdoms the military powers like their regional overlords and rivals needed financial expertise and the aid of men of capital to help the aspiring ruler to remit an initial revenue payment to an overlord. Some of the most impressive petty kingdoms therefore came to light as farms of revenue in which capitalist-warriors began to exercise kingly powers. The Raj of Benares adopted many of the styles of patronage and worship supposedly characteristic of ancient Hindu kings. Yet in practice the reason that Mansa Ram was able to survive as revenue farmer and later maharaja in the Awadh domains (from 1738) was that he had the financial support of the Hindu bankers of Benares and the military support of his rural clansmen. Some eighteenth-century magnates of Bengal – notably the great zamindari of Burdwan – originated as similar bundles of revenue-collecting rights acquired in the service of Mughal governors.

Finally, there was a range of local powers which still lay largely outside the Hindu and Muslim polities which were built up on the rich produce of the valleys and plains. The distinction between 'tribal' and Hindu India was never simple or static. But throughout north and central India and the Western Ghats (hills) were peoples only lightly touched by the major cultures and religions who lived in part by the skills of the pastoralist, the slash-and-burn farmer or the hunter and gatherer. Some of these peoples had chieftains who were designated rajas by outside potentates, though often the individual nomadic camp or hunting family was the key political unit and the state hardly existed as an entity.

The relationship between these petty kingdoms and local forms of production varied greatly. Sometimes as in the newly powerful state of Travancore on the south-west coast or Maratha Tanjore on the east coast, rulers intervened very closely in the production of rice or other valuable crops, controlling them through royal granaries and monopolies. In some cases rulers even controlled their own bands of ploughmen to increase the resources of the king's 'demesne'. However, the general trend was towards something approximating to the Mughal system – payment of tax in coin and the predominance of peasant farming. Between about 1600 and 1780 for instance the old Hindu state of Mysore progressively upped its nominal tax revenue from under 10 per cent of the gross produce to about 40 per cent under Tipu Sultan in the 1790s. Of course much of the enhanced total was never collected, but the growing costs of warfare and a desire for a new grandiose form of kingship spread across the subcontinent. As in the regional dominions, therefore, literate and numerate service families became increasingly important in the affairs of these local kingdoms. Moneylenders and bulk traders set up in their domains as guarantors of revenue and provisioners of their courts.

Petty kingdoms continued to retain their identity, their cults and their own form of political organisation. Still, the outward forms of Mughal practice at least were widely adopted. In the same way the influx of service personnel from outside encouraged rulers to adopt the forms of worship and religious patronage common in the world of the larger states. As the Maravar and Kallar warlords of Tamilnadu fashioned themselves into Hindu kings, they imported Brahmins and Brahmin rituals from the great temple centres of the south. As Afghan rulers in the western Ganges plain and the southern Deccan gained a more stable hold on their realms, new Islamic seminaries and libraries were founded while the teachers of the Naqshbandi order of Sufi mystics fanned out into new territories. What emerged was not an orthodox or standard pattern of religious practice so much as a subtle and sometimes conflict-ridden accommodation between outside forms of religious practice and local deities and cult saints. The tendency was towards greater complexity and richness of religious and cultural tradition rather than towards homogeneity.

The eighteenth century did not therefore see a resolution of the old tensions between the regional and imperial hegemonies and local kingdoms, so much as an interpenetration of these forms of power. Despite the high level of violence and destruction this eased the path to dominion of the more enterprising warriors and their administrative and capitalist clients. There were, however, two important conditions for the survival and even development of complex states and administrative forms. First, there needed to be some degree of stability in the villages – some persistent authority to provide a link between the peasantry and the warriors who lived off them. Secondly, production and trade needed to survive at a sufficiently high level to provide a constant supply of services and cash for the élites. The chapter now turns to these issues.

## POWER IN THE COUNTRYSIDE

Regional kingdoms and petty states were built up and collapsed quickly but there was more continuity of power in the villages. Throughout southern and western India local leadership remained in the hands of the village headmen (the *patel/munigar*) and their subordinates the accountants (*kurnam/kanikapillai*) and record keepers who together with related families made up the village élite. Often those village leaderships were bonded together at a wider level by kinship or economic interest into domains controlled by local magnates (*deshmukhs* in the Deccan; *kavalgars* in Tamilnadu). The hereditary office-holding families could often be traced back many generations. They assigned land to landless villagers, fixed rents and were prominent in the village arbitration councils. In rice-growing areas they played a prominent part in the communal organisation of agricultural production. The state negotiated with the agrarian community through the office holders and they received payments and services both by virtue of their leadership in the village and their rôle in the state's revenue machinery. In western India an early British official said that 'the Patils are the most important functionaries in the villages, and perhaps the most important class in the country'.[6] The headmen also played a crucial role in the religious life and ritual of the villages. They were protectors of the village deities; they were honoured during the great village festivals. The traveller Francis Buchanan was told by farmers in Coimbatore District of Madras that even if the state were to deprive the headmen of their political power 'the real hereditary munigar [Tamil for headman] will always continue to enjoy his rank as a chief; for he is the only person who can perform the annual sacrifice to the goddess Bhadra Kali, to whom in every village there is a temple as being the Grama Devata or village deity'.[7]

The nature of the village élite was rather different in north India. Here joint or individual proprietors excercised lordship rights over villages, controlling the waste and access to land along with ponds, trees and other sources of income. As in the south, this élite was predominantly drawn from high-caste peasant communities with a tradition of warfare, and these village magnates were often linked together by kinship bonds to form tight-knit blocs of power which coincided with the lowest unit of Mughal administration, the *pargana*. But it was rental income from tenants, along with these proprietary perquisites, rather than the rewards of village office which provided most of their livelihood. In part this difference reflected the superior agriculture of the Ganges valley which could support a rental profit of this sort (there were parts of the south, too, such as rich Tanjore district which also maintained joint proprietary communities – the *mirasidars*). In part it resulted from the failure of the state to penetrate

[6] G. W. Forrest (ed.) M. Elphinstone, *Report on the Territories Conquered from the Peshwa* (London, 1884), p. 275.
[7] Francis Buchanan, *A Journey from Madras through the countries of Mysore, Canara and Malabar* (London, 1807), ii, 216.

beneath the armed peasant proprietor bodies. Even in the immediate environs of Delhi itself Mughal grandees had depended on the good-will of headmen of the warrior-farmer communities.

During the eighteenth century the village notables came under various forms of pressure. In their search for revenue the regional and petty states almost always tried to gain a closer control over the head-men or village proprietors. Sometimes direct representatives of the state acquired revenue-collecting rights at the village level and eroded the power and perquisites of the headmen families. This was particu-larly true where the state was strong as in the Maratha territories around Poona between 1751 and 1818, or in Mysore where Haidar Ali and Tipu Sultan tried to eliminate all intermediaries between them-selves and the peasant farmers, subjecting them to new demands for the punctual payment of revenue. Elsewhere the absence of powerful authorities outside the village enhanced the authority of the élites as protectors and petty rulers of the villages.

In addition the village offices in the south and west were influenced by economic change. Village office as a source of profit could be shared, mortgaged or sold; through the offices of the headmen and the élites villages could borrow from moneylenders on security of their revenue. A brisk market developed in shares in the patel's right, in the joint mirasi tenures of the south and to a lesser extent in shares in vil-lage proprietors' rights of north India. The people who bought into shares in village office were usually other peasant leaders or local mer-chants. Interestingly, around Poona there is evidence that some of the great families of the Maratha state also built up bundles of rights of this sort to increase their local economic control. Such commercialisation had not yet created a village élite independent of moral status and pol-itical power as it came to do under the British. Nor had it created a market for individual peasant land as such. Yet it was an indication of the deep penetration of the money economy into the countryside and the fact that commercial change was compatible with political fluidity in pre-colonial India.

What is most striking about the meagre record of conditions in the villages at this period is its variety. Even during the worst period of the Anglo-Maratha wars observers noted that one village could be entirely desolate while the next, secure in the protection of some potentate, was dominated by prosperous farmers. A study from indigenous sources in Rajasthan reveals a rich peasant élite which accounted for about 10 per cent of the rural population.[8] The existence of such a group would clearly be dependant on well-developed internal markets and relative political stability. Given basic protection, though, it is not surprising that the subcontinent would support bodies of rich farmers and local magnates. Population density was low and there was much good land still to be taken under the plough. In areas of expanding agriculture it was not unusual to find agrarian magnates who owned and worked up to 200 acres of dry farm land through share-croppers or day-labourers and owned many plough teams. Such were the *jotedars* of north and east Bengal who actually controlled agriculture as inferior holders beneath the more famous *rentier* landlords – the zamindars. Rural magnates of this sort were also found in parts of south India where much smaller peasant holdings were the order of the day a century later after population pressure had worked its course.

It was shortage of labour rather than shortage of land which acted as the main constraint on agriculture. This helps explain the rather flexible society of the eighteenth century. 'Traditional' India has sometimes seemed to be hierarchical and static. But this was true of the ideal order of society rather than its actual workings. Men and skills were in short supply so that marriage outside caste groups was common. Great peasant caste-clusters such as the Kunbis of western India and the Jats of the north allowed their males to take concubines from related or lower caste groups. The sons of these liaisons were considered Jats or Kunbis in the next generation. Even some Rajput subcastes which were rigidly endogamous in the colonial period married outside caste in the eighteenth century. Caste status in the countryside was in fact a rather fluid matter. To some extent it was determined by how closely people adopted the ideal model of Brahmin or Warrior purity. More often than not the distinction between superior and inferior rural castes turned on the bearing of arms. In Gujarat at the end of Maratha rule the term Maratha with its connotation was generally applied to men of the Kunbi or peasant caste who carried weapons.[9]

Labour and skills could not always be acquired through marriage or domestic alliance. The force of political and religious power was also used to secure clients. This was all the more true since, as we now

[8] Dilbagh Singh, 'Local and land revenue administration of the state of Jaipur, *c.* 1750–1800', unpub. Ph.D. diss. Jawaharalal Nehru University, 1975.

[9] W. Hamilton, *A geographical, statistical and historical account of Hindustan and the adjacent countries* (London, 1820), p. 307; cf. R. O'Hanlon, *Caste, conflict and ideology* (Cambridge, 1985), pp. 22–4.

know, the ideal order of village-level caste dependencies (called the *jajmani* or *balutadar* system) only supplied the most refined specialist craftsmen and ritual servants. Eighteenth-century Indians were not tied into immutable village bodies or always dominated by hereditary divisions of labour. So agrarian clients had often to be actively sought. Serfs were secured from tribal groups by war or through bonds of indebtedness contracted with the large bodies of inferior labouring caste people, notably the Chamars in the north and the Paraiyans in the south. The dependence of such groups was maintained not simply by force and economic disadvantage but also by subtle systems of belief which gave high-caste gentry an important role in the life rites of their dependants and *vice versa*.[10]

Did the dependence of inferior groups therefore increase in the eighteenth century? The evidence is both meagre and contradictory. Probably it is best to speak of this century as a period of widening regional differences, compared with the more coherent trends which have been discerned in the Mughal and British periods. Warfare and the problems of money supply in the late eighteenth century may well have reduced many poor peasants – 'seekers of protection' – to greater dependence on rich farmers, moneylenders, office-holders and sub-Mughal grandees. This was probably the dominant trend. On the other hand, the very lack of skilled labour and the desperate desire of petty régimes to enhance their cash revenue for military purposes meant that agrarian labourers prepared and able to migrate retained a good deal of bargaining power. Throughout the subcontinent day-labourers were said to have been better rewarded than established occupancy tenants who would not abandon their fields for reasons of sentiment. There are even some examples of labourers and share-croppers resisting landholders and yeomen by desertion or by participation in millenarian movements claiming to improve their lot on earth.

The same paradox can be seen in the relations between the agrarian states and unsettled, semi-nomadic or tribal peoples who occupied such a large part of the map of the subcontinent before colonial rule. Indian society as a pioneer society inevitably impinged on such groups. The Maratha rulers of the Deccan and central India pushed further into the forest homelands of the Bhil and Gond tribes, convert-

[10] Gyan Prakash, 'Reproducing inequality: spirit cults and labour relations in colonial eastern India', *Modern Asian Studies*, xx, 2, 1986.

ing their tribal leaders into petty rajas and their tribesmen into bonds-
men or tribute-givers. The great peasant communities continued their
age-old migrations into the forests of the western Ghats or the jungles
to the north and south of the Ganges Valley. Haider and Tipu in
Mysore invaded the tribal lands of the Coorgs in the 1770s and 80s and
dragged many of them off to be Islamised and settled as agricultural
servants near their capitals. But arable India and the state did not have
it all its own way. With the weakening of the authority of Mughal rule
and its clients in the north 'headless' nomadic and pastoral societies
such as the Bhattis and Rangars in Haryana and Rajasthan managed to
extend their tribal grazing grounds and areas of plunder once again.[11]

Even in the Deccan and the south where the Mughal type of state
was making some headway during the eighteenth century, the effect
on tribal and nomadic groups was complex. The Bedar archers earned
large sums of money from service as guerrilla fighters in the armies of
Mysore. Northern followers of the Arcot Muslims were astonished by
the Kallar tribals whom they saw as 'black complexioned people ...
not pleasing to the eye who ate the raw flesh of animals such as the
horse'.[12] Later the Arcot rulers and their allies of the French and
English East India Companies recruited many Kallars and Maravars as
irregulars. This speeded the development of a money economy and
created more marked differences of wealth and power among the
tribesmen.

Indian society in the eighteenth century was typical of other frontier
societies in that the internal extent of the state's influence and of the
arable economy with its more hierarchical landed society was constantly in flux. Migration was followed by counter-migration,
especially across the great empty lands of the Deccan. Settled society
and its values were not irrevocably divided from the frontier; they
were in a state of mutual dependence. The tribesmen and nomads furnished the settled with beeswax, honey, spices, carriage, milk and
soldiers. The settled provided the fringes with money, cloth and grain.
The forest continued to play a part in the artistic and religious system
of the settled. Muslim mystical teachers often started as 'forest
fathers', while the unsettled and its peoples remained powerful carriers

[11] G. L. Devra, 'Efforts to check the problem of desertification in the north-west region of
Rajasthan' unpub. paper, Department of History, Dungar College, Bikaner.
[12] Jaswant Rai, 'Sayeed Nama', tr. S. A. R. Bokhari, 'Carnatic under the Nawabs as revealed through the Sayeed Nama of Jaswant Rai', M.Litt. diss. University of Madras, 1965,
p. 95.

of magic even for the Hindus who worshipped the high gods. On the other hand Brahmins and Muslim soldiers and administrators played a part in the rituals and beliefs of most of the tribal groups as they had done for many centuries. Brahmin administrators worked for the 'tribal' rajas of Coorg. In the Gond lands a superficial Hinduisation had been symbolised by an injunction by the new Maratha rulers of the late eighteenth century against the slaughter of holy cattle. Still, the old tribal gods were still worshipped and human sacrifice was recorded from time to time even in the colonial period

## ECONOMIC FOUNDATIONS OF POLITICAL POWER

The main forces working on any agrarian economy are population, the diffusion of basic forms of technology and management and the buoyancy of demand which set prices. Very little is known about any of these indicators for eighteenth-century India. What is known paints a more varied picture than the one of total decline which emerges from earlier literature. This is consistent with the political record of the century. The decline of Mughal hegemony allowed the further development of powerful commercial forces in the regions – a huge burst of entrepreneurship in power and money. Such interests often became locked in destructive conflict. However, there were forces partly independent of local political power which affected the political economy of eighteenth-century India – population growth, external trade and the seasons. It is to these influences that the chapter now turns.

Population growth was held back by epidemic disease and by periodic mortality from the failure of monsoon rains. In the long run the evidence from Mughal India suggests a gradual growth of population which may have reached 180 million for the whole of the subcontinent by 1750. Famines are recorded in central and western India for the 1680s and for 1702–4. But the first sixty years of the eighteenth century appear to have been relatively free from widespread famines, though the records of the Madurai Jesuit mission speak of severe distress in 1709 and 1733–5,[13] and there were local scarcities in north India. Prices rose slowly through to the 1750s, at least in central and north India, and this probably reflects limited population growth

[13] R. Venkatarama Ayyar, *A Manual of the Puddukotai State* (2nd edn. Puddukotai, 1938–44), I, 312.

more than the growth of bullion imports from overseas since both rice and dry grains moved up. Some indication of population expansion may also be found in the inability of Bengal to supply its weavers with raw cotton by the 1740s. The scattered records of internal migration point to continuing expansion of settlement and arable farming in north and east Bengal, in the jungles of southern Bihar and the Ganges Valley. In the south the great peasant lineages appear to have slowly colonised the plains and hills, moving out from the already populous rice basins.

The terrible Bengal famine of 1769–70, when excessive rains led to crop failure and the death of at least 25 per cent of the population, broke this trend. There was also a severe famine in north India in 1783 and local scarcities in Rajasthan and the south in the following decade. Warfare in the years 1773–1810 also damaged agriculture, particularly in the Delhi region and the Carnatic. Armies spread diseases to populations already affected by malnutrition. Still, there are good reasons for doubting whether an earlier trend of population growth was decisively reversed. Population picked up rapidly in south Asia, particularly when, as in 1783, much of the livestock survived. In Bengal, at least, the labour market appears to have begun to turn against the unsecured peasant farmer before the end of the century, suggesting population recovery. Quite high population densities are recorded in many of the famine districts in the early British censuses carried out in 1812 and 1813, though there were also patches of permanently 'deserted villages'.

Slow agricultural improvement continued in many parts of India through to about 1760, and in some areas even after that date. This was despite political fluidity. There were of course significant examples of collapse. The great Mughal canal system north of Delhi fell into disuse sometime after 1740, while the sugar cane and indigo agriculture of this region and adjoining Punjab suffered from the tribulations of the Mughal élite and its merchant clients who had once put in stone wells in the environs of towns such as Panipat or Bayana. In the south the conflict between the Nawabs of Arcot and the Hindu rulers of Tanjore in the 1770s also damaged the delicate system of labour upon which the southern rice bowl subsisted.[14] On the other hand there was new investment and expansion. The main roads of the growing state of

[14] But production stayed high until this point and revived again after 1785, Appendix 21 to the *Fourth Report . . . on the Affairs of the East India Company* (London, 1783).

Awadh were lined with new irrigation ponds and wells constructed by its aspiring gentry. The evidence also points to a substantial intensification of agriculture in the great warrior states of the south and west. Unbiased observers constantly praised the excellent agricultural management of the Maratha heartlands where low initial revenue rates encouraged expansion and investment. Haider Ali's Mysore was regarded as 'a garden from end to end' and there was a great expansion of road and irrigation canal building. Most important, there was a continuing painful advance of pioneer peasant cultivation on the fringes of the arable economy which compensated for the fall-back of high farming in areas such as western Rajasthan or the eastern Punjab where the domain of nomadic and plundering groups seems to have temporarily increased after 1760.

This expansion and patchy growth was reflected in the vitality of demand in early-eighteenth-century India. Price series are quite fragmentary but those few that do exist indicate a steady trend, and in some cases movement upward until mid-century, albeit interrupted by the effects of periodic wars and local scarcities. Thereafter the series suggest great volatility connected with both political and climatic shocks, but significantly, a clear downward trend is not recorded until the beginning of the nineteenth century. Even if it is accepted that disturbances in the Mughal heartland of north India diminished the capacity of its élites to consume and protect, the nobility of the new political entities went a long way to make up for the decline. The Marathas acquired large quantities of grain, cattle and cloth from the Gangetic plain by trade; this has been obscured by the constant references in British and Mughal sources to their looting campaigns. Large volumes of cotton wool and hides from the northern Deccan, sugar from the Benares region and cloth from the Carnatic were sucked into the Mysore of the Sultans in the last thirty years of the century.

Foreign demand also persisted in adversity. Crises in western Asia combined with the impact of the initial Maratha invasions to damage the trade of the great Mughal seaport of Surat as early as 1720. There were also temporary setbacks in the trade of Bengal and the Carnatic as a result of the Anglo-French conflicts occasioned by the War of Austrian Succession and the Seven Years War, but the volume of cloths, saltpetre and other trade goods acquired by the English Company and other European merchants increased steadily through to

1770. By the 1790s new commodities – cotton wool from Gujarat and central India, Malwa opium and indigo – had partially made up for the decline of some of the old staples. Indian-owned shipping and Indian exporting merchants were under pressure everywhere and had gone into a steep decline after 1780. Indian merchants were excluded from free trade in many valuable commodities by British monopolies, especially after 1763. However, Indian goods were still transported in British, French and Arab shipping.

Demand from Europeans continued to be supplemented by that of the Indonesian archipelago which took large quantities of Madras cloths; west Asian demand in the form of the trading empire of Muscat had also revived by 1790. The greatest purchaser, the English East India Company, drastically changed its form of payment after 1757 with considerable implications for the internal economy. After Clive's conquest of Bengal the British increasingly used the proceeds of their new Bengal revenues to pay for the goods acquired from Bengal and eastern India. No longer did they need to bring in bullion from external sources on anything like the same scale. With the decline of Surat and the atrophy of the Mughal revenue system this presumably accounts for the complaints of dearer money and trade recession which were heard throughout north India in the 1760s. However, this down-turn should not be viewed as an apocalypse. The resulting tightening of money supply did not amount to an actual demonetisation of the economy, except possibly on the fringes. Indeed, the 'scarcity of money' may be connected with the even stronger incentive to maximise cash revenues and mobilise new agricultural resources found among rulers and élites during this period. Massive stores of precious metals had built up in India between 1600 and 1750. The dispersion of old hoards may have eased the money supply, while bullion continued to come in through Bombay, Madras and many smaller ports. Indian bankers and revenue farmers with ready cash consequently increased their importance in the political system.

The acid test of the capacity of India's huge internal economy to resist severe pressures of war and poor external trading conditions is the fact that revenue continued to be paid in cash in the second half of the eighteenth century. This indicates that peasants continued to produce for markets and that traders continued to pay them in silver rupees or other coinages. The volumes of collection in the Mughal empire's northern heartlands do not appear often to have fallen below

65 per cent of the *nominal* demand of the later Mughals while agricultural production probably intensified in the domains of the Marathas and Mysore.

It may be better to conceive of economic change as the interpenetration and conflicts between several levels of activity. These levels were closely related to the different levels of political power. The economy can be divided into three interlinked elements. First, the world of the great cities, of external trade and the trader-financiers who moved wealth around the subcontinent in the form of bullion and credit notes. Secondly, the 'intermediate economy' of mass artisan production, of small country towns, and of the petty farms or assignments of revenue, or shares in office which proliferated in the wake of state-building and expansion. Thirdly, the vast bulk of India's internal agrarian economy. This responded to changes in the other elements since it was affected by money supply, demand and protection. Yet it always retained a great deal of autonomy – as the petty village markets and local cattle fairs were only spasmodically and poorly linked to the subcontinental economy. How far did these elements demonstrate the capacity for development as opposed to a simple resilience in the face of adversity?

The pan-Indian economy of the towns and great trade routes undoubtedly suffered disruption and flux after 1707, though its stability before this date should probably not be overestimated. About 10 per cent of the population lived in towns of above 5,000 in 1800, but estimates of the percentage of urban dwellers under the Mughals vary from 7 per cent to 15 per cent.[15] Key commercial towns of the earlier period – Surat, Ahmedabad, Maslipatnam and Dacca – suffered rapid decline. However, these were rapidly compensated for in the rise of British-controlled Bombay, Calcutta and Madras which will be discussed in the next chapter. Inland cities also suffered great vicissitudes. Delhi, Lahore, Agra and Burhanpur, which may have accounted for two million people in 1700, supported 500,000 at most by 1800. But several important new centres had established themselves in the meantime, sometimes on an earlier urban base. Lucknow, Hyderabad, Benares, the Maratha capitals, Mysore, Srirangapatam and Bangalore grew rapidly during the century as a reflection of the power of the re-

[15] Irfan Habib and Tapan Raychaudhuri (eds.), *The Cambridge Economic History of India*, i (Cambridge, 1982), 169. But Stephen Blake has much lower percentages, see his forthcoming article in *South Asia*.

gional dynasts. Trading cities such as Mirzapur, Kanpur or Baroda also sprang into life to service new external trades. The loss of services and accumulated wealth in these movements was probably considerable, but it is significant how quickly demand and production was made up from new sources. New overland trade routes emerged to compensate for the clogged Mughal trade arteries; production of Dacca and Murshidabad fine cloths held up remarkably to supply both Indian courts and the requirements of European companies. New commercial and credit networks run by mercantile castes in both east and western India acted as creditors both to Indian rulers and to the British. The great concentrations of military and urban populations under Aurangzeb may have dispersed. But urbanisation was more widely spread across the subcontinent by 1800.

In some of these centres there is evidence that merchant entrepreneurs gathered bodies of dependent weavers into something that approximated more to the conditions of wage-labour in factories. The cheapness of labour and relatively low technological level of weaving appears, however, to have perpetuated the tried system of advances and piece-work. Signs of a technological or institutional breakthrough in the weaving sector are too scattered to suggest any trend. The growing dominance of Europeans in India's external trade and of the English Company in the internal capital market suggests a clear limit to the autonomy of its capitalists.

A more important source of wealth for Indian trader-bankers was investment in political and military activity. Indigenous bankers were closely connected with the great families of revenue farmers, giving them advances on the security of their holdings. In several of the smaller eighteenth-century states trader-bankers were a key political group by the 1760s. Under the Mughals they may have been vital to the working of economy and society, but they never held open political power.

The problems of the great grid of subcontinental markets, production and capital does not necessarily imply that decline or disruption was universal or persistent in the other two elements of the economy. In fact, the presumption that the decline of a powerful, extractive all-India state in the form of the Mughal Empire brought misery seems a curious reflexive shadow thrown by the imperialists of the following century. In theory it is possible that the decline of such an empire could have led to a more intensive and efficient use of resources in the still large regional entities that survived its demise. The record on the ground, once cleared of the biases of contemporary discourse, provides some evidence of economic growth. Rural fixed markets (*ganjs* in north India; *pettas* in the south) were being created in great numbers in the first half of the eighteenth century. In the much less favourable conditions after 1750 such markets were still appearing in Awadh, Maharashtra and peninsular India. The presence of substantial yeoman-magnates cultivating their lands with day-labourers, share-croppers and large teams of ploughs has already been noted in Bengal, Benares and the south. This sort of development was often associated with growth of new centres of artisan production directed at mass regional markets.

The fine spread of new élites and flexible political institutions across the country following the waning of Mughal power sometimes intensified such changes. The puttting out to 'farm' of revenues – denounced by the old school of Mughal political economist was associated with growth in western Awadh under the great manager Almas Ali Khan and the Maratha territories under the peshwas even in the last quarter of the century. Elsewhere military magnates and gentry encouraged the settlement of agricultural specialists in order to raise the revenue potential of their fiefs. Trader-bankers, far from being unproductive usurers, invested in shares in the open and flexible village economies of Rajasthan and western India, providing relief in the event of bad seasons.

To understand the political economy of eighteenth-century India, we must therefore make a distinction between economic institutions and economic cycles. After 1760 many unfavourable trends began to operate on regional economies, though these were certainly not universal. However, long-term development of commercialisation in India – of credit, of markets and of the significance of traders and moneylenders – continued. It was these forms which facilitated, even attracted, British intervention and conquest.

## INDIAN CULTURE IN THE EIGHTEENTH CENTURY

In the commercial world the decline of Mughal hegemony gave free rein to forms of entrepreneurship throughout the subcontinent, but the result was to intensify conflict. An analogy can be made here with developments in religious and social life. The creation of successor states allowed to deepen the existing synthesis between the 'high religion' of the Brahmins and the Kuranic schools and particular forms of worship in different regions of India. However, rapid change also led to religious conflict and the creation of strong religious identities whose consequences flowed over into the colonial period.

Eighteenth-century Europeans were still impressed by the richness of the high traditions of Hindu and Muslim civilisations in India and intrigued by their popular forms. Sir William Jones who founded the Asiatic Society of Bengal (1784) and the Frenchman A. Anquetil Duperron venerated the Hindu scriptures as manifestations of antiquity comparable with the relics of ancient Greece and Rome. But discourse about Indian culture was already set into trends which would produce the early Victorian denunciations of 'superstition and barbarism'. The supercilious William Tennant condemned the domestic economy of Hindus for corruption and superstition which he thought laid the basis for 'public tyranny'. Francis Buchanan whose topographies and accounts provided models for later amateur British ethnographers compared Hinduism unfavourably with the ascetic Buddhism which he had encountered in Burma. More modern oriental scholarship has ignored or dismissed the record of the eighteenth century since it apparently threw up no great devotional poets and teachers of the Hindu tradition comparable with those who had flourished in the fifteenth and sixteenth centuries: notably Chaitanya in Bengal and Kabir in north India. Even the doctrinal vitality of Sikhism seemed to diminish after the death of Guru Gobind Singh in 1708.

Yet for all this the eighteenth century was a period of creativity in Indian religious and cultural life, not a sultry pause before the 'rediscovery' of Hinduism and Islam in the next century. The centres of the learned and philosophical Hinduism retained great vigour. Contemporary political change provided its own incentive for cultural reinterpretation. In the south the Maratha court of Tanjore presided over an outpouring of poetry, religion and dance in the first half of the century which resulted from the fusion of the ancient Vaishnavism of the south with the Shaivism and north Indian influences of the new rulers. Benares, strengthened by the continuation of all-India pilgrimage patterns, was vitalised by the influx of southern and Deccan Brahmins: its teaching institutions were likened to a university by European visitors. New centres of learning also grew up. In Bengal the patronage of local magnates enhanced the ancient Vaishnavite centre of Nadia as a centre of scholarship in Sanskrit and the Dayabhaga Hindu law. It was these flourishing traditions which were taken as exemplars of Hinduism by the scholars of the later part of the century who worked for British patrons or who had knowledge of the western critical textual traditions. So Henry Colebrooke worked with a Nadia Brahmin when he sought to draw up a 'code of Hindoo law'. Jonathan Duncan, British Resident of Benares, elicited fitful and suspicious interest from Benares pandits when he tried to establish the Benares Hindoo College. In the south Raja Serfoji of Tanjore, who had been educated by Danish missionaries, resurrected the literary and musical traditions of his immediate predecessors with the eye of an enlightenment scholar.

Eighteenth-century Muslim learned men also propagated a vigorous, developing tradition. This was not surprising in view of the rapid changes which took place in the political and economic circumstances of Indian Islam. The growing influence of the Shia sect, expressed particularly in the new court of Awadh, combined with a sense of unease among Sunni Muslims throughout the world to provoke a major reassessment of thought and practice. In Delhi the famous teachers Shah Waliullah and Shah Abdul Aziz spanned the century with their flow of tracts and analyses of Islam's contemporary weakness. Naqshbandiya sufi teachers sought to strengthen the faith through a *rapprochement* of the learned and mystical patterns of Islamic practice and had established a large number of teaching institutions in the imperial capital and its environs before 1800.[16] In the Punjab there was a vigorous development of the Chishti sufi order associated with a series of famous teachers whose shrines became the moral heart of the lives of Punjab's Muslims. The expanding Muslim states of the Deccan and southern India also drew in learned men from the north. The Nawab of Arcot venerated and maintained Maulana Abdul Ali Bahr-ul Ulum, teacher from the famous Lucknow seminary of Firangi Mahal,[17] as well as Maulana Baqir Agha, representative in Arcot of the learned traditions

---

[16] W. Fusfeld, 'The shaping of sufi leadership in Delhi: the Naqshbandiyya Mujaddidiya, 1750–1920', unpub. Ph.D. diss., University of Pennsylvania, 1981.

[17] F. C. R. Robinson, 'The *ulama* of Firangi Mahal and their *adab*', in B. D. Metcalf (ed.), *Moral conduct and authority. The place of adab in South Asian Islam* (Berkeley, 1984).

of the Deccan.[18] Everywhere the state-builders of the eighteenth century sought the solace of holy men and built up Islamic libraries. Rohilla Afghans, for instance, maintained a close link with men of the Naqshbandi order. Everywhere the Afghans established petty kingdoms from Rampur in the north to Nellore in Tamilnadu the chain of pupil-teacher relationships was expanded.

But it was not just the formal, learned traditions within Hinduism and Islam which took on new patterns. Popular cults and shrines displayed remarkable vigour, often in accommodation with practices drawn from the high traditions. All Indian rulers sought to secure their domains by linking themselves to centres of religious power, Hindu, Muslim and even Christian. Again the mobile warrior bands of the age were particularly favourable to the syncretic styles of religious practice which crossed the boundaries of the great faiths. In the north the Marathas supported the important shrine of Sheikh Muin-uddin Chishti in Ajmer, already a shrine of popular veneration for the Hindus of Rajasthan. In the south the Hindu Rajas of Tanjore and the severely Calvinistic Dutch merchants supported the shrine of Shaikh Shahul Hamid of Nagore, centre of an integrated network of Hindu, Christian and Muslim shrines which attracted veneration from the mercantile people of the Coromandel coast. On the south-west coast the expansionist rajas of Travancore adopted ceremonies of kingship representing the highest Brahminical aspirations. Yet in the coronation ceremony of his neighbour, the Raja of Cochin, local Jewish and Christian merchant people played an important symbolic rôle.

Developments in the religious practices of the ordinary townsmen and countrypeople are most difficult to chart for the eighteenth century. Among Hindus the devotional or *bhakti* cults appear to have maintained the popularity they achieved in the preaching phase of the previous two centuries. Ordinary people became followers of the popular cults associated with the Rama and Krishna cults of north India. Based on towns such as Brindaban, Ajodhya and Muttra, devotional religion was spread through the medium of the developing Hindi language, popular festivals and popular art. Local warfare seems even to have enhanced the popularity of these cults and the ascetic orders associated with them. Ascetics (Gosains and Bhairagis) had

---

[18] M. Y. Kokan, *Arabic and Persian in the Carnatic* (Madras, 1976) p. 148; Zakira Ghouse, 'Baquir Agha's contribution to Arabic, Persian and Urdu literatures', unpub. M.Litt. diss., Madras University, 1973.

forged themselves into powerful armed brotherhoods; they were also able to accumulate large quantities of capital because of their corporate organisation. Peasants and farmers looked to them for protection and finance in adversity and even donated their children to them in times of famine. In the same way the deification by ordinary Hindu and 'tribal' peoples of eighteenth-century Muslim and Hindu warriors speaks again of the capacity of ordinary Hindus to incorporate into their belief and imaginative world dangerous forces from the outside.

Of course, it has been said that developments such as these were no more than the sterile elaborations of traditions which were incapable of creativity. But this too needs examination since it echoes the missionaries' castigation of the 'meaningless ramblings' of the Brahmins, besides assuming the need for modernisation along Western lines. In fact, several of the traditions elaborated in the eighteenth centuries had distinctly practical applications. The Islamic teaching course, the Darz-i-Nizamiya developed at Firangi Mahal, Lucknow, owed its popularity in part to the fact that it provided an excellent education for the type of man of business needed in the contemporary courts as registrars, judges and revenue agents. The Delhi reformers similarly spent much of their time debating matters of inheritance, usury, relations with non-Muslims, particularly apposite to a period of rapid change. Again, the Usuli branch of Shia Islam which became established in the Awadh court emphasised rationalistic discrimination in matters of religious practice, an approach well suited to a kingdom grappling with problems of finance and British penetration.[19]

Nor was Hindu learning and religion 'otherworldly' to the point that it stultified beneficial social and economic change. Literacy in parts of north India may have been low by wider Asian standards.[20] However, letters supposedly from a Brahmin to Danish missionaries in Tranquebar and observations from a century later describe a well-developed system of pandit schools throughout the Tamil country. If a boy picked up the arithmetical forms taught here:

He may do anything in accounts, and may earn a very handsome maintenance in these countries, especially if he is capable of being an accountant in the

---

[19] J. R. I. Cole, 'Imami Shi'ism from Iran to North India', unpub. Ph.D. diss., University of California, Los Angeles, 1983.

[20] J. R. Hagen, 'Indigenous society, the political economy and colonial education in Patna district. A history of social change, 1811–1951', unpub. diss., University of Virginia, Charlottesville, 1981, p. 284.

Pagods [local silver coins], where receipts and disbursements are very different, and therefore the more difficult [1717].[21]

This widespread practical literacy is consonant with the mobility of men of the ordinary Tamil agricultural castes into the position of managing agents (*dubashes*) for both the incoming Mughal government and later the British.

A similar picture emerges from art. This was not a period of unrelieved stagnation despite the collapse of the culture of the great Mughal cities. It was during these years that the great schools of Indian music entrenched themselves in the regional power centres in both north and south India. Carnatic music was given a great impetus in the courts of Tanjore, while the Afghans of Farrukhabad also established a major tradition. The representation of devotion to God Krishna within the small states of the north is attested to by the vitality of the painting of Kangra and Rajasthan which broke away from the formalism of Mughal miniature painting. Even the architecture of the new centres such as Lucknow or Hyderabad or the Arcot palace at Chepauk, once considered 'baroque' or 'degenerate', can be regarded as a creative response to western European styles and an abandonment of the sombre formalism of the Mughal tradition.

Along with this vitality went conflict. The foundation in 1699 of the Sikh warrior brotherhood, the Khalsa, gave an added edge of communal solidarity, sometimes even aggression, to a movement which hitherto had been syncretic and lacking in militancy. The decline of empire saw an increasingly bitter conflict between the Sunni and Shia branches of Islam, while the implications for relations between Hindus and Muslims of the many and varied movements of Islamic reform were doubtful. As in the realms of politics and the economy, creativity and conflict were deeply interconnected.

The eighteenth century in India was neither a period of universal collapse nor one of easy social transformation. It saw rather a resilient adaptation to political and economic conflict by élites, merchants, peasants and artisans which favoured some of these groups at the expense of others. The myth of universal anarchy and the fall of the Mughal empire has proved persistent in part because it seems to offer an easy explanation for the speed with which the British were able to

[21] 'Mr. Phillips', *An Account of the religion, manners and learning of the people of Malabar* (London, 1717), p. 66.

penetrate and dominate a subcontinent which had held them at bay for so long. But a more balanced and less pessimistic view can also help to explain western domination. For these positive changes in Indian society also helped the British. The growing divorce between the authority and the power of the Mughal helped the East India Company to establish legitimacy within the Indian system. In the same way the military and commercial sophistication of the Indian scene could be turned to the Company's advantage. By paying regular and generous wages its agents could sweep into service men of the north Indian soldier castes; its protection could procure the support of merchant credit-networks; its formal adherence to the science of Indo-Persian justice and revenue management attracted the service of the literate gentry both Hindu and Muslim. At a humbler level the spread of the skills of management, of money-changing and money-use provided the colonialists with the keys to unlock the wealth of Indian rural society. By buying into revenue-farms, monopolies and the political perquisites which had been the stock in trade of the eighteenth-century kingdoms, Company servants and free merchants effectively made the transition between trade and dominion before the authorities in England knew what was afoot. It is to these developments that the next chapter turns.

## CHAPTER 2

# INDIAN CAPITAL AND THE EMERGENCE OF COLONIAL SOCIETY

Europeans had been domesticated into the Indian scene since the early seventeenth century. Like the great Arab, Asian and Jewish trading communities, the Europeans – Portuguese, Dutch, French and English – were attracted to the Indian trade by her fine manufactures of cloth and silk and her agricultural raw materials, notably indigo, pepper, cardamum and other spices. Around their coastal settlements, particularly Portuguese Goa, Europeans already exercised considerable local influence in the wars and politics of the maritime states. However, under the great Mughals their trade had even begun to affect the inland economy in one important respect. Europeans paid for their commodity purchases in silver bullion from the New World, in Japanese copper and sometimes in gold. Precious metals were only found in India in small quantities, yet India's revenues and much of her rents were paid in cash. Europeans therefore filled an important function in providing the raw materials for the coin which made the internal economy – indeed the Mughal hegemony as a whole – function smoothly. In this sense India was already linked to and partly dependent on the European world economy from earlier than was once thought.

The European rôle did not begin to grow significantly until the war of the Austrian Succession, 1744–7. In their attempt to destroy each others' trade and political influence on the southern (Coromandel) coast, the English and French East India Companies became embroiled in the factional conflicts between Muslim military leaders, and these intensified following the death of the Nizam of Hyderabad, Asaf Jah, in 1748. Superior British naval strength and larger capital resources allowed them to beat off the French challenge and at the same time to consolidate their hold over their Indian client, Mahomed Ali, Nawab of Arcot, who was officially a subordinate of the Hyderabad régime. By the time of the Peace of Paris (1763) which ended the Seven Years' War between Britain and France, the French had been reduced to minor intrigue and impotence throughout India.

In 1757 Robert Clive used the now greatly augmented forces of the English Company at Madras in a dispute with the Nawab of Bengal.

This had arisen over the fortification of Calcutta in response to a resurgence of French power, but it escalated when the Nawab, Siraj-ud Daula attempted to expel all the English from Bengal and its riches. Clive's victory at Plassey in 1757 followed by the defeat of the client Nawab Mir Kasim and his north Indian allies at Buxar in 1764 made the position of the British in Bengal unassailable. Hereafter they were able to use the land revenues of Bengal to support a yet larger army, to intervene in the internal politics of other Indian states and decisively to check the threat from the new, more militarily alert Indian kingdoms, notably Mysore and the Marathas, which rose to prominence in the later half of the century.

A critical condition for British success was naval dominance in the Indian Ocean and Arabian seas. By 1760 Bombay and Calcutta both had large merchant fleets involved in inter-Asian trade which could be stiffened by flotillas of the Royal Navy and used to supply hard-pressed coastal settlements throughout the subcontinent. British ships now carried much of India's most valuable external trade to west Asia and the Far East. But the English Company servants also had large corporate and private interests in the inland trade of India. Unable to violate the Company's monopoly on direct trade to Europe, they invested their earnings in the so-called 'country trade'. This created a myriad of ties between them and the Indian merchant communities and made their commerce critical to the finances of Indian states. Indian rulers derived between 5 and 15 per cent of their income from taxes on internal trade. Besides, flourishing trade was essential to the workings of the land-revenue system and the functioning of the agrarian economy as a whole.

The next two chapters discuss the reasons for the British conquest of India between 1757 and 1818 particularly from the vantage point of the indigenous conditions which made it possible. In the past (though not always by contemporaries themselves) Indian politics and trade were seen as irremediably disorganised and self-destructive. Yet from another perspective the British were drawn into internal trade and politics precisely because they were buoyant, volatile and immensely profitable. The large artisan industrial sector was linked through flows of commodities to the agrarian hinterlands and through flows of money to Indian administrations and armies. Trade, politics and revenue were so closely intertwined that any successful entrepreneur had to work in all these fields. The British were sucked into the Indian economy by the dynamic of its political economy as much as by their own relentless drive for profit. In turn, the Company was forced to build an army and develop new administrative methods to contain not so much India's crises of degeneration, but the crises which arose from its long-term expansion. Chapter 2 shows how indigenous entrepreneurs and the late Mughal commercial and fiscal systems were a formative influence in the emergence of British India. Chapter 3 shows how some Indian states were undermined by the pressure of the system of alliances which the Company constructed to contain these intensified economic and political conflicts. It also shows how other states were forced into reconstruction and into powerful resistance which was only narrowly defeated by the Company's political cohesion and gathering military strength.

## BRITISH EXPANSION AND INDIGENOUS CAPITAL

The first chapter has shown that India in the eighteenth century was a dynamic, though conflict-ridden, society. During the years 1680–1750 the waning of the Mughal hegemony had allowed the lower ranks of India's 'hierarchy of kings' to achieve greater autonomy. Following the strengthening of regional centres of power the typical Islamic system of farming out the state's revenues extended in the north and spread to areas of central and south India where it had made little impact before. Military entrepreneurs farmed revenue, engaged in local agricultural trade, and tried to build up holdings of zamindari land in the countryside. The magnates' great households were usually closely linked to merchant houses of Hindu or Jain origin. These firms were essential to political dominion. They could mobilise large reserves of liquid capital at times other than the harvest period because merchants alone participated in all-India chains of trade and credit. Busy markets for agricultural produce and for rights and offices continued to develop in the villages and fixed bazaars of areas which had survived or prospered in the political flux.

These actors – the petty kings, the revenue and military entrepreneurs, the great bankers and the warrior peasant lords of the villages – all represented forms of indigenous capitalism. All derived wealth from commodity trade; all speculated in money profit. The revenue farmers and rural lords were dependent on trade and the operation of rural markets because peasants had to sell their produce in order to pay rent in silver rupees. However isolated they were, even the rural Hindu lords needed cash to buy cannon, muskets, elephants and other badges of power and status.

Yet the interests and culture of these different types of entrepreneur were often in conflict. The Mughal emperors had sought to control local officials through a delicate system of checks and balances. As this system atrophied the way was left open for more severe conflict. The growing intervention of merchants in military finance and soldiers in trade, usury and revenue management provided many occasions for such conflict. Rulers and revenue farmers needed credit to tide them over the periods between harvests as they were required to equip and pay armies month by month throughout the year. This encouraged them to squeeze the merchants and village magnates. Merchants for their part avoided direct management of agrarian taxation and were reluctant to disburse resources which they might need in commodity trades. It was in the interest of the village magnates to husband their resources from all outside interference and to construct their own networks of credit in the countryside. Above all, the successor states to the Mughals were often in conflict with each other, fighting for cash revenues and for the still limited pool of agricultural and artisan labour.

The English East India Company was the great beneficiary of this age of war, flux and opportunity. The Company was able to play off one state against another and offer its own formidable services for sale in the all-India military bazaar. At the same time its own interests in the textile trade encouraged the Company to support the Indian mercantile interests in their periodic conflicts with military entrepreneurs and revenue farmers. The very flexibility and sophistication of these networks for making money inexorably drew the Company and its servants into politics. Politics, warfare and land management all delicately interpenetrated each other. And since the British inherited the expansive but fragile system of Mughal revenue management, the Company soon found itself in conflict also with the Hindu warrior lords of the countryside. The need to 'pacify' this second key element of Indian society forced the European merchant adventurers to construct a larger and larger army, and the framework of an administration which could sustain trade and bring in ever-growing quantities of tribute and revenue.

## THE ENGLISH COMPANY AND POLITICAL
## CONFLICT IN BENGAL

It was in Bengal that the British most clearly exploited the conflicts of the Indian body politic. From the early eighteenth century the Company had emerged preeminent on India's external routes. The disruption of trade on the west coast resulting from turmoil in Iran and Arabia and the Maratha attacks on the old Mughal seaport had encouraged western Indian Hindu merchant groups to rely increasingly on the protection of the British fleet during the 1730s and 40s. The growth of the export of textiles from Bengal between 1690 and 1740, and the burgeoning profits to be made on the triangular trade between India, China and Britain, had gradually built up the importance of Calcutta at the expense of its Mughal counterpart, Hughly. The English Company was much more heavily capitalised than its nearest rival, the French, and was usually able to beat the competition in the Bengal textile market. Since the Company paid for its goods with silver until Robert Clive's coup of 1757, it had developed close relations with the great banking houses of the Bengal Nawabs, especially the famous Jagat Seths and another north Indian banker, Omichand. The desire of the Company (and of its servants trading on their own account) to control textile supplies at source, also encouraged them to try to get direct control of local merchants and weavers in inland towns such as Lakshmipur, Dacca and Patna.

The politics of Bengal in the 1740s and 50s were volatile. Beginning in 1704 when Murshid Kuli Khan was appointed diwan Mughal provincial government had been reorganised. His successors became virtually independent dynasts or nawabs. In their desire to streamline revenue administration they encouraged the consolidation of about thirty great zamindaris. Some of these were long-established Hindu chieftains whose social influence selected them out as useful intermediaries between the nawabs and local society. But several, such as the magnates of Burdwan and Rajshahi, originated as servants of the court who had amalgamated land grants and made permanent earlier farms of the land revenue. They were typical late Mughal fiscal lords in fact, and such magnates were at risk from the envy of a cash-hungry ruler. Even more at risk were the Jagat Seths and allied banking interests whose extraordinary wealth marked them out as milch cows. The Seths' influence had increased as the nawabs themselves removed the checks and balances of the Mughals. The Seths and Omichand gathered all aspects of state and zamindari finance into their hands. They now controlled the Bengal mint, they remitted the periodic payments to the Delhi court; they advanced money on the outturn of the harvest; increasingly they became financiers and through their networks of smaller dealers, purchasers for the British in inland markets.

So a conflict between the different actors in Bengal politics inevitably brought in the British. This was all the more so because, since the Maratha invasions of Bengal in 1742 and 44 and the European war between the British and the French, trading profits in Bengal had been less secure.

The accession to power of the young Siraj-ud-Daula following the death of the 'old Nabob' Alivardi Khan in 1756 provided the occasion for crisis. The new ruler, in an attempt to consolidate his power, began to squeeze resources out of the large zamindars and the Jagat Seths. Siraj-ud-Daula's relations with the British also soured rapidly as the British, fearing a French attack, fortified Calcutta. This and the refusal of the Company to send the customary presents to the Nawab was taken by him as a virtual declaration of war. The British were forced to flee from Calcutta but, for the Indian merchants and zamindars this expulsion could not be borne long; their own interests had become far too closely intertwined with the fate of the Europeans who imported silver and bought the productions of their zamindaris and their trade goods.

The British and the alienated Bengali factions therefore plotted the nawab's overthrow. They could employ detachments of the Company's troops from Madras which had been augmented by the Anglo-French conflict around Madras. On 30 April 1757 Robert Clive, who had been commanding the Company's forces in Madras, noted the conspiracy against Siraj-ud-Daulah led 'by several of the great men, at the head of which is Jugget Seit himself'. In June of that year following Clive's commitment of British support to the conspiracy, he remarked about Jagat Seth that 'as he is a person of the greatest property and influence in the three *subas* [Provinces: Bengal, Bihar and Orissa] and of no inconsiderable weight at the Mogul's court, it was natural to determine on him, as the properest person to settle the affairs of this Government'.[1]

Clive's coup of August 1757, which installed Mir Jaffar as ruler and delivered into the hands of the Company control of the court and £4 million of Bengal revenues and presents, was a fortuitous revolution. A key feature had been the estrangement within Bengal of the court and the fiscal and trading groups which sustained it. In this the coup

---

[1] Clive to Select Committee, Calcutta, 30 June 1857; Clive to Pigot, 30 April 1787, S. C. Hill, *Bengal in 1756–7* (London, 1905), ii, 457, 468. cf. J. Nicholl, 'The British in India, 1740–63: A study in imperial expansion in Bengal', unpub. Cambridge Ph.D. diss., 1973, pp. 81–3.

resembled many other incidents in Indo-Islamic history, the replacement of Mir Rustam Ali as revenue farmer of Benares by Mansa Ram in 1738 or the military and fiscal conspiracy which put Haidar Ali in power in Mysore in 1761, for instance. But there was one critical difference. All this had happened within the context of a system of world trade in which the British were rapidly becoming dominant. The Bengal revenues could therefore be used to counterbalance the Company's trading performance which had been deteriorating since about 1740 as a result of war and competition from the private trade of its own servants. The revenues could also be used to pay for the Company's ever-growing army.

Bengal, which had probably been the wealthiest province of Mughal India, proved an extraordinary prize for the British. It put the Company and its servants at an enormous advantage in dealings with all other states and economies in the subcontinent. The massive Rs 30 million land revenues, secured by good natural irrigation, were deployed throughout the later part of the century to support the poorer presidencies of Bombay and Madras which at this time had no similar rich hinterlands. After 1765 when the Company took over direct administration of these revenues as diwan it was able to support its embarrassed trade profits by channelling them into the annual 'investment' in Bengal goods destined for the London market. Bengal was also a rice surplus area except briefly during the terrible famine of 1769–70. Its produce was shipped up the Ganges to support British inland garrisons. During the second Mysore war (1780–4) and the ensuing famine, rice was despatched to Madras; even Bombay was fed by sea from Bengal during 1791. Besides its weaving industry which was still at a high level of production as late as 1790, Bengal supported a large class of literate Hindu gentry who had early showed themselves adept in both commerce and revenue management.

Yet from the point of view of both the Company and its servants seeking to amass private fortunes it was the particular form of commercialisation in late Mughal Bengal which stood out as their greatest advantage. Buoyant commodity trade and the inroads of fiscal entrepreneurs under the nawabs had resulted in the farming out or marketing of 'shares' of a whole range of enterprises. The Company secured control of monopolies of valuable produce such as saltpetre, salt, indigo and betel nut. Its servants penetrating into the interior after 1757 built up huge fortunes by using political influence to gain privileges and to exempt themselves and their servants from Mughal

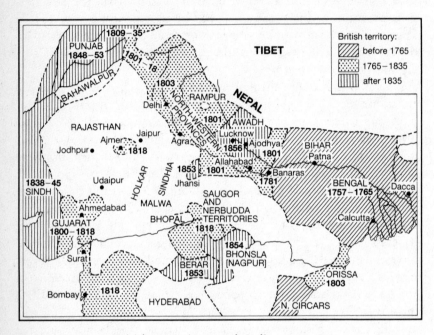

2 British expansion: north India, 1750–1860

custom dues. It was this development which brought to a head the conflicts between the Company and its 'client nawab', Mir Kasim in 1763. The subsequent war against Mir Kasim and his ally the Nawab of Awadh and their defeat at Buxar (22 October 1764) allowed Clive to achieve complete control in Bengal. In 1765 the Company began to administer the revenues of Bengal as diwan of the Mughal Emperor.

A further bonanza by the Company and its servants ensued. When in 1772 Warren Hastings allowed European officials into the hinterland as revenue collectors, they were able to exploit the market in rights and privileges to the full. So, for instance, the Hon. Robert Lindsay became revenue farmer of the district of Sylhet. Aided by the local monopoly of catching elephants and supplying the bazaars of Calcutta with oranges, he was able to acquire a large fortune during the 1770s.[2]

The unstable commercialisation of late Mughal India was, however, modified in one crucial respect. The Company's profits in land-revenue management and private individuals' fortunes built up through the purchase of nawabi perquisites were now used to sustain a system of world trade which stretched to Canton and London. After 1757 the Company virtually ceased to import bullion into Bengal, which precipitated a severe credit crisis in eastern India. Instead it used the proceeds of political power – cash revenues – to finance its trade. Private merchants and Company servants invested much of their earnings in inland trading, so opening up new pressures on the up-country powers of Benares and Awadh. But fortunes were also remitted to Europe by covert means, through Portuguese, Austrian or Dutch agents in Canton and Macao.

Indian capital represented by the Jagat Seths and Omichand connections, along with the zamindars of west Bengal and dissident military entrepreneurs, had provided the support and the occasion for the British coup in Bengal, just as similar groups had supported earlier schisms and rebellions in Indo-Muslim history. They also exploited new fields for entrepreneurship opened up by the coups of 1757 and 1763. True, the Jagat Seths themselves were rapidly deposed from their controlling influence over the revenue and trade of the province. But other indigenous capitalists quickly filled their rôle, though now fronted by and subordinate to the vast system of British peculation and inland trade. The inheritors were men who controlled the skills of administration, literacy and commercial management, as often from the

[2] W. Seton-Karr, *Rulers of India. The Marquess Cornwallis* (Oxford, 1893), p. 29.

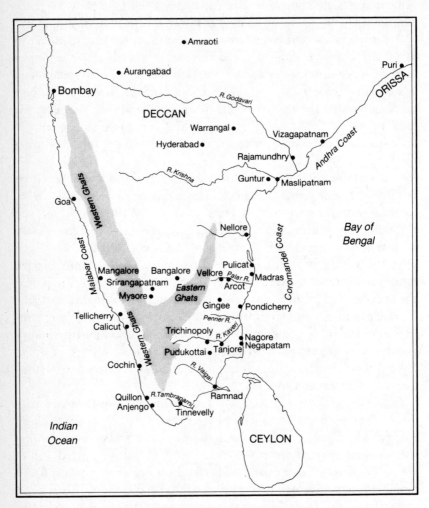

3 South India: physical and towns

literate Brahmin, Vaidya and Kayastha gentry as from the professional Hindu and Jain commercial castes. Most effective were the banians or commercial agents of the most influential British officers who built up large fortunes in trade and revenue management while beginning to buy up land rights in the environs of Calcutta. These were not simply creatures of the British. A man like Krishna Kanta Nandi ('Cantoo Babu'), banian of Francis Sykes and Warren Hastings, was already a successful estate manager and silk trader before he came into direct European employment. Of course, the banians and agents of the later eighteenth century were not fundamentally different as a social group from the *mutsaddis* or men of business who had served the Muslim magnates and revenue farmers and were found in all the eighteenth-century successor states. Yet there were differences. The operation of the new British courts which came into being after 1772, and the greater access to landed income afforded by the early colonial régime, offered them a much more secure base than the uncertain alliance-making and alliance-breaking of the indigenous polities.

Ultimately, pressures from London combined with the need for regular revenues in time of war forced the Company to inhibit the dynamic flow of resources from fiscal through military to trading entrepreneurship. This was the aim of the Permanent Settlement of land revenue in Bengal of 1793, the gradual end to the practice of revenue farming, and the prohibition on private trading by Company servants. First, however, this section will trace the relationship between different forms of indigenous capital and the expansion of British power in other parts of coastal India.

### MONEY AND POWER IN THE SOUTH

In southern India the two centres of Company influence before 1760 were Madras and the rich provinces of the rivers Krishna and Godavari known later as the Northern Circars. The Northern Circars had been the scene of some of the English Company's earliest trading and diplomatic ventures as towns such as Maslipatnam and Vizagapatnam rivalled Bengal in their production of fine cloths and printed designs. The interior of the country was held by large numbers of well-armed Hindu zamindars whose fortresses dominated local market villages. The whole tract was highly productive and commercialised. A British report of 1776 noted that 'the forests to the west produce teak and other valuable woods; they have mines which might furnish iron for many useful purposes; saltpetre is made on the borders of Guntoor Circar; the sugar cane grows luxuriantly in Rajamundhry Circar, and over the whole country are weavers in great numbers'.[3]

Muslim powers in search of revenue and produce had long been influential in this territory, battling with the Hindu zamindars for control of labour and resources. But as in Bengal the early eighteenth century saw the agents of regional powers – in this case the Nizam of Hyderabad – intensifying their pressure. Between 1732 and 1739, for instance, Rustam Khan, local governor of Rajamundhry, fought many campaigns against the Hindu chiefs, forcing them to pay regular revenue and putting over them revenue farmers from among client Muslim and Hindu families whom he rewarded with grants of revenue-free lands. In the following decade Charles de Bussy, a French general fighting on behalf of Hyderabad, warred down more of the Hindu chiefs and expropriated rights and trade privileges.

The new, more intense pressure generated by Muslim entrepreneurs and their Hindu servants for cash-revenue provided the context within which successive British commercial residents in the coastal towns of Maslipatnam and Vizagapatnam penetrated into the market for monopolies and perquisites, both on Company service and for their own private business. While the country was still formally a coastal province under the control of the Hyderabad régime British officials were already working with a combination of Hindu revenue entrepreneurs, such as Jogi Pantalu of Rajamundhry and big Gujarati banking houses, to secure rents of salt, saltpetre and other monopolies and gain control of its forts, the key to local politics. In January 1765, for instance, John Pybus, Chief of the Company factory at Rajamundhry, wrote to Pantalu that the Company must gain control of the district of Mustafanagar 'for it is not only a country very capable of improvements but has so many of its towns so intermixed with those of the Nizam's districts as to give frequent cause for disputes among the inhabitants but the business of the Company's merchants which is chiefly carried on there is liable to interruptions and impositions.'[4] Once again, the lure of a rapid profit attracted the Europeans to the trade of the

---

[3] Fort St George Consultations, 26 July 1776, cited in, *Copies of papers relative to the restoration of the King of Tanjore* (London, 1787), ii, 361.

[4] R. Subba Rao, 'Correspondence between the Hon. The East India Company and the Kandregula family', *Journal of the Andhra Historical Research Society*, ii, parts 3 and 4, 1927, p. 61.

interior, but it was indigenous social conflicts which encouraged their direct intervention.

The Company seized on the growing desperation of the Hyderabad rulers in their contests with the Marathas to prize these valuable provinces out of their hands by promises of regular tribute and military aid. Still, in the first instance it seems to have been the private interests of Company officials which benefited most from the acquisition. During the 1770s men such as Anthony Sadleir of Maslipatnam took farms of produce and rents throughout the Circars. The Collector of Ganjam had a lucrative business in cloth on his own account. Agents (dubashes) of the British drawn from the Komati commercial community of Andhra made large fortunes like the banians of Bengal. The profits of this and the huge private fines taken from the zamindars contributed to a system of peculation which reached as high as Sir Thomas Rumbold, Governor of Madras (1777–80). In essence practices of this sort did not differ greatly from those of Rustam Khan or earlier agents of the Muslim powers. However, there was one important difference: here again revenue farming and the market in perquisites was tied into an international system of commercial and fiscal profiteering. Much of this private wealth appears to have been exported in the form of silver to Macao and Canton through the agency of private British captains and Portuguese commercial houses.[5] Here it was put to use to make further fortunes for the European expatriates.

It was further south in Madras, however, that the triangle of tensions and alliances between the Muslim state, British private capital and the Hindu entrepreneur found its most dramatic form. The Coromandel coast and the rich deltas of the rivers Kavery, Vaigal and Tambraparni had long supported high agricultural production and flourishing external trade. There were old-established Tamil merchant communities, but men of ordinary peasant caste and Brahmins had also become entrepreneurs within the bounds of the petty Hindu states which dominated the river valleys. Other agents or dubashes aided Europeans to secure and strengthen their grip over the region's large and skilled weaver population. Until the 1730s British trade in cloths on public and private account had encountered fewer vicissitudes here than in the north and west, secure in good relations with local rulers and their distant Deccan overlords. But increasingly the reverberations of Muslim state-building were felt on the Coromandel coast. Lieutenants of the rulers of Hyderabad began to increase their

[5] *Fourth Report* (1773), p. 100.

hold on the region's agricultural resources, pushing south and east from the fortress towns of Vellore and Arcot. A savage battle for dominance between the Awadh family of Anwaruddin Khan and his son Mahomed Ali Wallajah, on the one hand, and Deccani Navaiyits, a major administrative service family led by Chanda Sahib, along with northern Afghans, on the other, flared up in 1743. In an effort to protect and enhance their trade during a period of European war, the British had supported the Wallajah family, the French, Chanda Sahib who was ultimately defeated and killed in 1752.

By 1763 British naval and financial superiority had virtually banished French power from the coast and had helped Mahomed Ali Wallajah to consolidate his position as Nawab of Arcot. In the meantime, powerful bonds of dependency had been tied which were ultimately to strangle Arcot and draw the British into direct administrative control of the Tamil country.

In the first place the British had adopted and perfected the mechanism of the subsidiary alliance, which they had copied via the French from the practice of Indian powers. In return for a tribute – a 'subsidy' in eighteenth-century parlance – or the lease of productive territories, the Company engaged to support Mahomed Ali against his enemies and to maintain their own troops in his lands as garrisons. This sort of scheme was to be adopted many times over the whole subcontinent in the next half-century as a mode of securing a stable frontier for British commercial interests and payment for Company troops. In the north, for instance, the Nawab of Awadh acquiesced in a subsidiary treaty in 1765. In practice, however, alliances put intolerable strains on fragile Indian states whose rulers were never likely to be certain of the outturn of the revenue from month to month. Shortfalls in subsidiary payments faced the British with mutinies among their own unpaid troops and led to piecemeal annexation in order to stabilise the financial situation. It is ironic that the subsidiary alliance system, designed to set bounds to British territorial intervention, in fact pointed to its unlimited extension. This issue will be taken up in greater detail in the next chapter.

In Madras the mire of the finances of the subsidiary alliance with Arcot was particularly clinging. For British personnel in Madras had privately lent vast sums to the Nawab, helping to fund his military expenditure and his lavish attempts to establish authority among his Hindu and Muslim subjects. By the early 1760s, therefore, there had developed on the southern coast a tangled series of relationships between British interests and the authority of the indigenous state. Three broad groups of revenue and commercial entrepreneurs were involved. Based on Madras were the Nawab's British creditors, a collection of military officers, contractors and traders chief among whom was the architect Paul Benfield. The capital of these men was derived from salaries and perquisites, trading ventures to south-east Asia, connections in Bengal and above all, from Indian moneylenders. It seems that smaller Indian financiers felt it was safer to lend money indirectly, through powerful British creditors. Here then was a paradox typical of eighteenth-century India: indigenous capital penetrated into the emerging Muslim state system through the good offices of British speculators. A smaller group of Europeans had even lent money to the Raja of Tanjore, inveterate enemy of the expansion of Arcot.

It appears that Nawab Mahomed Ali had gone so heavily into debt to Europeans in part because large scale Indian bankers were less in evidence in the Tamil country than they were in north India, but also because the Nawab hoped to build up a party favourable to his own independence among Company servants in Madras and Bengal. In this he was quite successful. The Arcot creditors consistently put their own interests above those of the Company; in 1776 they were powerful enough in the Madras Council to imprison Lord Pigot, the Governor. Pigot had sought to return Tanjore, which had been invaded by Arcot, into the hands of its own Raja, and so fell foul of the rapacity of the creditors. Pigot's subsequent death as an indirect result of his captivity, was another scandal which drew the unwelcome attention of the British home government to India affairs.

Secondly, there were the military men, revenue-farmers and fiscal entrepreneurs connected with the Arcot court, who acted much as did similar groups elsewhere in the post-Mughal régimes, building up blocks of financial interests, trading in commodities derived from payments-in-kind and providing new entrées into the Indian countryside for their own European creditors. Lastly, there were the Hindu men of business – the dubashes – who plied an uneasy course between service of the Europeans in their private capacity, the Company as a corporate body and their Muslim overlords. One such was Venkatanarayana Pillai whose family on both his father's and mother's side had served the English and French companies since about 1680. Venkatanarayana had been servant to Warren Hastings. He had secured the protection of the Nawab and had helped manage the Company's land-revenue holdings in the environs of Madras. Another relative had been a dubash of George Stratton, member of the Madras council, and later became revenue under-manager of Ramnad district in the far south where he is said to have made a fortune by disposing of government grain at a profit during a famine. Several other relatives and descendents of Venkatanarayana had invested heavily in the bonds sold by the Nawab to accommodate his debts.[6] Agents of this sort played a crucial role as intermediaries between the Arcot and British rulers and the markets and credit networks of the villages. It was the growing confusion of private interests and state-revenue demands which forced the British in the 1790s to reorganise the revenue systems of the Madras area to create a more permanent set of relationships between the state and village headmen.

This skein of peculation was coming to be seen as 'corrupt' in both England and India. It might have survived had not the further development of the Muslim state in south India exposed the impossibility of reconciling the interests of European creditors, the Company and the many varieties of indigenous fiscal and commercial entrepreneur. The Sultanate of Mysore, the major threat to British power in the South, became the catalyst for change. In 1769 and again in 1781–3 Mysore forces penetrated and ravaged the coast. Until its final defeat in 1799 Mysore was a sword of Damocles suspended over the Madras revenues. Throughout a generation of campaigns the Company had difficulty in procuring supplies and military aid from the Arcot régime despite the subsidiary treaty. In 1781 Sir Eyre Coote, the Commander in Chief, wrote of the 'bad consequences arising from the exercise of a separate authority, and the support of a divided interest in the country at so very critical a time',[7] when Mysore forces were poised to take Madras. The Nawab's attempts to husband his remaining resources arose from a pathetic desire to maintain independence and the scarcely concealed Anglophobia of his son Umdat-ul-Umara. Yet it was powerfully reinforced by the incessant demands of his European creditors for repayment. Here then the Company's public interest and that of its servants and European associates were directly at odds.

There was another sense also in which the Company was divided against itself. Until 1785 the Court of Directors in London still in-

<hr/>

[6] S. K. Govindaswami, 'Some unpublished letters of Charles Bourchier and George Stratton', in H. Milford (ed.), *The Madras Tercentenary Volume* (Madras, 1939), pp. 28–9.

[7] Coote to Madras Council, 13 November 1781, cited, Lt Col. W. J. Wilson, *History of the Madras Army* (Madras, 1882), i. 98.

sisted that the first priority in Madras was the maintenance of the annual investment in Coromandel cloths for sale in the European market.[8] Military security and the payment of the army were definitely of secondary importance. As a direct consequence garrisons of the Madras army were constantly in mutiny. The short-term expedient was for the Madras authorities to take over 'direct' management of wealthy parts of the Arcot lands during the long periods of war. This occurred between 1781 and 85 and again in the early 1790. But the cure was as bad as the disease. Direct management merely encouraged profiteering by Company officials and their dubashes, undermining the structure of the Arcot government further and in some cases actually diminishing the land-revenue yields. It also drew the attention of London to Madras in an era when Warren Hastings himself was on trial for 'corruption' and arbitrary acts. Ultimately it was left to Richard Wellesley as Governor-General in 1799 to sweep away the whole ambiguous and irritating façade of Arcot rule. However, world war, a potential threat from Mysore, and a new spirit of interventionist government was required before the piecemeal erosion of indigenous authority by the Nawab's creditors and Indian dubashes became fatal.

## EUROPEANS AND INDIAN MERCHANTS ON THE WEST COAST

In the case of Bengal, Indian mercantile capitalists allied with revenue entrepreneurs and disenchanted soldiers to encourage the expansionist ambition of Company servants. In the Northern Circars and the Carnatic the trading and money-lending activities of the British helped undermine the finances of indigenous states, while Indian entrepreneurs provided the skills and means by which they could appropriate local rescources. On the west coast again the priorities and fate of Indian merchants were to prove a critical spur to British expansion.

On the Malabar coast the process of commercialisation had gone even further than in Bengal or Madras. Bonded serf labour was widely in evidence, but there were large commercial farmers, very high land prices and a flourishing market in mortgages. This resulted from well-developed external and inland waterborne trade routes, down which were carried valuable items such as teak wood, coconut produce and,

8 Ibid., i, 141–2.

above all, pepper. The coast was controlled by a constellation of petty Hindu kingdoms ruled by the Nayar warrior caste and several coastal Muslim states. These petty kings were also entrepreneurs in pepper. But their desire for monopolies and transit duties had often brought them into conflict with the major pepper-trading interest, the Moplah merchants, supposedly the descendants of Arab traders and Indian women, who were linked into the wider west-Asian commercial world. In the south, the state of Travancore had succeeded by 1750 in establishing a viable pepper monopoly and a large army.

The British, based on coastal fortresses such as Anjengo and Telli-cherry, had established a foothold on the coast in the footsteps of the Portuguese and Dutch. Their factors at Tellicherry had acted like a small Indian state seeking control of pepper lands through a series of petty wars against other states and, from time to time, the French. The weak and isolated British authorities at Surat and Bombay did little to encourage their local territorial ambitions. Yet as in other parts of India the decisive turning point in the second half of the eighteenth century was brought about by the expansion and consolidation of a new Muslim state, Mysore. Haider and Tipu desired to control the rich trade of the coast, as much to further commercial links with Muslim west Asia as to break down dangerous dependencies on the Euro-peans. For a time the British in Bombay and Tellicherry held off the Sultan by satisfying his desire for European weapons, but between 1785 and 1789 they were effectively cut out of the pepper trade when Mysore had succeeded in stalemating Madras during the second Anglo–Mysore war.

Mysore rule in Malabar resulted in the further spread of systems of renting monopolies and by an array of new taxes on valuable agricul-tural produce, such as coconut and palmyra trees. The Mysore auth-orities also tilted towards the Moplah merchant community and against the recalcitrant Hindu chieftains. There had long been conflict between local rulers and the Moplahs, most particularly because 'the nobles of the country, having frequent resort to the Mapelets [sic], who lent them large sums of money at exorbitant interest, sometimes upon pawns and sometimes in advance upon the harvests of pepper, cardamums and rice'.[9] With their narrow defeat of Tipu Sultan in the third Mysore War (1791) the Company and private British interests in a now reinvigorated Bombay were enabled to reconstruct their lucra-

[9] N.M.D.L.T. (de la Tour, Hyder's French commander), *History of Ayder Ali Khan Nebab-Behadur* (London, 1784), i, 95.

tive trade in peppers and cardamums. Yet why should they have opted for direct administration of Malabar rather than an indirect rule through the Nayar chieftains? Here the position of the indigenous merchant community was once again crucial. The Moplahs were agents in the pepper trade for the British; they alone had contacts with growers in the interior. However, the reaction of the Nayars against Mysore rule was savage. There were frequent massacres of Tipu's assumed collaborators, the Moplahs. The British appear to have felt that working through the Nayars as independent rulers was an inadequate security for political stability or for the pepper trade, hence the situation necessitated 'the interposition of Company authority to enforce law and order and protect the Moplahs who are a very useful merchant class'.[10] Private traders working within the ambit of the Company's influence also appear to have favoured a 'forward policy' on the coast.

Further north in Bombay's sphere of influence similar considerations caused the British authorities to play a more interventionist rôle. Since the first decade of the century the great Mughal port of Surat had been subject to continuous external threats from the disruption of west Asian trade and also from the expansion of the Marathas against its inland routes. The powerful and influential Hindu and Parsi merchant communities had increasingly sought the protection of the British merchant marine and the safety of British shipping in their voyages to west Asian ports. But the position in Gujarat itself was unsatisfactory. The port of Surat was controlled by a condominium of Maratha and declining Mughal interests. In 1758 the Indian merchants and a faction of Muslim notables urged the British authorities to take the initiative and seize control of the strategically important Surat castle from the weak Mughal grip. This took place in 1759. Indian merchant communities were able to influence Company policies towards expansion on this and later occasions in part because it was they who kept the bankrupt and exposed Presidency alive by remitting money from Bengal through the inland town of Benares during the wars of the later half of the century. After 1784 their economic rôle increased further as the growth of the trade in cotton between Gujarat and China greatly enhanced the importance of western Indian settlements in the financial calculations of both the Company and the growing number of British private traders operating in the area. The Hindu merchants were now not only financiers for Bombay and Surat, but

[10] Abercrombie to Dick, 21 November 1791, cited in B. Swai, 'The British in Malabar, 1792–1806', unpub. Ph.D. thesis, University of Sussex, 1974, p. 133.

also inland purchasing agents for its most valuable new commodity, raw cotton. For their part the merchants and the European houses of agency needed the military protection of the Company and feared the muscle of the Maratha magnates in the Gujarat cotton markets. In this way there developd a consensus for territorial expansion in western India.[11] The Indian merchants, the Company, and the British private traders all desired a more secure Gujarat cotton-growing zone, free from the intervention of Maratha renters and agents which tended to diminish their profits. The wars of Lord Wellesley's era provided the excuse for such surreptitious territorial expansion, his insatiable demands for extra revenue a further justification. Broach, Kaira and Ahmedabad districts were seized in 1803.

## SETTLING THE COUNTRYSIDE

The conflicts between different styles of European and Indian entre-preneurship provided the occasion for British expansion in seaboard India. These conflicts also forced the British to intervene more directly in the countryside. By 1794 the Permanent Settlement of the Bengal Revenues and Lionel Place's settlement of the Chigleput district of Madras anticipated many of the features which marked out the admin-istrative practices of the mature colonial systems. By 1795 Alexander Reade and Thomas Munro had adapted the system developed by Haider Ali and Tipu Sultan to British purposes in the districts which had been seized from the sultans after the war of 1791.

The hectic pace of renting, farming sub-renting and division of revenues, monopolies and royal perquisites which had characterised the later stages of Mughal rule drew in many varieties of enterprising individual; Hindu banians, Muslim grandees, British military officers and Company servants trading privately all made fortunes during the years 1757 to 1784. Three sets of conditions, however, made it imposs-ible that this heyday of the 'nabobs' could continue. In the first place, there was a pervasive feeling and much evidence to suggest that Bengal's hitherto buoyant rural society was in clear decline. The Com-pany ceased its imports of silver in 1757, secure in Bengal land revenues; this precipitated a number of commercial crises as the money supply of eastern India was tightened. In addition to this, the

[11] Lakshmi Subramanian, 'The West Coast of India: the eighteenth century', unpub. Ph.D. thesis presented to Viswa Bharati University, 1984.

Bengal famine of 1769–70, in which up to a quarter of the population perished and many of the survivors were made vagrant, severely diminished production over the next few years. The decline of indigenous authority seems to have exacerbated the problem of banditry and led to a general feeling of malaise. This concern about decline was transmitted to England by enemies of the Company's monopoly and confused with the notion that Indian government was seized by some grave moral and administrative weakness which might, if allowed to proceed unchecked, infect the metropolitan body politic itself.

Secondly, the commercial free-for-all rapidly undermined the pretence that the indigenous political system could survive. The collusion between Indian men of capital and Company supervisors in engrossing further rights and privileges after 1765 forced Warren Hastings to withdraw European agency from revenue collection once again by 1773. But the following years failed to provide a stable system of Indian collection either. In effect too much of Bengal's cash revenue was still being syphoned off into private Indian and European hands in the form of presents, perquisites, remissions and revenue-free grants. Finally, the pressures of the American and French wars of 1780–3 made the need for drastic change irresistible. Lord Cornwallis was sent to India in 1786 with a brief from the directors of the Company to reform the administration of Bengal and also to make British India's external boundaries safe. The Company was faced with a financial crisis since its revenues could not support both its civil and military establishments and the annual investment in Indian good for the European market. Cornwallis argued that the Company's trade itself was in danger 'because agriculture must flourish before its [Bengal's] commerce can become extensive'.[12] The way to create a flourishing agriculture was to stabilise a hereditary landed aristocracy. This would also allow the rapid extension of the cultivated area in north Bengal and the lower deltas and repair the scars left by the mortality of 1770. The notion of a stable aristocracy accorded well with both vulgar Whig notions of the sanctity of property and the more refined doctrine that land was the basis of all wealth, propounded by the French physiocratic philosophers and propagated in India by Philip Francis, member of the Calcutta Council. Moreover, dispensing with 'native agency' and its replacement by a disciplined cadre of European collectors of rev-

[12] Cornwallis to directors, 6 March 1793, cited in A. Tripathi, *Trade and Finance in the Bengal Presidency, 1793–1833* (rev. edn, Calcutta, 1979), pp. 17–18.

enue and judges would hasten the demise of what Cornwallis saw as 'Asiatic tyranny'[13] and the corruption of public office.

Did Cornwallis's settlement abruptly terminate the revenue entrepreneurship of late Mughal India? Certainly, there were some important changes. Great Indian revenue-farmers or Muslim grandees who had previously transformed political service into land-holdings and had moved easily between the worlds of military finance, trade and revenue-farming disappeared from the scene. British 'nabobs' also disappeared as revenue collectors and other public officers were forbidden to trade on their own accounts or surreptitiously to hold farms of revenue rights and monopolies. The British also welded together two forms of property which had been kept separate in Mughal India: the rights to collect and to profit from the collection of state revenue on the one hand, and the rights of proprietory dominion – rental profits, profits on ponds, trees and waste land – which zamindars held at village level, on the other. Henceforward if a man failed to pay his state revenue, his proprietary rights might be put on sale by government, something that did not happen under the nawabs.

On the other hand, speculation in these modified land rights continued to provide the opportunity for rapid advancement as they did under the nawabs. The Permanent Settlement fixed the revenue in perpetuity at 286 lakhs of Company rupees. In the early days of the settlement this brought a large volume of land rights onto the market, as proprietors were unable to pay this high and inflexible demand. The gainers were, however, very much the sort of people who had rapidly increased their wealth over the previous hundred years. Literate and high-caste servants of the older proprietors, particularly Brahmins and Kayasthas of the writer caste bought up zamindari rights as did banians of the British. Pressure on the great estate owners descended from the servants of the nawabs also led to the creation of many subordinate revenue rights. Though they were more likely to remain in the hands of one family this was not a markedly different form of property and profit from the proliferating revenue farms of the old régime.

The effect on Bengal's peasantry is more obscure. Certainly, the provisions of the Settlement gave few rights to tenants, concerned as it was to stabilise a land-owning class. But the prosperity of the ordinary farmer continued to be determined more by ecology, price levels and

---

[13] See, e.g. Cornwallis's minute dated 18 September 1789, in G. Forrest (ed.), *Selections from the state papers of the Governors-General of India. Lord Cornwallis* (London, 1914), ii, 79.

population growth than by administrative fiat. As population pulled back from the great famine, the large farmers (jotedars) of north Bengal were gradually put in stronger position in regard to their share-cropping tenants and day-labourers. Falling prices in the early nine-teenth century did little to improve the lot of the more homogeneous peasantry of central Bengal. The picture here is one of continuity. Many of the institutions of Mughal Bengal, notably the petty rural market places (ganjs) founded by earlier revenue entrepreneurs were drawn into networks of export trade in indigo, opium, mulberry or saltpetre. But social relations based upon share-cropping and control of credit which were already well-established at the beginning of the eighteenth century were perpetuated within the wider world of col-onial trade.

The 1790s also witnessed the experiments designed to stabilise rural society in the environs of Madras. The Company's aim was once again to control the conflicts between different types of rural and tax entre-preneurs which had become increasingly disruptive to regular revenue returns. In particular the Company hoped to eliminate some conflict by diminishing the role of revenue-farmers and dubashes. Once again it was forced to work with some elements of the old régime. In gen-eral the renters and revenue farmers of the Arcot nawabs had failed to gain the grip on rural resources clinched by their counterparts in Bengal. The farming system was therefore swept away. An effort was made to transform payments in kind which had been much more characteristic of the south, into payments in cash. This tended to sever government officers from the volatile internal traffic in grain. Yet, as in Bengal, the British were inclined to enlist in their system men they saw as natural leaders of the people. Here the southern Hindu chiefs – the poligars – were pressed into service. Where these warrior leaders had actively opposed the British or their surrogate, the erstwhile Arcot court, new men were drafted to fill the breach.

There was one exception to this. In the territories conquered in 1791 from the sultans of Mysore (the Baramahal territories) settlement with the poligars or other intermediaries was out of the question because the Muslim rulers had already severely diminished their power across much of the countryside. Reade and Munro, later luminaries of the Madras revenue system, were forced to adopt the practice of making settlements with village leaders, either declining village proprietors (mirasidars) or individual peasant farmers who were called ryots. By 1820 it was this system rather than settlement with larger magnates which had become the norm for the new Madras presidency. The reason for this was not so much the triumph of Munro's deeply held ideal of peasant individualism as an acknowledgement of the rapid changes which had overtaken rural society in the south during the previous century.

## THE BIRTH OF COLONIAL SOCIETY:
### CALCUTTA, BOMBAY AND MADRAS

The accommodation between British power and indigenous capital – a relationship in which Indians were rapidly becoming subordinate – was forcefully illustrated in the coastal cities. By 1800 Madras and Calcutta probably had larger populations than all other Indian cities. The sharpest periods of growth in Calcutta and Hughly were in the aftermath of 1757 and in the decade after the end of the Napoleonic wars. The first period of expansion was based on the immense private fortunes accumulated as British private traders and their Indian banians gained control of the most lucrative sectors of Bengal's economy; the second followed the boom in sales of cotton and opium to China after 1801. Calcutta's total population appears to have advanced from about 120,000 in 1750 to 200,000 in 1780 and 350,000 in 1820. The early counts of Madras population are unreliable, but there was an estimate of 300,000 in 1802.[14] Much of the growth of Madras had taken place after the defeat of the French on the Coromandel coast and the peace of 1763; after this, population appears to have stagnated. Bombay probably had a population of about 80,000 in 1780, though its arsenals and the growth of the cotton trade from Gujarat to China rapidly increased its importance. By 1825, when Bombay had also become educational and administrative capital of a large hinterland, its population had also grown to about 200,000. Probably only Lucknow, Lahore and Hyderabad could equal that figure, while Delhi was barely more than half of it.

At first the Company's Indian settlements reproduced patterns of indigenous urban growth around a small core of European fort and factory. Calcutta in 1760 was still a conglomeration of riverine landing stages, fishing and weaving villages and Hindu holy places such as Kalighat. Communities of weavers (tantis) and small merchants (seths and bysaks) acted as agents, purchasers and commissaries for Com-

[14] A. K. Ray, *Census of India, 1901* (Calcutta, 1902), pp. 59–62; H. Dodwell, *Report on the Madras Records* (Madras, 1916), pp. 59–61.

pany ships. They founded residential communities around the fort just as similar groups had built up Mughal Murshidabad or Hughly. Outside there was little obviously colonial about Calcutta before 1780. Madras was much the same. It remained a stretch of waterside markets and villages typical of settlement patterns along the Coromandel coast. Telugu warriors (the nayaks of Kalahasti) had given the original grants to the Company in 1633, as other inland warriors had patronised the region's diverse merchant group. In turn Tamil merchant communities and men from the Andhra Coast (Komatis) where the Company had early settlements flocked to secure positions as brokers and agents in the business of cloth export. Portuguese convert communities (at San Thome) and Brahmin temple towns (at Triplicane and Mylapore) clustered promiscuously along the coast in the environs of the British fort. After 1763 the Nawab of Arcot settled in Triplicane, adding a community of about 20,000 northern Muslims to the old population of Tamil-speaking Muslim merchants of the coast, the Marakayyars.

The formative rôle of Indian merchant communities in the growth of Madras was expressed through the building and endowment of temples. Indian merchants also took part in the rituals of the European city burgesses, filling several offices in the Madras Corporation which had been founded in 1688. For their part, European officials up to the governors were often involved in the power-play, and even religious contests, of their Indian subalterns. On the west coast the pattern also remained an indigenous one in the early eighteenth century. In Surat the English Company increased its control over its European and Indian rivals after 1730, but it still acted out its rôle of corporate grantee within the carcass of the Mughal city, not openly assuming the rôle of sovereign until 1802. In Bombay patterns of settlement were caste-based, though lightly influenced by Portuguese patterns of town planning and ethnic jurisdiction. Headmen of Gujarati merchants, Parsis and later, Marathas from the interior, established themselves among existing groups of fishing villages, clustering around what is now the site of Mamba Devi temple, later taken to be patron goddess of the city.

Outside the fort enclaves exclusive racial zones and European dominance in city government were quite slow to develop. However, between 1770 and 1800 the easy symbiosis between Europeans and Indians began to decline under the pressures of world war and commercial rivalry. Multi-racial corporate cities in which Indians were justices, members of civic bodies and in which a variety of Mughal offices retained honour gave way to colonial cities in which an exclusively European executive dominated both Indian and European commercial communities.

The change was particularly sharp in Madras where the threat from the French and, later, Mysore, encouraged the local government to redraw the city in its own image. In 1781 following famine and incursions from Mysore, up to 10,000 poor Indian residents (and some say many more) who held no written titles to land were forced out of the city to north Arcot district in order to conserve local food supplies which were barely being maintained with rice from Bengal. Sporadic attempts to create a police force were invigorated by the notion that 'Blacktown swarmed with ... spies in the service of European as well as Asiatic powers'.[15] Government intervened to regulate prices charged by Indian merchants and artisans and in 1787 a Board of Regulation was set up. A campaign against 'dubashism' – that is, the supposedly corrupt association of European officers with Indian capital – was initiated. As late as 1776 European private interests, feeding on the wealth of indigenous magnates through the Nawab's debts, could imprison a governor who acted against them. But by 1800 the executive had greatly strengthened its power against both European and Indian merchants. In 1800 private British merchants were expelled from the Fort and in the next year Government swept away much of Arcot's influence and began to tackle the running sore of the debts.

Alongside these attempts to build an untrammelled European executive went various forms of social control initiated by European residents. There was concern over the 'growth' of the half-caste community, thought to number more than 11,000 in the British coastal settlements by 1788. Protestant charitable organisations hoped to transform these people from carriers of popery and impure blood into a 'Protestant colony of useful subjects'.[16] An orphanage was designed to deal with the problems of the foundlings of the European poor. Conservancy measures funded by a wall tax were imposed on members of Blacktown and the original 'Portuguese' half-caste militia was gradually subordinated to British executive control. The rapid loss of power and status by Portuguese Asian communities both here and in Calcutta was a consequence of the fear of Catholic subversion during the French wars and also of the decline of the powerful Portuguese

[15] Capt. Popham, 1786 in H. D. Love, *Vestiges of Old Madras, 1640–1800* (London, 1913), iii, 323.

[16] Richard Wilson, surgeon, 1778, ibid., iii, 179.

trading houses which had once dominated the routes from the Indian ports to Manila, Macao and Canton. It was reinforced by the trend of official policy which in 1793 barred people of mixed race from government service and emphasised the growing racial separateness of European residents. The British spilled out from the Fort enclave into Blacktown. However, the most notable feature of the years after 1770 was the creation of a market in land within the mirasi villages which surrounded Madras. It became possible for Europeans to buy up large tracts of land for conversion into Palladian-style garden houses which emphasised the new grandeur of white domination within the city and its new colonial character.

In Calcutta too the European population asserted its dominance and within it the executive separated from the commercial community, though the timing was somewhat different. Calcutta's first crisis occurred during the period of the Maratha invasions in the first half of the century and the struggle with the Nawabs between 1756 and 1764. The response was a remodelling of the town's defences and the destruction of the Bengali village of Govindpur to make way for a new fort in the 1760s. Thereafter the European residents (who may have numbered 3,000–4,000 in 1790) gradually spread out from the central Tank Square area of the city to salubrious suburbs such as Chowringee and Garden Reach, so cutting themselves off from the other merchant communities. Wellesley's autocracy saw the creation of a neo-classical Governor-General's mansion and the building of new roads and other public buildings which had the effect of splitting off European from Indian residential areas. Calcutta's second period of growth between 1815 and 1837 was to see the creation of a Lottery Committee which spent money on conservancy and policing among Calcutta's Indian residents. Even Bombay, where European commercial ventures on a more equal basis with Indians persisted much longer than in Calcutta and Madras, had thrown up by 1800 a separate European society, dominated by heads of the Agency houses and Bombay administrators. These features were by slow degrees exported to other towns where British commercial and administrative influence became paramount before 1800: Patna and Mirzapur on the Ganges trade route, or Surat and Tellicherry on the west coast, had small and exclusive communities of expatriates, particularly Scots and Anglo-Irish.

While the British sought a new dominance within 'their' cities during the years 1770 to 1820, Indian society was also changing its form. One striking feature was the decline of Muslim influence and the rise of a more segregated and hierarchical society amongst Hindus. Muslim power had once been considerable in both Madras and Calcutta. In Madras the Arcot palace and its associated bazaars formed a centre of power which at times threatened to overwhelm Fort St George itself. The Nawab had perhaps 500 highly paid staff in 1790 and each of these supported about another ten dependants. European clerks, surgeons, builders and soldiers fronted for a large Indian network of power and perquisites. In Calcutta too members of the Muslim clerical classes and wealthy artisans dominated the middle level of city life as late as 1780 and made up nearly 40 per cent of the population. But in both cities Muslim influence was on the wane. In part this reflected the dismantling of Mughal administrative forms in Bengal and Madras; in part the failure of Muslims to participate in the new commercial opportunities which the Company and European private trade had opened up. On the west coast the decline of the Mughal port city of Surat in the face of rising Bombay marked an even sharper break with the past. In both Surat (1795)[17] and Calcutta (1789)[18] riots by sections of the Muslim artisan communities against the new dominance of Hindu capital and British administration marked the passage of the old order.

At the same time the basis of influence within the Hindu community had changed. In the mid-eighteenth century banians, brokers and factotums connected with senior Company servants had dominated Hindu society in Calcutta. Some of these men had been Brahmins, but the general picture is of rapid social mobility by men of quite humble origin, largely unconnected with the control of land. By the beginning of the nineteenth century there had emerged a much more stratified society based on the control of landlords' rents both within and outside the city. Some banians had made money from the Permanent Settlement and become landlords in the districts adjoining Calcutta. Other families of middle-level literate estate servants had used landed property in the interior as a basis for invading the city in search of service in the expanding British administration. Such, for instance, were the Babus or 'gentry' of Bishnupur, high-caste landowners from Bankura District who bought up land after 1793 and soon created a successful

---

[17] L. Subramanian, 'Capital and crowd in a declining Asian port city', *Modern Asian Studies*, xix, 2, 1985.

[18] *Calcutta Gazette*, 9 April 1789, *Selections from the Calcutta Gazettes*, i (Calcutta, 1864).

pool of patronage for office jobs in the city. The rising value of land in Calcutta also encouraged the development of an Indian urban landlord class. The old community-based divisions of the city broke down. Magnates like the famous Malik family built large suburban palaces in an ornate Italianate style and became rack-renting landlords of the tenement buildings which surrounded them.

Similar developments took place in Madras. After 1802 the rapid expansion of the Madras Presidency attracted numbers of literate Tamil- and Telugu-speaking Brahmins to the city. Such families combined with propertied dependants of earlier dubash entrepreneurs such as the Pachaiyappa family to create a magnate class less dependent on trade and more dependent on office and rents. In Bombay Parsi families (total population about 13,000 by 1813) whose ancestors had been Surat shipwrights and carpenters two generations earlier matched a cheerful westernisation with the construction of large houses in the European style and the acquisition of valuable city property. Bombay's urban élite was to remain mercantile – a reflection of the persistence of openings in trade not completely controlled by Europeans. After the expansion of the Presidency from 1805 onwards increasing numbers of Maratha and Gujarati literate people came to the city in search of service in government offices and new educational institutions.

So cities which had begun as settlements of merchants and artisans within the broad ambit of Mughal rule were transformed into administrative centres dominated by separated European enclaves, now supported by land-owning and money-lending Indian élites. Naturally, these new Indian oligarchies sought to define their relations with the Europeans and with the burgeoning Hindu populations of their cities. This was particularly important because the power of the old ruling families who had guaranteed castes and statuses in rural society were largely absent. Problems of ranking, definition and ritual became even more pressing. Temple-building, the feeding of Brahmins and elaborate death-ceremony rituals represented the pious aspirations of these new rich, so contributing to what a British official characterised as the 'more rigid form of the modern Hinduism'. Yet how were distinctions of ritual to be maintained in these melting-pot societies? In Madras newly urbanising families were absorbed into the ancient divisions of 'right-hand' and 'left-hand' castes. This delicate hierarchy of ceremonial honours and precedents was shaken from time to time by riot and contention, notably in 1707, 1716 and in 1787. But these were patterned and controlled conflicts which allowed magnates connected with the East India Company to build up support and reputation.

In Calcutta problems of ritual and leadership were also acute. In the mid eighteenth century Calcutta had a series of caste courts (*cutcherries*) to adjudicate on matters of ritual and marriage. These were presided over by caste-elders – often magnates associated with Company officials. By the end of the century a looser pattern had emerged with the appearance of multi-caste factions (*dals*) centred on a leader who helped resolve conflicts of caste, inheritance and marriage among his adherents and provided a centre of cultural activity for them. This was the latest of a series of institutions which Bengali society had thrown up over the previous millennium in the face of rapid political change which might bring about a 'mixing of blood' and degeneration of the caste order. Thus the local caste associations (*sabhas*) of the fifteenth and sixteenth century may themselves have been responses to the decline of Hindu kings under pressure from Muslim invasion. Still, these dals or factions were something new. They represented the formation of a new type of social power combining control of land in a capitalist property market with literacy and tenuous commercial connections to the world economy. Dals were to be not only the basis of the newly defined caste order of colonial Calcutta; they were also the basis of the political and cultural associations which articulated the Bengali response to western ideas and British dominion. Associations such as the reformer Rammohun Roy's Brahmo Samaj (1828) and the neo-orthodox Dharma Sabha which fought the religious and social battles of the next generation drew on links and sympathies created through the dals.

Multi-caste factions of this sort in Calcutta and the patterned disputes over temple and processional honours in Madras drew in members of inferior groups and impinged on the lives of the urban poor who lived in large shanty towns in the cities' suburbs. Yet it would be wrong to see these institutions as monolithic tools of control or to see the early colonial period as an era of calm before the era of ethnic and class conflict at the end of the Raj. Calcutta, Bombay and Madras were all the scenes of continuous riots, affrays and demonstrations against authority. In Calcutta the execution in 1775 on charges of conspiracy of the administrator Nandakumar, popularly considered a man of probity, caused a powerful demonstration against the authorities. Within the city regular conflicts took place between mixed gangs of 'Portuguese' and Bengalis associated with liquor shops and brothels. European soldiers often took part in incidents of looting and rape in the port areas. Sir William Jones advancing his view of the need for tougher policing in his address to the half-yearly sessions in 1788 asserted that 'the alarms of burglaries, riots and assaults were almost constant.'[19] Other evidence of severe social tension included regular fire-raising which devastated whole communities of a city where two-thirds of the population lived in thatched straw shanties. No doubt the new concern of the European population for order – reflecting changing social mores in Britain – and concern for their property on the part of newly wealthy Indians tended to exaggerate these events. Yet the high level of communal rioting, affrays and burglaries do give the impression of the strains of rapid urbanisation.

One feature which increased the physical instability of the early colonial cities was the settlement in them of large communities of migrant workers and specialists on a seasonal basis. While the cities' links to their immediate hinterlands were sometimes rather weak, people came from considerable distances to work there. In Calcutta were settled doormen and guards from Patna (four hundred miles away) and from Benares whence the Company recruited its soldiers. Palanquin bearers came from Orissa and many tradesmen came from the Afghan hills. The north Indian population of Calcutta was as high as 30 per cent in 1830 and the population of Madras drawn from the Deccan, Kerala and the north may also have been as high.

Though the Indian sections of Calcutta, Madras and Bombay were increasingly separated off from the European, institutions within the European cities were already having a powerful influence on indigenous intellectual and social life. Indians were associated with the new Calcutta Supreme Court created by the 1773 India Act. The form of law created for these courts was also influential. Hastings, guided by oriental scholars such as Nathaniel Brassey Halhed considered that Indians should be subject to Hindu and Muslim laws. But the very fact of finding and consolidating the wide range of variable practice and custom into monolithic codes of law created new interpretations. Works such as H. T. Colebrooke's compendious treatise on 'Hindoo Laws' always tended to draw on textual and high caste interpretations and to propagate these through Anglo-Indian courts. In this way

[19] *Calcutta Gazette*, 11 December 1788, ibid.

European influences and the British concern for stability helped consolidate the desire of Indian élites for hierarchy and control. The recovery and editing of Islamic and Persian texts by teachers at the Calcutta Madrassah founded by Hastings in 1781 had a similar effect on the Muslim learned classes, reinforcing the search for pure, authoritative and codified statements on law and religion 'to qualify the sons of Muhammadan gentlemen for responsible and lucrative offices in the state.'[20]

So while the legislative assault by the British on the 'corruption' of Indian society was not initiated until evangelical Christian and utilitarian pressures became stronger in the 1820s, European norms had begun to influence the conduct of Indian élites from an earlier period. Indians had become acquainted with notions of positive law, judicial process, western science and, above all, with the notion of linear historical change before the turn of the nineteenth century.

## THE RENOVATION OF COMPANY ADMINISTRATION

It was during the last thirty years of the eighteenth century that there came into being the administrative structure which survived, little modified, until the end of the colonial period. Parliamentary control was asserted over the East India Company at home and in India. Three pieces of parliamentary legislation, the Regulating Act of 1778, Pitt's India Act of 1784 and the Charter Act of 1793 limited the power of the Company and created the India Board of Control by which governments sought to control Indian affairs in London. At the same time the home authorities sought to rationalise relations between different authorities in the subcontinent. The governor-general emerged paramount in his own council in Calcutta. Calcutta in turn gained the upper hand over Madras and Bombay. A central secretariat was created and a professional civil service of collectors and district magistrates emerged from the reforms of Lord Cornwallis.

This administrative consolidation was a continuation of the process of British expansion itself. Territorial acquisition was a response, directly or indirectly, to the complex manoeuvring between forms of Indian capital and revenue entrepreneurs. The danger was not only

[20] H. Sharp (ed.), *Selections from Educational Records*, i, *1781–1839* (Calcutta, 1920), 7.

from Indian powers and principalities engaged in the constant redistribution of resources of taxation and Indian labour, but from Europeans who were also drawn into the process. The subordination of Madras to the authority of Calcutta in 1786 was a response to the gradual entanglement of private Europeans in Madras in a typical Indo-Muslim system of fiscal state-building and military entrepreneurship – what came to be known by the British as the 'Nawab of Arcot's Debts'. In the same way Cornwallis's settlement of 1793 was an attempt to freeze the dangerously volatile processes of revenue farming and fiscal fief-building in Bengal. He worried that otherwise India, already a scene of 'native corruption' would become 'the resort of all the most unprincipled ruffians of the British dominions.'[21] Only a commercial system acceptable to the English landed gentry, creditworthy and separated from political entanglements could be allowed to flourish in India.

For not all the pressures for reform came from within Indian agrarian society. A rationalisation of Company government was also required by the vast growth of Indian country and international shipping and by the slow change in India's commercial relations with the rest of the world. For instance, the Company's stake in western India had to be reorganised and put on a firmer footing after 1784 when the cotton (and later opium) trades to China from Gujarat through Bombay dramatically increased, bringing new profits to private British traders and welcome relief for the Company's own battered finances. This trade was made possible by an act of Parliament of 1784 which reduced the British excise tax on tea from 129 per cent to 12.5 per cent at a stroke. Since raw cotton was the only commodity which the Chinese would buy in large volumes in return for their teas, a secure and well-protected Bombay became an essential feature of imperial policy. The need to supply funds for Company armies, protect British private trade now burgeoning again on the west coast, and to provide funds for its continuing investment in Indian cotton manufactures increased the pressure on the Calcutta authorities to experiment with new systems of revenue management.

Finally, the virtual creation of the British Indian bureaucracy after 1784 was a response to changes of opinion in Britain as well as Indian practicalities. Enlightenment approval of the stability of Asian civilisations was tempered by a chorus of vilification of Indians for the sup-

---

[21] Cornwallis to Dundas, 7 April 1790, cited, W. Seton-Karr, *Cornwallis*, p. 78.

posed corruption of their 'public affairs'. In particular the 'economical reform' of Indian government under Cornwallis was infused with what the editors of the later *Fifth Report* on Indian affairs called 'the strong objections entertained by Lord Cornwallis against the principles and practices of the native Asiatic governments'.[22] The corruption spreading from Hindu merchants and Muslim 'tyrants' to the personnel of the Company – as exemplified by Hasting's career – was in danger of undermining moral integrity as the basis of good government. Cornwallis therefore sought to remove Indians from all but minor offices, to remove Company servants from the corruption of 'dubashism' and to demote the people of mixed race who had hitherto been an underpinning of European power in the Orient. At the same time the executive of government seemed to acquire new lustre. As late as 1785 Company servants had petitioned Parliament as free and equal members of a series of collegiate institutions in the form of presidency councils. They were men imbued with the 'liberties of Englishmen' and jealous of the power of the state.[23] After 1793 patriotism expressed in the form of public meetings in support of the King became commonplace.[24] Some of these changes of view originated in the conflicts between British businessmen and Indian banias and rulers. They also reflected a wider reformation of morality in British society which resulted from the threat of war with revolutionary France and the emergence of evangelicalism among Protestant Christians. Cornwallis and, later, Wellesley fostered a climate of opinion in which drinking, gambling, liaisons with Indian women and gross peculation were no longer admired or tolerated.

[22] W. K. Firminger, *Fifth Report from the Select Committee ... on the affairs of the East India Company* (Calcutta, 1917), i, 80.

[23] 'Resolutions ... by the officers of the Third Brigade stationed at Cawnpore' against the 1784 Act, cited, V. Harlow, *The Founding of the Second British Empire, 1763–93*, ii, (Oxford, 1964), p. 211.

[24] E.g., Memorial of public meeting of the British inhabitants of Calcutta, 17 July 1798, Home Misc. 481, India Office Library, London.

# CHAPTER 3

# THE CRISIS OF THE INDIAN STATE,
## 1780–1820

The British had been drawn into the politics of coastal India by lust for profit and the intricate connections between markets in produce and markets in revenue and political perquisites. The need to control the conflicts of a society in the process of rapid change forced them to elaborate their own style of Indian government. Their success at the art of combining the sale of military services with entrepreneurship in the management of cash revenues embroiled them further in indigenous society. But Indian powers were not hypnotised victims of the cobra's strike. Those which drew on the strength of the subcontinent's tradition of military sultanates and mobilisation of peasant warriors, notably Mysore, the Marathas and the Sikhs, remained a challenge. For these states also had the capacity to put together flexible combinations of cash and men. Moreover, the changes which these martial régimes wrought on rural India were as much formative influences on the Company's nineteenth-century empire as the British revenue settlements. This chapter examines the working out of the processes of expansion both of the British and of the last independent Indian states. First though, it turns to the new pressures on the Company's Indian establishments which finally forged a European military despotism out of the loose congeries of independent mercantile corporations and creole armies which it had been in Hasting's time.

Richard Wellesley's period as Governor-General (1798–1805) represented a new phase of British imperialism in India. The ambition of the Wellesley 'family circle' – his brothers Henry and Arthur along with an assortment of younger military acolytes and Orientalists – was strident. It was complemented by a new aggressive spirit in an embattled Britain and the 'voracious desire' for lands and territories announced by Henry Dundas, President of the Board of Control established to oversee Company affairs under Pitt's India Act of 1784. Wellesley had a clear plan for British India when he arrived in Madras in April 1798 and foresaw two great problems. The first was how to stabilise the military organisation of those Indian states with which the

Company had contracted subsidiary alliances in the previous generation: Awadh, Hyderabad and the Carnatic. Against the background
of world war with the French, the activities of Frenchmen at Indian
courts and an imminent Afghan invasion of north India, Wellesley decided to cut the Gordian knot by outright annexation in the case of
Awadh and the Carnatic, and by engineering a coup favourable to the
Company in Hyderabad.

The second problem was how to deal with the new, expansionist
Indian states, notably Mysore and the constituent parts of the Maratha
'confederacy' which were adapting their fiscal and military organisation to confront the power of the Company. Conquest seemed the
only option in the case of Mysore, still a threat to the rich lands and
trade of Madras. The Governor-General hoped that the Maratha
problem could be dealt with more subtly by concluding a tributary
alliance with the Peshwa, whom he took to be the 'head of the Mahratta nation'. A subsidiary alliance would also, it was hoped, help to
solve the Company's crippling debt problem which had arisen from
the succession of wars. A subsidiary treaty with the Peshwa was finally
achieved at Bassein in 1802.

In the event, British interference in Maratha affairs simply forced
the major Maratha chieftains Scindia and Holkar into direct confron-
tation with the Company. The Marathas were narrowly defeated by
the tactical brilliance of Arthur Wellesley. But the longed-for stability
was not achieved. The Company's debt tripled between 1798 and 1806
despite the huge accession of territory. In addition, Wellesley
bequeathed his successors, Cornwallis (Governor-General again,
1805–6), Minto (1807–13), and the Marquess of Hastings (1813–23), a
formidable problem of pacification. Large bands of mercenary
soldiers (the Pindaris) who had been dismissed from Indian armies
roamed the Deccan plateau, complicating the relations between the
Company and its new Indian client states. The Company's moves
against these raiders and peasant rebels with whom they were associated panicked the remaining semi-independent Maratha states into resistance in 1816. The outcome was their final defeat and the
dispossession of the Peshwa by Hastings.

These events in India were now part of a world-wide strategy dic-
tated by the unprecedented demands on Great Britain for resources
during the Napoleonic Wars. The seizure of Dutch territory in Ceylon
and southern Africa (1795–6) and Java (1811) was brought about by

the alliance of France with the Netherlands. Indian military questions were now debated in an international context. The Cape of Good Hope and Egypt became vital spheres of influence for the Indian Empire. Bengal troops were despatched to Java and the Bombay marine to the Red Sea, while their use in the Caribbean was canvassed. So began the rôle of the Indian army as an imperial reserve, a position which it was to hold down to 1947.

## PRECONDITIONS FOR EMPIRE

The political theory and practice of the Wellesley circle represented the first coherent imperial policy in British Indian history. Clive was an opportunist. Warren Hastings had sought to protect British trade by refurbishing the Mughal successor state of Bengal. Cornwallis and his men were pragmatists, shoring up the Company's defences while purging its administration along the lines of Whig 'economical reform'. The Wellesley generation made fewer far-reaching changes in the structure of administration, but they infused it with a new single-mindedness which emphasised the power and dignity of the state, the morality of conquest and British racial superiority. Just as the French wars saw the emergence of true Toryism in England, so in India the combined threat of Indian reaction and local Jacobinism nurtured true imperialism.

Richard and Arthur Wellesley both asserted Britain's right to India by conquest. The Company, they argued, had saved Bengal by its military protection. Besides, Britain's exploitation was 'founded upon the policy usually adopted by modern and ancient nations in regard to conquered territories'.[1] The summary execution of resisting petty rulers in southern and western India was justified by similar appeals to quasi-Roman precedents. A second order of legitimation was supplied by the notion that most contemporary Indian rulers were tyrannical usurpers of previous dynasties and rights, and could therefore be dispensed with at will so that 'this ancient and highly cultivated people' could be 'restored to the full enjoyment of their religious and civil rights'.[2] This line of reasoning reached its pinnacle in the elaborate denunciations of Tipu Sultan of Mysore who 'violated the law and

---

[1] 'Memorandum on Bengal', S. J. Owen (ed.), *A Selection from the Despatches relating to India of the Duke of Wellington* (London, 1880), p. 503.
[2] *Asiatic Annual Register* (London), 1798, p. 37.

intercourse of nations' while at the same time destroying the basis of landed property under the 'ancient Hindoo constitution'. According to Mark Wilks, one of Wellesley's new political agents and resident in Mysore, the aim of British policy was to restore this ancient constitution and the Hindu Wodiyar house which had existed before Haidar Ali's takeover in 1761.[3]

As yet there was no attempt to deny the legitimacy of properly constituted Mughal authority. The Mughal emperor should be accorded 'reverence and respect' so that the Company could secure possession of the person and continue to participate in 'the nominal authority of the Moghul.'[4] All the same, for Wellesley and his supporters it was essential that the Company and particularly the governor-general should stand forth as sovereigns in dealing both with Indian powers and their own servants. The governor-general 'should have the power of summoning a privy council and should act in it as the King or the Lord-Lieutenant of Ireland'.[5] The ancient corporate nature of the Company councils with their near equality between members should be dispensed with for these 'had the character of an aristocratic republic rather than a monarchy'. It is notable that though Wellesley's successors discountenanced the semi-royal character of the governor-generalship, they nevertheless stressed the need for the Company to be seen as an Indian sovereign in matters such as public ritual and the creation of irrigation works, kingship's traditional duties.

Wellesley never received the backing of the home authorities for a thorough reorganisation of government, but he achieved much through patronage and reorganisation in Calcutta. Through his brother Arthur and a loyal commander-in-chief, Gerard Lake, he laid a firm hand on the Indian army. He kept control of the new administrative service through his brother Henry and jealously circumvented the Court of Directors in London by appointing his own men not only to political office but also to the circles of orientalists and publicists surrounding the new 'court'. He kept direct control of the Political Department concerned with British India's foreign relations and dispensed with the services of the governor-general's council in this area. His private governor-general's office became the training ground for a

---

[3] Mark Wilks, *Historical Sketches of the South of India* (Mysore, 1930), i, esp. 176–87.
[4] Wellesley to Lake, 27 July 1803, Martin (ed.), *Wellesley Despatches*, iii, 214.
[5] E.g. Mornington to Dundas, 1 October 1798, E. Ingram (ed.), *Two Views of British India* (London, 1969), p. 93.

creative new generation of administrators and political agents, notably Sir Charles Metcalfe, Sir Richard Jenkins, and W. B. Bayley.[6] Wellesley also tried to rationalise training for the civil service and infuse it with a new spirit. The Fort William College, which he founded against the opposition of the Court of Directors, was to foster the teaching of oriental languages and to extricate the young public servants from the 'habitual indolence, dissipation and licentious indulgence' which were the 'natural consequence' of living in close proximity to the 'peculiar depravity of the people of India'.[7] The young were also to be distanced from the commercial character of the Company. The old designations of office – writer, factor and merchant – were abolished and the private trade of civil servants was even more firmly discountenanced. Open concubinage with Indian women was disapproved. Gambling and drunkenness censured, and the social life of Calcutta cleaned up. Two Calcutta editors critical of the Governor-General were denounced as 'jacobins' and deported. The Company's old right to make regulations, akin to the by-laws promulgated by English corporate bodies, had been codified by Cornwallis. It was now used vigorously in the settlement of newly annexed territories.

This new emphasis on the power and dignity of the executive might appear to be in contradiction to the concern for free trade expressed by Wellesley's friends and patrons and to the constant denunciation of restraints to trade operated by Indian rulers. But free trade always worked in symbiosis with state power and imperial expansion in India. Wellesley and his circle certainly wanted to open Indo-European trade to British private merchants and resisted the interests within the Company and metropolitan ship-owning circles which wished to continue strict monopoly. The immediate aim was to grab back from neutral nations the trade which they had won since the beginning of the French wars. This in turn was expected to improve the Government of India's capital position and credit. In addition English shipping could be 'more easily controlled and regulated' than sundry Danish, American or Arab fleets. Ultimately the policy was to make 'London the throne of commerce of the world' as he had declared in a parliamentary debate on Irish affairs in 1787.[8] Yet the Wellesley circle did not espouse the doctrinaire type of free-trade phil-

[6] Personal narrative of N. B. Edmonstone, Venn papers, Centre of South Asian Studies, Cambridge.

[7] Minute in Council at Fort William, 18 August 1800, *Asiatic Annual Register*, 1802, 129.

[8] R. Pearce (ed.), *The Wellesley Papers* (London, 1914), i, 15.

osophy. They were too concerned for the power and dignity of the state in India. If government intervention was required this was perfectly appropriate according to free-traders, including Adam Smith himself, who saw state control to be essential in times of war. So in internal policy Wellesley continued Cornwallis's policy of reducing multiple duties on trade and rationalising bazaar taxes. Yet his government also continued monopolies in salt and saltpetre and forced Indian merchants into the service of British armies. In the interior Henry Wellesley and his contemporaries founded markets through state power, making vigorous efforts to facilitate the transport of raw cotton to the seaports and to sell British goods at fairs and markets in north India. In practice the Company's monopolies survived through to 1833 (when it lost the monopoly of the China trade) largely unscathed while the Company itself became more of a government and less of a commercial enterprise.

The Company's rule in India had come to rest primarily on its military despotism. In the 1780s it had been fought to a draw by both Mysore and the Marathas. Cornwallis's much-heralded defeat of Tipu Sultan in 1792 was really only a local war in which Mysore preserved its richest revenue-bearing areas. Circles close to Wellesley ridiculed the possibility of an overland French attack on India and the Duke of Wellington later stated that French naval equipment was not adequate to the task of sea-borne Asian warfare. Yet there was fear that up to two hundred assorted European, Catholic and 'Jacobin' advisers at Indian courts might enhance the military capability of Indian states to the point where they could defeat the British. This was more likely since the Company's army had its weaknesses. Its European officers formed a tight-knit body, jealous of their rich perquisites and a system of promotion which favoured seniority rather than ability. An attempt by ministers in London to gain control of the Bengal army through the agency of Sir John Shore (Governor-General, 1793–8) was fought off in a near mutiny in 1796.

Yet even before the final showdown with Tipu in 1799 the Bengal army had displayed strengths on which the Wellesleys were to build. From 1765 the Company had begun to recruit from the major breeding-ground of India's infantry in eastern Awadh and the lands around Benares. The high caste Bhumihar and Rajput squireens of these areas (known as *purbias* or 'easterners') had been recruited by Muslim powers since the fifteenth century. The waning of Mughal power and the limits placed on the armies of its allies demanded by the Company forced them to seek British service if they were to retain their village status. By 1800 recruiting agents were at work in the region which was to provide up to eighty per cent of Bengal troops until the rebellion of 1857. Retired soldiers in turn created links between the distant European rulers and the Indian countryside which were to underpin the British systems of rural control.

The Bengal army was a reserve of manpower for operations elsewhere in the subcontinent. When Cornwallis sent Bengal troops south in 1791 there were some desertions. Yet the force was critical in stiffening the back of the weak Madras army which had yet to find a reliable recruiting ground, and comprised a less cohesive body of Eurasians, Telugu warriors and Muslims who had failed to get service in Mysore. Bengal soldiers were also used in the Ceylon, Java and Red Sea campaigns. But Bengal was important to the emerging Indian army in another sense too. Company sepoys' pay was high; infantry received about Rs 80 per annum, several times the pay of a specialist field worker. The regularity of this pay which distinguished British from indigenous Indian armies was crucially dependent on the Company's possession of the rich revenue-bearing lands of the Bengal Presidency. Seaborne support and access to new musket technology doubtless gave the Company a slight edge. Yet the mystique of the Bengal army's prowess was also an important if unquantifiable asset. The carefully drilled red-coated sepoys and their white officers inspired a kind of awe in their adversaries. In Maharashtra and in Java the sepoys were regarded as the embodiment of demonic forces, sometimes of antique warrior heroes. Indian rulers adopted red serge jackets for their own forces and retainers as if to capture their magical quality.

After 1790 the pace of British military expansion in India speeded up notably. Between 1789 and 1805 the Company's total strength increased from about 115,000 to 155,000, making it one of the largest European-style standing armies in the world. More important, the Company, which had been at the mercy of Indian light horse in earlier wars, created a strong cavalry arm. Not only were the numbers of cavalry tripled but the state itself provided horse and arms, a system which was imposed on Britain's tributary allies over the next generation. Indian troopers who owned their own mounts had been reluctant to risk them in close encounters. The importance of cavalry was two-fold: first, it protected and helped supply cumbersome infantry and artillery columns; secondly, it made possible quick pursuit and control over a fractious countryside. Wellesley, for instance, attributed his speedy defeat of the Maratha chief Daundia Waugh, 'heir to Tipu' in 1800 to cavalry pursuit, and cavalry was later to be crucial in mopping-up operations against the Pindari raiders. Cavalry power was thus an important guarantee of the capacity to extract revenue. Bringing in strong horses from Europe and southern Africa the Company's army was able to build up an excellent pool of mares, while the decline of pasturage and the loss of horse-breeding skills in British India tended to weaken the cavalry capability of its enemies. Along with cavalry, there was a clear improvement in the equipment and training of the Company's artillery and the quality of its musketry. This was important because the Indian powers were themselves rapidly increasing their ordnance and because effective gunnery was vital to siege warfare against small fortresses as the British strove for mastery in the interior.

Another major improvement in the Company's army can be attributed directly to Arthur Wellesley. No formal commissary's department concerned with feeding and supplying the army was constituted until the following decade. But Wellesley insisted on detailed control and regular payment of the vast private enterprise of pack-bullock herds which attended Indian armies. By this means he was able to ensure the provision of fodder for and transport of the long-range field guns which he regarded as so crucial for success in battle. Clearing large swathes of jungle and building roads into the eyries of rebellious Nayar chieftains, Arthur Wellesley also pioneered the use of ecological warfare by Europeans against Asians. In turn success brought greater efficiency. The defeat of Tipu in 1799 left in the Company's hands nearly 250,000 strong white Mysorean draught cattle which proved vital in the Deccan campaigns of the following decade.

The development of military organisation had its repercussions in the field of government and politics. Despite the Wellesleys' stated desire to keep military and civilian, judicial and executive powers separated, they recognised that Company rule was a military despotism outside Bengal. The revenue systems adopted by Munro and Reade in the areas seized from Tipu in 1792 (the progenitors of the *ryotwari* system) were simple adaptations of the revenue systems of the Sultans, designed to provide money to pay for armies. Military personnel filled the vital office of resident at the Indian courts. The young

soldiers despatched by Wellesley into Mysore and the Maratha territories and to Delhi transmitted vital political and military information
which was stored in the reorganised Foreign and Political Depart-
ments in Calcutta. Whereas Hastings had often worked in the dark his
successors after 1792 had at hand detailed family histories of most of
the ruling families in India, assessments of their military capabilities
and notes on their commercial resources. A Persian Secretariat dealt
with correspondence in Indian languages and acquired great com-
petence in bending to British advantage the systems of precedence and
ceremonial gift exchange among the Indian powers. The Persian Secretary, N.B. Edmonstone, was appointed as superintendent of Wellesley's 'Governor-General's Office' which collated information and
dealt with 'those branches of the administrative government which the
Governor-General deemed it proper personally to conduct'.[9]

Much of the information which enabled the British to control and
tax their Indian possessions was gathered by army and naval officers
and resulted from the growing military character of the Company after
Cornwallis. Officers accompanying residents on their postings extended the techniques of the great cartographer James Rennell to the
Indian interior and drew the maps which were later filled out by the
revenue surveys of 1814–35. Investigations of Indian resources, particularly on the west coast were driven by the need to find suitable
sorts of timber for the Bombay marine. Yet not all of this explosion of
information on India in the last ten years of the century resulted from
military and practical incentives. There was also a change in the orien-
tation of European knowledge about Asia. As late as 1770 there had
been a preoccupation with issues regarding Brahminism and the
Indian scriptures. Hastings' Calcutta Madrassa signalled a greater interest in Indian languages and literature among the rulers, but it was in
the last fifteen years of the century that the real change came. The
Permanent Settlement brought officials for the first time directly into
contact with problems of Indian village organisation and concepts of
right. Colebrooke's *Remarks on the Present State of Husbandry in
Bengal* (1795) with its quantification and concern for peasant production became the pattern for future domesday books of parts of the
Indian empire, providing a standard against which future topographers, Francis Buchanan and Walter Hamilton, assessed the societies
they investigated.

[9] Edmonstone narrative, Venn Papers.

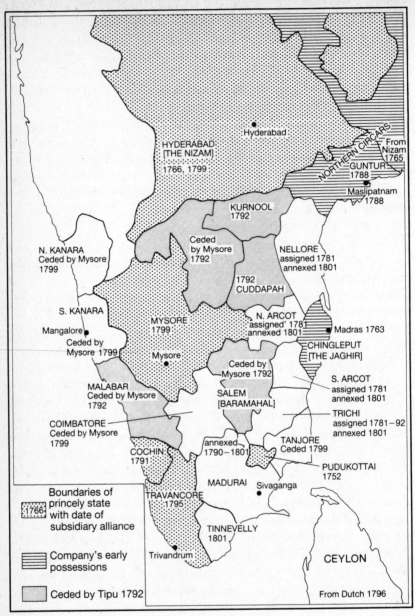

4 British expansion: south India, 1750–1820

These developments mirrored the contemporary passion in Britain and Europe for social statistics, itself a harbinger of the emergence of the modern state, but it was also something with independent scientific origin. The eighteenth-century concern with belief and systems of value gave way to the empirical documentation of known facts, the creation in social studies of analyses and taxonomies which distantly reflected the norms of Linnean botany. Just as Captain James Cook's aides had been schooled in the new botany, so the greatest of the Anglo-Indian topographers, Buchanan, was a medical doctor and botanist by training.

## THE DECLINE OF THE SUBSIDIARY ALLIANCE

The rôle of commercial, financial or strategic considerations in this great wave of expansion is best analysed region by region. The crisis which the Governor-General saw among his allies, and the danger from his enemies resulted largely from the corrosive effect of the British military presence on the delicate politics of the Indian states. 'Anarchy', military weakness and 'corruption' were not as the Victorian historians considered, the consequence of effete rulers and oriental despotism. They resulted quite often from British fiscal and diplomatic intervention in Indian affairs. The subsidiary alliance system, as noted in the last chapter, had been pioneered by the French in their dealings with Hyderabad during the 1740s. It was adopted by the Madras council in treaties with the Nawabs of Arcot and in 1765 imposed by Clive on the Nawabs of Awadh. Under these treaties the Indian ruler paid for the presence on his soil of Company troops which 'protected' him against internal and external aggressors. The arrangement was presided over by a Company official (later resident) at the court of the Indian ruler who was given privileged access to him and was able to influence his relations with peers and overlords. The essential advantage for the Company, of course, was that it limited the costs incurred in the defence of its own borders.

Yet the subsidiary alliance system posed great problems both for the Indian states and for the British. British military supremacy rested above all on the Company's ability to pay its Indian troops regularly. However, the Mughal revenue system had been flexible, even unpredictable from month to month. It depended on the outturn of the crops, adaptable systems of credit and revenue remissions along with the mutual cooperation of (or bargaining by conflict between) a host of rural intermediaries, revenue farmers and moneylenders. Indian rulers subject to a British subsidiary alliance all fell rapidly and irremediably into arrears. The stronger became the British pressure to pay, the more it impaired the rulers' ability to produce a regular subsidy for the troops. As Arthur Wellesley noted, since the tribute was

generally the whole or nearly the whole disposable resource of the state, it is not easy to produce it at the stipulated moment. The tributary government has to borrow at usurious interest ... to take advances from aumildars [revenue farmers] and to sell the office of aumildar.[10]

This in turn led to avarice, extortion and a decline in respect for the indigenous régime. Ultimately the British government was 'obliged to interfere in the internal administration in order to save the resources of the state' and to avoid 'employing the troops in quelling internal rebellion and disorder, which were intended to resist the foreign enemy'.

The manner in which stringent demands for tribute or subsidy could lead to revolt and British annexation was first seen in 1781 when the British stepped deeper into the Ganges valley after the defeat of Raja Cheyt Singh of Benares. Benares had become a major crossroads for trade and finance in north India. But since 1775 it had also provided Rs 45 lakhs per annum to the Company's treasury as an annual tribute which had been paid to Awadh before 1775. Hastings pressed relentlessly for regular payment as war spread through India in 1779. But the system of revenue farming which was now common throughout the region was unpredictable in times of crisis. Poor harvests occurred and the Raja found himself squeezed between an implacable Governor-General and an intractable countryside. A revolt broke out in the city and hinterland which put at risk the life of Hastings, who was temporarily in Benares. Cheyt Singh's revolt was, however, quickly snuffed out and a new Raja subservient to the British was installed, with the resident now virtual ruler of the territory.

Much the same happened on a grander scale in Awadh itself. Awadh was the classic Mughal successor state. The dynasty which had established itself here after 1720 was nominally subordinate to the Mughal court and continued to remit a diminished quantity of revenue to the

---

[10] Memorandum on Awadh (c. 1798), Owen (ed.), *Wellington Despatches*, pp. 476–7.

centre until the late 1780s. A small élite of Mughal warriors, literati and gentry stood poised over a vast Hindu countryside ruled by petty chieftains of Rajput origin. In order to guarantee regular income the system of farming out revenue had been generalised in the early part of the century and about two dozen great magnates accounted for most of the state's revenue and much of its military strength.

The British had, since 1765, received a large annual tribute of Rs 75 lakhs or more in payment for the Company troops now stationed at three places in Awadh to 'protect' it from internal and external enemies. Using their political clout, the British officers associated with these garrisons grabbed a monopoly in several of the most important items of trade in the realm, thus reducing the ruler's income from customs and transit duties. More seriously, the pressures of the huge annual demand disrupted the fragile and multi-layered political system. At times the rulers connived in a process of decentralisation which hid the true revenue resources of the state. At times pressures from revenue contractors forced local notables into revolt, while peasants and merchants moved to areas of lower taxation. In 1781 attempts by British temporary collectors under the direction of the resident at Lucknow to extract a larger revenue resulted in a mass rising of Rajput landholders and their liegemen in southern Awadh, an explosion which foreshadowed the rebellion of 1857. A chastened Hastings drew back, and over the next fifteen years British demands on Awadh were reduced. A new commercial treaty negotiated by Cornwallis in 1788 struck at the worst abuses of the private trading system.

However, the damage to the power and credibility of Awadh was already too great. The state's pressure for enhanced revenue gave rise during the 1790s to several revolts. The most serious were in the west where the proud Rohillas and their Rajput allies sought to recreate the independence they had enjoyed before the Nawab and his English supporters invaded the territory in 1774 in a search for loot and revenue. The Awadh soldiery was in a state of constant disaffection because of massive arrears in pay. Meanwhile some of the richest areas of the realm were controlled not by the Nawab but by great revenue farming magnates such as the eunuch Almas Ali Khan who in the 1790s could mobilise more troops than his master in Lucknow.

The situation worsened after Asaf's death in 1797. Sir John Shore suspicious of the 'loyalty' of Asaf's supposed son, Vazir Ali, engineered a succession dispute and managed to have Vazir Ali declared illegitimate, replacing him with the more pliant Saadat Ali Khan who had been long under British tutelage. Barely had Wellesley set foot in India in 1798 than Vazir Ali, who had been exiled to Benares, murdered the district collector and fled the city to raise rebellion in alliance with Rajput warriors of the Awadh hinterland and with the connivance of some of the rulers of the northern frontier. It was the nagging fear of Awadh as a dangerous frontier for British Bengal and Benares which determined Wellesley to push for the abdication of the new Nawab Saadat Ali Khan during 1799 and 1800. It seemed possible that the ruler of Afghanistan, Zeman Shah, who had already invaded the Punjab in 1797, might proceed into Hindustan picking up support from the Rohilla Afghans and even from Almas Ali Khan. The Nawab refused to abdicate in the manner of his peer in Arcot, but was eventually forced to cede all his western territories and those along the rivers Ganges and Jumna. The rump of Awadh survived until it too was annexed in 1856. But the realm, cut off from its most valuable trade routes, subject to continued interference from the British resident and suffering a great outward haemorrhage of its capital to British cities and into Company bonds, became little more than a backwater of the silver age of Mughal culture in north India.

What was the rôle of commerce in this story of erosion and annexation? It is quite clear that Europeans were in control of a significant sector of Awadh's economy before 1800. They had little presence in the most important trades – salt, grain and inferior cloths. But army officers before the commercial treaty of 1788, and private merchants afterwards, dominated a large part of the trade in finer cloths and the powerfully expanding commerce with Bengal in items such as raw cotton. This European commercial penetration affected Awadh in two ways. Firstly, free passes and privileges extracted by Europeans and their Indian allies denied important sources of a revenue to the state so aggravating its fiscal and political crisis. Secondly, the alliance between powerful British commercial interests and semi-independent magnates strengthened the forces of decentralisation against Lucknow. Almas Ali Khan, for instance, lent money to British private merchants on a large scale and helped them with their purchase of cloth in the inland markets. Groups of these traders influenced the British resident at Lucknow to keep the centre's hands off their ally. It does not seem that private traders intrigued for or even welcomed the direct cession of large parts of Awadh in 1801–2. And it is certainly clear that the Governor-General was not himself motivated by simple commercial interests in his decision. Yet the buoyancy of British trade had certainly acted to further weaken Awadh's ailing polity.

In the autumn of 1800 Wellesley's government forced Nawab of Arcot to cede to them the districts which later formed the heart of the Madras Presidency in return for a small fixed pension. The arrangement followed the pattern already set in the relations between Madras and the small but rich state of Tanjore which had been annexed in 1799. The Company had been in Madras since 1639, and, as the previous chapter showed, the slow expansion of its cloth exports to Europe and south-east Asia had put the British in a dominant position on the Coromandel coast as early as 1756. The question then arises as to why the Company allowed the semi-independent state of Arcot to exist so long in the heart of its second most important enclave and why it finally annexed these territories in 1800. The answer to both these questions seems to lie in the weakness of the Arcot régime.

Compared to Awadh or even to Mughal Bengal before 1757, Arcot was a dependent régime. It was a fragile conquest state on the fringes of Muslim India, poised uneasily over a Hindu society dominated by warrior chieftains. Only in the ancient areas of rice cultivation on the Penner river and in the environs of the great fortress town of Trichinopoly had the Nawabs' revenue agents established a firm grip over the countryside, and his control over them was never sure. As a client of the ruler of Hyderabad, himself only an agent of the Delhi Emperor, the Nawab of Arcot's legitimacy rested on conspicuous Islamic piety combined happily with the active patronage of the religious institutions of his Hindu subjects. He had survived the wars against the French and their allies as a result of the self-interested support of the British in Madras. With the rise of aggressive and capable rulers in adjoining Mysore the very survival of the state rested on the uncertain support of the Company's Madras army which was secured under the initial alliance of the 1740s. But as in the case of Awadh the financial demands of the alliance merely served to erode the basis of the state, and ultimately to provide the conditions for British annexation.

The longevity of Arcot compared with the Nawabs of Bengal was a reflection of the ease with which the state could be suborned by private European interests. In their capacity of exporters of cloth the Company and its servants could use the Nawab's authority to coerce the hinterland weavers and create monopolies of their produce. In their more important capacity as usurers living on the Arcot revenues Company servants had an interest in keeping the state formally independent. But this was not a situation which recommended itself to Wellesley. The wars of the 1780s and 1790s, revenue peculation by British dubashes or Arcot officials and the emigration of weavers and farmers to Mysore had irreparably damaged the state's revenues. The Arcot debts continued to provide a transfusion of blood to sustain the private interests of old Madras into the age of 'economical reform' pioneered by Cornwallis and Wellesley. Private interests were even conspiring with dissident factions at the Arcot court to play off the Company against the Crown by instituting a long series of plaints and petitions to the Prince of Wales in London. An alleged correspondence between the new Nawab Umdat-ul-Umara and Tipu Sultan during the Mysore war of 1799 and a further failure by the Nawab's officials to provision British forces effectively sealed the fate of independent Arcot. The state was swept away in January 1800. Here once again the expansion of British commerce on the Coromandel coast had been a precondition for British annexation. The conflict between different groups of indigenous and European capitalist and fiscal entrepreneur had drawn British influence deeper into the fabric of the indigenous state. Yet it had been the pressures of the subsidiary alliance system which rendered indirect rule unviable by straining Arcot's authority to breaking point.

The final buffer state in Wellesley's *cordon sanitaire* around the Marathas was Hyderabad. Here the cost of administering the vast and thinly peopled uplands of the Deccan prohibited formal annexation. A new subsidiary alliance in September 1798, along with a subsequent commercial treaty (1802), clamped home the Nizam's dependence and expelled the French battalion which had given him a little room for manoeuvre in his relations with the British. Of course the Nizam's options had long been limited. Since 1766 the Company had occupied the rich coastal weaving districts of his domain and in 1788 it had secured control of the district of Guntur. Hyderabad's own control over the Telugu warriors of its outer districts was so weak that the annual tribute which the Company continued to pay for these districts was crucial to its survival. The British already had a powerful group of supporters at Hyderabad. The party led by the diwan was made up largely of minority Shia Muslims and north Indian Hindus; it tended to look to the British for support in internal factions and for protection against the Marathas. The anti-British party based on local notables and centred on the ruler's household corps was more distant from financial and administrative control within the domain. As Hyderabad lost more of its outlying districts in 1800–1, it was drawn firmly into the British orbit as a succession of powerful residents built up this alliance with the diwans of the day

## MYSORE AND THE MARATHAS

Wellesley's annexations were mainly the longer term results of the erosion of the pluralistic polities of the Mughal successor states by the British connection – and in particular by the pressures generated from the subsidiary alliance system. But the occasion and justification for these annexations were attempts by the militarily stronger states – Mysore and the Marathas – to escape from the same trap. The society and administration of these two powers were rather different. The Maratha states rose as a loose alliance of Deccan agriculturalists and pastoralists seeking the status of Hindu warrior kings though still operating within the Mughal political system. The Mysore of Haidar Ali and his son Tipu Sultan was, by contrast, a Muslim conquest state created in 1761 by a coup against the Hindu ruling house, which drew on the support of the army and Hindu bankers. The new Mysore was maintained by rigorous revenue management and a growing emphasis on the power of the sultan. Both polities were seen as a threat to British dominance because they had begun to develop a capacity in infantry and gunnery which challenged the Company's army.

Mysore was based upon an ancient core of royal power in south India. The black soils of its northern districts grew excellent cotton. To the west the land was watered by streams from the western ghats and through the heartland ran 1,000 miles of the river Kavery and its tributaries. In addition ancient irrigation works provided a further 1,200 miles of canals and large numbers of irrigation tanks.[11] The natural products and crops of the region were well balanced and easily supported its relatively sparse population. Mysore in the time of Haidar Ali (d. 1782) also had a large artisan population and a flourishing entrepôt trade. Srirangapatam, the capital, and the newly founded Bangalore were a crossroads for the south, receiving goods from the east and

[11] *Mysore and Coorg. A Gazetteer Compiled for the Government of India* (Bangalore, 1877), i, chs 1–2.

west coasts and from Hyderabad in the north, and exporting its own wood, grain and cloth in return.

Haidar and Tipu both struggled to bring a larger share of this wealth under the direct control of the state. Haidar followed the policy of earlier Hindu kings (notably Chika Devarayya III, 1672–1704) of attempting to discipline the Telugu warrior chieftains and raise the state's revenue portion to something more like the supposed Mughal 30–40 per cent of the agricultural product. The Mysore rulers pushed for money taxation in areas where there had customarily been only grain assessments. Haidar Ali had sought to attract into his realm outside merchant communities. He also encouraged peasant farmers to migrate from nearby territories, including those of the Company. This policy succeeded because until the last days of Tipu's reign the state's increment was drawn not from the cultivators but from the elimination of poligars and intermediate revenue agents. These policies brought Mysore a degree of prosperity which even its English enemies could not ignore. A British observer wrote of it as 'well-cultivated, populous with industrious inhabitants, cities newly founded and commerce extending'.[12] Yet by the last decade of the century the strains of war and the huge indemnity squeezed out of Mysore by Lord Cornwallis in 1792 was beginning to tell. Tipu Sultan was determined to pay off the indemnity as soon as possible to avoid falling into a state of indebtedness such as that which had crippled Arcot or Awadh. He pensioned off the old revenue managers, instituted a new system of tax collectors and tried to push up the land revenue over much of the country by a further 25 per cent. Suspicious of the older Deccani nobility he sought to promote new families into his administration and to create an army of Arab and African mercenaries or personal dependants. Forced loans from merchants and rigorous monopolies in agricultural produce and rural industries contributed to the picture of savage despotism which English apologists loved to paint. But even in the 1790s Mysore's economy had points of growth while still supporting an army of well over 60,000 men.

The Mysore army was strong in those areas where the Company, and especially its Madras contingents, was weakest. The Mysore light cavalry was 'the best in the world' according to Arthur Wellesley and

---

[12] Edward Moore, 1794, cited A. Sen, 'A pre-British economic formation in India of the late eighteenth century', in Barun De (ed.), *Perspectives in Social Sciences* (Calcutta, 1977), i, *Historical Dimensions*, 46.

its harrying of Cornwallis's army in 1792 was one reason why the Governor-General had come to terms with Tipu and achieved only a limited victory. Mysore also had a useful force of irregular marksmen who were drawn from the Telugu huntsman caste (the Bedas or Beydaru). These had been settled by Tipu in the north of his domains where they could dominate the countryside, but were ready for military service.[13] Irrigation specialists from the villages also provided a good supply of sappers and miners. But the most valuable of all Tipu's military resources was the huge bullock 'park' of white Deccan cattle which was later used by the British in their war against the Marathas.

Under the pressure of British encirclement, Haider and Tipu sought to invigorate their state. Both rulers fought for access to the Indian ocean on the west; this was the rationale for their intervention on the Malabar coast. As Haidar is supposed to have said, 'I can defeat them [the British] on land, but I cannot swallow the sea'. Tipu in turn realised that the decline of Muslim-controlled trade in the Arabian Sea and the rise of the Company's pepper interests on the west coast presented an insidious threat to all the Indian states of the region. Accordingly he tried to stimulate trade with Arabia and Persia by setting up state trading institutions in the port towns. He also ravaged the spice bushes of the Keralan coast and dispersed the Hindu and Christian populations attached to the foreign trading posts. Most of all, Tipu seems to have understood the political weaknesses of Mysore when confronting the surrogate of a powerful European nation state. This perhaps lay behind his attempts to establish himself as an 'emperor' (*padishah*) independent of Mughal authority and, latterly, stress the Islamic features of his state (which he called the 'God Given Kingdom'). This policy, of course, had to be applied with caution. Mysore was too dependent on Hindu warriors and on Tamil Brahmin administrators for Tipu to institute a general holy war. He carefully distinguished between Hindus and Christians who might be the stalking-horse of British influence and the majority of his non-Muslim subjects whom he treated with consideration.

Tipu died fighting Wellesley's armies at the gates of Srirangapatam true to his adage 'better to live a day as a lion than a lifetime as a sheep'. His realm was not a decaying eastern despotism, but an attempt to face European mercantilist power with its own weapons: state monopoly and an aggressive ideology of expansion. It failed because the re-

[13] Buchanan, *Journey into ... Mysore*, i, 178–9.

sources of the British were expanding faster than those of Mysore, fuelled as much by Indian merchant capital as by European control over the most productive parts of the countryside. For all his rigorousness Tipu still only had limited success in penetrating beneath the powerful poligar lords of the countryside.

In this respect the Marathas posed a yet more dangerous threat because they above all represented the fusion of the power of the Hindu warrior landholders with the techniques of the Muslim administrators. To Richard Wellesley the Maratha kingdoms represented an empire or 'confederacy' whose 'head' was the Peshwa. If the Peshwa were brought into a subsidiary alliance, his subordinate chiefs would also submit and the last dangerous frontier of British India would be closed. But the Treaty of Bassein concluded between the British and a Peshwa weakened by internal opposition in 1802 had very different results. The major chieftains, Scindia, Holkar and the Raja of Berar saw this alliance as a clear challenge to their own independence and drifted into war with the Company. Between 1803 and 1806 large areas of central India were laid waste and the Marathas shackled more tightly to the British alliance. At the same time the Company's debt doubled and a series of military reverses undermined Wellesley's position with the authorities in London.

In the case of Awadh or Arcot the instability which the British perceived on their frontier was itself a consequence of the pressures of subsidiary alliance – and to a lesser extent of the corrosive effects of British trade. In the case of the Marathas, the alliance of 1802 forced the Maratha magnates into opposition while the growth of trade on the west coast had progressively put the hard upland areas of the Deccan at an economic disadvantage. Yet the volatility of Maratha politics also derived from the rapid social changes which had occurred in the region since the beginning of the eighteenth century. By 1780 what the British called the 'Maratha empire' referred not to a state or even to a culture but to a loosely bonded range of Hindu warriors and related agriculturalists who had achieved dominance within the heartland of Mughal India. Maratha hegemony resembled Mughal hegemony in many respects and used its methods of alliance-building and breaking. Poona had begun to resemble the rôle of Delhi as a moral centre, though Delhi retained much of its aura. The Peshwa (a Chitpavan Brahmin), and, more distantly, the Maratha descendants of Shivaji, their first great war-leader, had attained legitimacy as high-kings among the Marathas. But as in the case of the Mughals a complicated process of expansion – of subdividing and sharing in rights and honours – had tended to put chiefs in the outer regions at an advantage in their dealings with the centre. Like the Mughals too, the power of the ruling group was dependent on the support of non-Maratha magnates and mercenaries. Around Poona, of course, the Maratha ruling class was supreme and the villagers 'have some pride in the triumph of their nation, and some ambition to partake in its military exploits'.[14] But outside this heartland, Marathas formed only a thin ruling group. In the other tracts of Kanara, for instance, Marathas only accounted for 8–10 per cent of the population, a small élite of soldiers, revenue-managers and brahmins. In north central India and the Ganges Valley where the great war leader Mahadji Scindia had created a powerful domain in the 1780s within sight of the walls of Delhi, Maratha influence and culture were an even thinner veneer. A majority of Scindia's troops were 'easterners' – Rajputs and Brahmins from the great breeding ground of soldiers near Benares, or Muslim troopers from further west. His officers were British or French and his state reared on the expertise of Mughal revenue managers.

Even in 1800 the old Maratha society of the upland valleys of the north west Deccan had not been completely absorbed into the orbit of Mughal north India. The valley of the Tapti, home of the Shivaji still bred 'most of the horses in the Mahratta country' and most of the 'military adventurers'.[15] The peasant culture of the old Maratha movement still survived. Sturdy western Indian warriors rose rapidly to become kings. The great cavalry leader Tukoji Holkar was only a generation or two removed from his pastoralist ancestry and still maintained the traditions of predatory cavalry warfare to the discomfiture of the Wellesleys. Women displayed their independence by riding their own mounts in camp and the Maratha countryside still boasted weak caste distinctions and a homogeneous religious culture infused with the devotional worship of the god Shiva. But the transformation of this society by the forces of commerce and Mughal style state-building was proceeding rapidly. It was this which the British considered the increasing 'anarchy' of Maratha politics.

The expansion of the Maratha polities and the development of local

---

[14] G. W. Forrest (ed.), *Report of the Territories conquered from the Peshwa* (London, 1884), 261.
[15] Ibid., 259.

centres of power in Gujarat and north India was accompanied by monetisation, the growth of urban centres, production and trade. Maratha rulers had always used revenue-farming leases and revenue concessions as a way of bringing new areas into cultivation and this had encouraged the growth of 'great families' of capitalists and men of business of Maratha and Brahmin origin. Commercial links with coastal ports such as Goa, Diu and Daman also seem to have expanded in the early part of the eighteenth century.[16] In the 1750s there was a sharp increase in the state's land-revenue claim and a rationalisation of management. Again in the 1790s and 1810s the desire of the peshwas for increased revenue to pay for their armies and their obligations to British allies caused an expansion of revenue farming and an increase in the state's demands. The greater complexity, maturity and monetisation of the Maratha domains provided the background for the growing influence of the Brahmin élites, notably the Chitpavan Brahmins who consolidated their influence after 1720, when the office of peshwa became hereditary to the family of Balaji Vishwanath. Alienations of land from the state and the careful husbanding of resources allowed this new managerial faction and their rural allies to gain a larger share of the produce of the villages and even in some cases to buy shares in the crucial office of village headman. At the same time towns such as Poona and Nagpur which had been little more than large villages before 1780 expanded fast as a new group of urban consumers came into existence.[17]

The military complexion of the Maratha polities also quickly changed. Their armies rapidly developed European-style infantry and artillery wings. Mahadji Scindia's attempt to establish himself in the Mughal heartland led to the creation of a powerful force of sappers and gunners to blast down the fortresses of its refractory princes. By 1785 he had established his own ordnance factories near Agra. These developments so alarmed the Company that it forbade Britons to serve as gunners with the Marathas and attempted to staunch the trade in muskets. French and Portuguese officers and gunners, however, quickly filled the breach. Contemporary military analysts sometimes argued that the move of the Marathas from irregular cavalry warfare to infantry battles proved their undoing. Yet on a number of occasions

---

[16] See, e.g., T. R. de Souza, 'Mhamai House Records', *The Indian Archives*, xxxi, i, 1982.
[17] Malet's report on Poona, proceedings of the Resident Benares, July 1788, U.P. State Archives, Allahabad.

they came close to defeating the British. A more convincing explanation for their ultimate failure is that the British were able to exploit the dissidence which arose from the rapid development of the Maratha polities. Maratha expansion within the shell of Mughal rule had always proceeded by 'faction' and apparent 'treachery'. The problem for the Marathas was that they could not fragment and split the British commanders and residents in the same way that they had once played on the rivalries between the Mughal generals.

The British on the other hand could exploit not only the personal rivalries which had been the epiphenomena of even the strongest Indian state, but also the deeper fissures between different social groups. First, there were persistent problems about royal succession especially as Maratha politics at the top retained a familial character. The ability to compromise conflicts by splitting the patrimony and creating shares in royal rights had given Maratha politics a good deal of flexibility. But in opposition to the rigid loyalties of the Company it rapidly became a weakness. The year 1762 saw the beginning of a long factional dispute between members of the peshwa's family. Raghunath Rao, one of the protagonists, had riven the Marathas when he had demanded partition of the Maratha patrimony. He had even enlisted British help in an abortive military effort to gain control of the young peshwa, Madhu Rao Narayan, in 1778–9. But the consequences of this family dispute reverberated to the end of the century and allowed the Company authorities to keep the Marathas permanently divided.[18] Secondly, there were conflicts over the authority of the peshwaship, originally no more than one of the ministers to the Raja of Satara, descendant of the seventeenth-century founder of the Maratha kingdom, Shivaji. Several Maratha chiefs, including the rajas of Berar and Satara, claimed a prior sovereignty within the polity. These conflicts were also exploited by the British.

Finally, the different functions and rôles of major social groups within the Maratha domains could provide the basis for political faction. The Brahmin administrative and commercial élite, the old Maratha aristocracy, and new military adventurers from the backward parts of the Deccan or from north India were three groups which underlay the whole structure of Maratha politics. Factions of all these groups combined and recombined with each other. But the cadre of

[18] For a detailed account of Maratha politics, 'Customs of the Marathas', *Asiatic Annual Register*, 1802, 55–67.

Brahmin men of business, led by the master statesman Nana Fadnavis did provide a holding alliance which conferred a degree of unity on the polities and held the British at bay for more than a generation. The death of Fadnavis in 1800 and the rise of military adventurers such as Sarje Rao Ghatke eclipsed the power of the bureaucratic and commercial élite and allowed the intensification of conflicts between the other groups.

The Marathas 'failed' in part because the rapid expansion of their polities created fractures which a European state and army could consistently exploit. Yet they also faced an underlying problem of resources reminiscent of the dilemma of the sultans of Mysore. The heartland of their power around Poona was, by the mid-eighteenth century, at the limits of development given the state of its technology. It was poorly irrigated and relatively sparsely populated and could barely support a landholding and warrior community above the body of the peasantry. After the breakdown of the Mughal revenue pump (itself partly a consequence of Maratha expansion) the balance of trade between the Deccan and the rest of India was severely disadvantageous to the Marathas. They did not produce enough to maintain imports of specialist goods, particularly weapons. This explains the persistent outward pressure of the Marathas into areas of stable agriculture like Tanjore in the south and Gujarat and the Ganges Valley in the north. But the very processes of social mobility and external conquest by which the Marathas sought to remedy this deficiency endangered the inner basis of resources on which the central élite subsisted. War took away men from agriculture; it also invited reprisal and faction. In 1752 the then Peshwa Balaji Baji Rao had spoken of the need to 'water' the dry lands around Poona with the flows of gold of north and south India.[19] By 1801 that dearth had intensified; Arthur Wellesley noted that there was not a tree or ear of corn left standing for 150 miles around Poona as the result of a factional dispute between the Peshwa and his 'lieutenant' Holkar whose cavalry had looted the region.

The lack of resources of Indian states led to external dependency. The cost of mercenary armies encouraged Indian rulers either to risk everything in one hazardous throw against their enemies or to bring in British aid. When war did break out there was always pressure to come to an accommodation. Many Maratha rulers, particularly those in Kanara and Gujarat, derived considerable income from levies on trade

[19] S. N. Sen, *Military System of the Marathas* (Calcutta, 1858), p. 60.

with their British rivals which was channelled towards Bombay. Their war effort could only be maintained for a few months. By contrast the Company could now redistribute resources from the most productive regions across the whole subcontinent and also draw on the capital of Indian commercial men.

Wellesley's campaigns succeeded in humbling the major Maratha war leaders but did not bring to a halt the struggle for succession in central India. A military setback against Holkar in 1804, combined with an escalating debt, gave the Directors an excuse to recall Wellesley in the following year. Under his successors Lord Cornwallis, Sir George Barlow and Lord Minto the Company limited itself to small wars of containment and used its resources in the East Indies as a contribution to the international struggle against Napoleonic France. But the British connection still acted as a dead weight on the Indian states. Sir Thomas Munro echoed Arthur Wellesley's sentiments when he wrote that 'the subsidiary system must everywhere run its full course, and destroy every government which it seeks to protect'. Subsidiary alliances forced some states like the Peshwa's to screw up the ratchet of land revenue even tighter which led to British complaints of misgovernment and oppression. Or else, as in the case of the chastened Holkar and Scindia, the desperate battle for resources led to border wars for revenue and agricultural labourers, also giving the impression of 'anarchy'. Constant intervention by the British residents, particularly in the matter of succession to the throne, frustrated the workings of the fluid political systems of the Indian states, exacerbating factions amongst dependant chiefs. Ultimately in 1817 fear of British intentions led the remaining Maratha chieftains into a final struggle for independence. British penetration of the warrior states of Rajasthan proceeded by similar, though somewhat less bloody, stages.

The occasion for the British mobilisation which panicked the Marathas into war was the Company's campaign against the so-called Pindari raiders. The Pindaris, bands of irregular cavalry who roamed through central India levying plunder, frightened the British because they resembled 'what the Mahratta power was in the decline of the Mughal empire of India'. They derived from several sources. Some were Afghan and other north Indian cavalrymen pursuing the ancient career of building states on the Deccan. Others were bands of 'easterner' Rajputs who sought service with rulers as their ancestors had done and found their sources of patronage limited by British restrictions. Yet others appear to have been leaders of peasant defence associations, lumped into the Pindari category by colonial observers who saw all dissidence as criminal. A mopping-up campaign against the Pindaris, and, if necessary, against the Maratha states who were suspected of harbouring them, was inevitable since the Company regarded them as dangerous rivals for land revenue and a potential threat to commerce in the settled territories of the Ganges valley.

The Company was drawn into conquest in the western Deccan and central India primarily because the demands of its fiscal and military machine, expressed through the subsidiary alliance system, was incompatible with the fluid practice of indigenous politics and taxation. However, there were examples along the west coast of India where direct commercial motives reinforced or even initiated the drive for formal empire. Since the early 1780s British private trade based on Bombay had become particularly buoyant. Pepper prices were high towards the end of the century and both the Company and private firms looked for secure supplies from the kingdoms of the Malabar coast. Cornwallis had legitimated the Bombay authorities' acquisition of Kanara in 1792 in order to stabilise the pepper trade. Hereafter merchants sought to extend the Company's interest in dependent states such as Travancore at the same time as they tried to frustrate its monopoly claims.

However, it was in the case of the cotton trade that commercial motives are clearest. After 1784 the Company needed larger and larger quantities of raw cotton for the China market. The House of Commons had reduced the duties on tea in Britain during that year. Increased quantities of tea could only be procured by boosting sales of cotton to the burgeoning population of southern China. So the value of cotton exported from Gujarat via Bombay increased from Rs 4 lakhs to Rs 35 lakhs between 1783 and 1802. This benefited the perilous finances of the Company which held the monopoly of the China trade, but also the new generation of Bombay-based agency houses such as Forbes and Co. and McKillop and Co. In Bombay private trading interests represented by men such as David Scott had a powerful voice in the Company's counsels and could manipulate the complaisant governor, Jonathan Duncan. An alliance of commercial forces was completed by the Hindu bania merchants of western India who purchased the raw cotton from the Gujarat markets and had helped keep the Bombay government's finances afloat during the Maratha wars through large loans and other services.

The continuation of the complex system of taxation sharing by which the British in Gujarat had subsisted with the Marathas and other regional powers was seen as a threat by all these interests. Usually the case was represented in lurid terms of Maratha 'misrule'. Actually the Maratha powers had as much interest in enhancing the produce of the cotton zones as did the Company. But the Marathas played politics with trade, interrupting it from time to time and putting pressure on growers and merchants in order to maximise their earnings. The Bombay government's decision to take over the government of Surat city and to annex the cotton districts of Broach and Surat proceeded from pure commercial motives, though it was carried out under cover of the subcontinental ambitions of Wellesley. In the words of General Stuart, the annexation of Gujarat 'would secure to us the best manufacture of piece goods, and the command of the cotton market, the most valuable staple of India.'[20]

In 1810 the East India remained a powerful mercantilist institution; free traders were growing in importance but not yet dominant. If there were some important areas such as Gujarat where private traders reinforced local pressures for political expansion there were others such as Awadh where private interests opposed Company expansion which might inhibit their freedom of action. British commercial wealth remained overwhelmingly based on the profits of trade and political perquisites acquired in India itself. The new cotton (and later opium) trades to China were only very indirectly related to industrialisation in Britain. The policies of administrators and governors-general were dominated by the military and fiscal needs of the Company as an Indian ruler and as a purchaser of Indian-manufactured piece goods. British political power in India continued to move forward because of the Company's demands as a military despotism. It was a despotism required not only to support an army but also to remit Indian manufactures to Britain. The attempt to find resources compatible with this dual rôle proved impossible to accommodate within the volatile politics of the indigenous Indian states. Rather, the Company's pressure on these polities had undermined them and created the direct conditions for annexation.

[20] Stuart to Wellesley, 31 January 1800, cited Pamela Nightingale, *Trade and Empire in Western India* (Cambridge, 1969), p. 177.

# CHAPTER 4

# THE CONSOLIDATION AND FAILURE
# OF THE EAST INDIA
# COMPANY'S STATE, 1818–57

The East India Company rose to power because it had provided a secure financial base for its powerful mercenary army. The land revenues of Bengal, combined with the capital – Indian as much as European – generated in the coastal trading economy, allowed the Company's Indian operations to sustain the massive debts incurred in its fight to the finish with the Indian kingdoms. However, political dominion did not solve the Company's financial problems. The ominous presence and constant pressure of this part-oriental, part-European state continued to tempt petty rulers within and outside its domains into revolt. Though aspects of the social and political conflict which had drawn the Company into expansion were suppressed under its rule, so too was much of the economic dynamism which had given rise to that conflict. India's huge agricultural economy was not performing well enough to underwrite the costs of European dominion. The East India Company's rule widely came to be seen as a dismal failure long before the Great Rebellion of 1857 blew up its foundations. This chapter demonstrates how the British maintained their fragile dominance over the subcontinent in the early years of the nineteenth century before considering this economic impasse and the attempts of administrators to escape from it.

## MILITARY DOMINATION AND POLITICAL
## SUASION

The development of a cavalry arm and efficient siege methods for use against small fortresses put the Company on the offensive again throughout India. The British could begin to suppress what Arthur Wellesley called 'the freebooting system' and corral those armed plunderers – Pindaris, 'Arabs', and Rohillas – who threatened the land-revenue yield in western and central India. The first principles of British administration were moulded by strong prejudices in favour of private property in land, but they were usually implemented with an eye to maximum military and financial security. Near the hearts of eighteenth-century principalities rulers had already warred down intermediary chieftains and magnates in order to deal with village élites. In the south and west British administration which was more military in character than in Bengal, followed suit. The famous ryotwari systems of Malcolm and Munro were developed in the Baramahal territories of Mysore where Tipu Sultan had already reduced the power of the warlords and come to terms with village headmen. Even elsewhere in the Madras Presidency where short-lived attempts to find zamindars like those of Bengal went ahead, the new rulers sought to end the system of 'military land tenures' which had prevailed under the poligars. The poligars' servants were 'excused' their service under arms and instead confirmed in ordinary tenures at low rates of revenue. Throughout the subcontinent petty chieftains were encouraged by cannonade and remissions of revenue to dismantle their mud forts and clear areas of forest which could provide harbour for bandits.

The British paid particular attention to their internal frontiers. In western and central India the Marathas had tried to regulate relations with tribal societies such as the Kolis and Bhils by awarding their chieftains royal honours and the right to control mountain passes and forests. In the same way the Nizam of Hyderabad had conferred titles on the *naiks* or headmen of the wandering Banjaras to release his lands from the danger of plunder and to secure their service for his armies. The Company tried to fix these fluid political arrangements. Once an area had been 'pacified' Bhil chiefs were separated off from their clansmen and recognised as rajas in return for a fixed tribute. In the north Deccan a special Bhil Corps was established in 1823 to drain off the military energies of young Bhils and to compensate their villages for the end of mercenary income. In the areas south of Delhi plundering bands of Mewattis were afforded the status of special police force by the British and brought formally within the bounds of the law. Measures like this took effect only slowly. Much of the Deccan and north Gujarat was affected by local warfare well into the 1840s. But the security of major towns and trade routes was secured.

Control and distribution of forest and waste land was another important tactic in the settlement of rural society. Here the British broke cleanly with the practice of earlier rulers who had not generally assessed the waste alongside village lands. Instead they sought to parcel out such lands and create forms of private property whose owners would both pay them revenue and aid in the containment of 'unruly' elements. Their aim was to break up unstable concentrations of power on the fringes of the arable. Officials acknowledged that the assessment of waste in ryotwari areas was designed to secure a fixed population and to 'limit the spirit of emigrating'.[1] If populations were to move it was to be the orderly emigration of wage earners from one district to the next, not the irruptions of armed peasant brotherhoods which had occurred in the previous era. These measures had a cumulative effect on agrarian society. Rates of interest fell quite sharply throughout India in the immediate aftermath of British conquest as greater security prevailed on major routes and in the commercial cities. House prices and the value of urban property in Delhi nearly trebled between 1803 and 1826, for instance, while the towns of rural Gujarat began to recover from the rigours of the Anglo-Maratha wars. The British repaired the Mughal system of fortified rest-houses on major roads and this encouraged marketing farmers and small merchants to make longer commercial journeys. Moneylenders such as the Bohras of Rajasthan moved into small towns as the security of loans and property was felt to improve. However severe the pressure of the Company's revenue assessments, however disturbed some parts of India remained, however buoyant parts of pre-colonial India's economy, the reality of Pax Britannica for much of rural society cannot be doubted. Countless Indian sources refer, grudgingly often, to the new security of life. The red-coated sepoy, like the Muslim warrior-on-horseback before him, was a figure of terror and destruction in some popular and artistic manifestations though as often he appears as protector.

Of course, the Company's aim was stability not equity. Almost everywhere the rural élite was consolidated or attempts were made to create one. Cornwallis's Permanent Settlement, for all its antecedents in eighteenth-century physiocratic philosophy, was primarily a device for guaranteeing revenue and military stability in time of war. It was avowedly designed to reinforce social control and help settle large and productive areas of north Bengal. Officials became discontented with the system not because of its aristocratic bias but because they ended up with the wrong sort of gentry. John Shore made it clear that they

---

[1] Collector of Chittoor to Board of Revenue, Madras, 7 August 1811, Abstract of papers relating to the settlement of 1811–12, North Arcot District, Madras Record Office.

had wanted an 'English gentry' with deep control over a deferential yeomanry. Instead they formed an 'Irish' class of non-resident and non-productive *rentiers* lording it over an impoverished peasantry.

Political and a military considerations dominated the decision on the merits of zamindari and ryotwari systems in Madras Presidency between 1790 and 1825, even though the debate was conducted in the categories of Burke's conservatism. As William Bentinck's minute of June 1806[2] makes clear, ryotwari was preferred in the south (and later the west) for three main reasons. First, to create a system of large 'estates' over the large areas of Tamilnadu where there were none before was to invite default in the revenue and political trouble; this clearly acknowledged the realities of south Indian society. Secondly, smallholding and a peasant élite was much less of a threat to the state monopoly of power than large blocks such as the Bengal zamindars or a landlord class of reformed poligars. Thirdly, the ryotwari system allowed assessment – and regular reassessments – of each farmer's fields in line with productivity and profit. This made it possible for government to increase its share of the value of agricultural produce in an era when its value had begun generally to decline.

This goal of progressively rising land-revenue returns often stood in direct contradiction to hopes of 'improvement' for the peasantry. For even in day to day administration early Company government everywhere sought to assuage and stabilise the rural community. Wherever possible a regular succession to larger estates was encouraged. Often this meant that collectors sought to impose primogeniture in defiance of local custom. The expansion of information about districts allowed officials to develop direct communications with the major landholding communities, to build up family histories and detailed methods of surveillance. A vast array of statistical information poured into the Calcutta Secretariat as the Company's charter came up for revision in 1813 and as new revenue assessments were introduced throughout much of the North-Western Provinces and Madras. By the mid-1820s almost all districts had revenue survey maps going far beyond the earlier Mughal route maps which had been designed simply for military supply. Slowly, too, the Company tried to gain direct access to the

[2] Cited in S. Balasundaram, 'Administrative policies of the Madras government, 1800–35', unpub. Ph.D. diss. Madras University, 1963, pp. 228–30; cf. ibid. 110–40, 248–52; for antecedents, see T. Munro to Board of Revenue, Madras, 9 October 1800, *The letters of Sir Thomas Munro relating to the early administration of Canara. Selections from the Records of the Collector of South Canara* (Mangalore, 1879).

village-level officials who controlled revenue papers and registered land permutations.

Of course, this was no simple question of the modern state intruding into the countryside for the first time. Indian régimes possessed subtle and efficient methods of gathering information. Sometimes the practice of kingship had extended to areas of religious and customary practice from which the colonial government actually withdrew, or which it hopelessly misunderstood. In outlying areas such as Guntur District in the Andhra country village leaders and subordinate officials could combine to reduce the European official to a cipher. Yet the range of the Company state, its monopoly of physical force, and its capacity to command resources from a peasantry now increasingly disarmed set it apart even in its early days from all the régimes which had preceded it.

The foundations of British rule in India consisted not only in direct administration but in the creation of a flexible and expert diplomatic system among its subordinate allies and dependants. Shorn of their military power the princes could still become magnets for disaffection. But conversely, if properly controlled, their resources could be used against rebels in directly controlled territories and their lands act as fire-screens to prevent the brush fire wars of consolidation becoming conflagrations. The eventual adherence of Diwan Purniya of Mysore to the civil power during the so-called 'White Mutiny' of Madras army officers in 1809 nipped a dangerous conspiracy in the bud.[3] During the British disasters of the Afghan Wars of 1839–42 the Company's resident in Nepal, Brian Hodgson, headed off a potentially calamitous revolt along the central mountain chain. In 1857 the resident held Hyderabad by a whisker. Otherwise the revolt might have acquired a crucial southern focus. So the further development of the residency system, an embryonic Indian political service and a series of techniques for neutralising disaffected Indian states, reinforced the administrative consolidation of British India.

Once relative security had been established in 1818 the main aim of the residencies was to regularise the fluid practices of Indian politics along lines laid down by the powerful Political Department in Calcutta. In view of the British assumption of 'paramount power', Indian states were not allowed to enter into bilateral relations. This put the

---

[3] 'A Field Officer', *Diary of a tour through southern India, Egypt and Palestine in the years 1821–2* (London, 1823), pp. 148–9.

British government into the position of arbitrator between them. Residents sought to control succession to the throne by eliminating the influence of royal women and military commanders. Unreliable successors such as Taj-ul-Umara in Arcot in 1799 and Vazir Ali in Awadh in 1797 were bypassed. But once residents had gained control over access to and the education of princes, an insistence on primogeniture was usually sufficient to guarantee subservience. Residents such as Mark Wilks at Mysore and Mark Cubbon in Pudukottai became 'stepfathers' to royal heirs, assuming the position of close personal adviser which had been occupied by uncles or royal mothers in the independent courts. Through carefully selected tutors, residents began to implant western notions of 'progressive' government in the minds of their Indian charges, so anticipating the model of the chiefs' colleges of the later nineteenth century.

The key to the residents' control of the direction of internal administration was close alliance with the chief financial officer, the diwan. Here again the British modified the tactics of the Mughal sovereigns who had controlled provinces until the eighteenth century by balancing the diwan against the provincial governors. In Hyderabad, for instance, Chandu Lal, a north Indian Khattri, formed the heart of the 'resident's party' in court politics. Diwans were often close to the local financial community and to the revenue farmers and holders of Company bonds who prospered under British rule. Sometimes they were outsiders, Hindustani businessmen, Brahmins or Muslim gentry in the Deccan, Tamil Brahmins in Travancore. Such men differed from the local aristocracy of the states by training and attitude, so they could be rallied against them by a clever resident. In some cases, however, British control penetrated more deeply. John Munro became diwan as well as resident of the state of Travancore in 1811. He suppressed revolt among the now declining Nayar warrior caste, but stirred to frenzy the squabbles between the state's St Thomas Christians with his bracing Anglican evangelicalism.

British military power cowed the Indian states and the policy of Company residents ruled out combinations among them. Yet the Company's success in holding the subcontinent in the face of persistent revolt and widespread popular hostility still requires explanation, particularly in view of the doubtful reliability of the Bengal army, on which so many officials remarked. One reason for this success was the wide discretion which the British allowed the Indian states and the

landed magnates within directly administered territories for the fulfil-
ment of their vital ceremonial, ritual and cultural functions – at least
until the 1840s. The magnificence and munificence of the early
nineteenth-century courts obscured their loss of power. Foreign hegemony may have swept away military élites but it provided ample
room for the scribes, brahmins and families of court officials who
served these domesticated monarchies.

This policy can best be illustrated by particular cases. The ruler of
the eighteenth-century poligar state of Pudukottai had long been a
Company ally. In 1794 Madras cancelled the tribute which the raja had
paid to the Nawab of Arcot and in 1803 'released' him from contributing to the Nawab's Muslim festivals, a move which pleased the growing faction of court brahmins. Later the resident dashed attempts by
the neighbouring king of Tanjore to treat Pudukottai's ruler as a 'mere
zamindar' and in his form of address implicitly recognised the state's
right to share in the ancient sovereignty of Vijayanagar which was so
important in the south. By this date the raja had acquired the right to
use the white umbrella and ceremonial maces, key symbols of royalty.[4] The British controlled the army and state policy but they
allowed the king sufficient resources to found temples and establish
Brahmins on rent-free forest land. Vaishnavite sect leaders were
patronised, as they had been in the old south; literature and music
flourished. As the royal house under Raja Rajasinha I (1780–1825) successfully asserted its right to high caste status, honour fell by reflection
on the families of the erstwhile 'tribesmen' – the Kallar military élite.

In nearby Tanjore the reality of British power was obscured even
more completely by the kingly munificence of Raja Serfoji, a major
patron of the arts. In 1799 he had given up the administration of his
entire rich kingdom in exchange for an annual pension of Rs. 12 lakhs.
Serfoji inherited the great tradition of scholarship, musical performance and religious devotion which had been nurtured by his Maratha
ancestors, especially Shahji (1689–1712). Serfoji's lavish donations
amounted in some years to ten per cent of the territory's entire revenue. He had his family history carved on the walls of the now reconstructed great Shaivite Brihadeshwara temple. The king also took care
to venerate the older Vaishnavite temples of the Tanjore delta and even
succoured the small but powerful Christian flock of the state's *éminence grise*, the Danish missionary Reverend Benjamin Shwartz. By

[4] R. Aiyar, *A general history of the Puddukotai State* (Puddukotai, 1916), i, 301–2.

achieving a neo-traditional revival in the realms of painting, dance and music, Serfoji appealed to a wide populace. The distance between courtly and popular arts was not great and in the institution of the north Indian Bhagwati Kava style of musical performance he involved ordinary villagers and townsmen in this cultural renaissance.[5] Applauding the popular veneration of their client, British residents stood masked in the shadows until Lord Dalhousie brutally stopped the show in 1856 and finally annexed Tanjore to British India.

A similar neo-traditional court style also emerged in Mysore under Raja Krishnadevaraja III (1799–1836) and his great financial officer Purniya (*flor.* 1782–1811). With the residents' help the court made the uneasy transition from Tipu's 'God-given state' to a dependent Hindu polity, partly by securing the adherence of the great Hindu and Jain religious institutions which received massive grants of land. Especially important was the powerful Vaishnavite 'monastery' of Sringeri which inherited the spiritual power of one of India's greatest religious sages, the seventh-century teacher, Shankaracharya. The 'abbot' of Sringeri played a major rôle in compromising conflicts in the villages where he had many followers amongst artisans and specialist farmers.[6] The court itself revived the pre-Muslim administrative system and emphasised the rôle of secular brahmins. The line of authority was traced back once again to the Vijayanagar kings and a court legend was created, with the help of the British resident, Mark Wilks (1799–1805), which crudely implicated Tipu in the destruction of Hindu temples. The court was brought back to Mysore from the Muslim city of Srirangapatam where it would be near to the Hindu dynastic emblems, the temple of goddess Chamundi and the giant Nandi bull. Yet care was taken not to offend the Muslims. Poor Muslims of Mysore were given a new mosque and several of Tipu's officers quietly moved into service of the new régime. While it is impossible to gauge the degree of popular support for all this, it is significant that the reinstated Dussehra festival celebrations quickly became among the most sumptuous and best attended in India.

In directly administered territories also the British were generally eager to foster the religious and cultural authority of their clients

[5] V. Raghavan (ed.) *Sridhara Venkatesa. Sahendravilasa* (Tanjore Saraswati Mahal series, 54, n.d.), introduction; C. K. Srinivasan, *Maratha Rule in the Carnatic* (Annamalai University Historical Series, 5, 1944).
[6] R. Narasimachar, 'The Sringeri Math', *Quarterly Journal of the Mythic Society* (Mysore), viii, 1917–18, 26–33.

among the petty rulers, large landlords and men of commerce. If necessary they were prepared to fulfil the ritual rôle of rulers themselves. From as early as 1690 governors of Madras had intervened to compromise disputes in the city's two great temples at Mylapore and Triplicane. They also built up the authority of the chief dubashes of the main merchant groups in an attempt to minimise the conflicts between 'right-hand' and 'left-hand' caste alliances. When direct rule spread across the south of the continent collectors became donors and protectors of Hindu temples as Muslim rulers had been before them. They allowed easy access to the great southern temple of Tirupati which was venerated by a wide range of people including local tribals and Gujarati merchant castes. In Orissa they were careful to encourage endowments for the great temple of Jagganath and fought off attempts by Christian missionaries to restrict some of its more exotic cult practices. The importance of this cannot be underestimated. The first clause in the deeds of administrative abdication, signed as rulers stepped aside in favour of the British, was often a solemn undertaking that the colonial authorities would protect religion, graves and shrines. Even if we cannot assume that the masses were casually manipulated by such policies, they did head off trouble. When in the 1840s the Company began to withdraw from the direct administration of Hindu places of worship under the pressure of evangelical Christian disapproval, there were major riots in south Indian towns and mass petitions were collected denouncing the government's abdication of its religious duties.

Throughout the subcontinent the new rulers tried to associate themselves with indigenous law-givers and centres of religious authority. The Muslim law officers (kazi, mufti, kotwal) were maintained when the Bengal Regulations were extended to north India after 1793. This was important because it allowed those Muslim learned men who remained neutral on the question of whether Christian rule posed a threat to Islam to argue that some of the basic conditions of Muslim religious life were still preserved. Few jurists considered that India had now become a 'land of conflict' where holy war was a binding duty. True, there were not many Muslims who would directly associate themselves with institutions such as the Delhi College (founded 1792) which sought to bridge the gap between Islamic and Western learning, just as there were few Hindu pandits who could associate themselves with the Benares Sanskrit College (founded 1791). But enough of the learned were prepared to offer guidance in the British courts to still the fears of the populace that spheres of family and customary law were being interfered with. Only after 1830, with the further infiltration of Christian missionaries and a self-consciously 'reforming' government, did these fears begin to assume wider proportions.

Some qualifications must be made, however. First, the intervention by British officers modified the very institutions whose character they sought to maintain. The management of Hindu temples in the south became notably more bureaucratic and rule-ridden. Hindu and Muslim law as operated in British courts became more rigid, reflecting the norms of the high castes and the most orthodox interpretations rather than the pragmatic and fluid ajudications of the pandits and jurists of the past. Secondly, while the British viewed their intervention as an attempt to order and control society, well-placed Indians were still able to manipulate British officers for their own purposes, as witness the periodic explosion of 'scandals' in princely courts, temples and trusts. At a humbler level village leaderships were sometimes able to exploit British misunderstandings or distortions of indigenous legal and social forms to entrench themselves in power. The mirasidar proprietors of Tanjore and Tinnevelly in the far south, for instance, put up a clever and well-orchestrated opposition to Sir Thomas Munro's ryotwari regulations in the areas which they controlled during the 1820s and 30s. The result was that they became recognised as 'ancient lords of the land' in those districts.

Finally, the tactics of cultural suasion were only partially successful. Many Muslim learned withdrew from the land of unbelievers to work in the more pristine environment of Hyderabad, or better still, Mecca and Medina. In Delhi the leader of one of the city's most important religious institutions, the Chishti Sufi hospice, turned his back on the visiting Sir Charles Metcalfe, Chief Commissioner of the City, 'an infidel stinking of alcohol'. Nor were all Hindus swayed by the cultural largesse of the new courts. The great south Indian singer and poet Thyagaraja refused the blandishments of Raja Serfoji. Altogether the balance was a delicate one. Popular revolt, cultural reaction and religious revitalisation could always combine into a combustible mixture as they did in the 1830s and more momentously in 1857. The final chapter considers in greater detail how Indian resistance in conflicts over both material and ideological issues also shaped the form of the colonial régime.

## THE CAPTURE OF INDIA'S ECONOMY

Britain's economic dominion in the east as much as her political power was built upon the foundations of the Indian land revenues. As early as 1765, Clive had hit upon the expedient of using Bengal's revenue yield of £3 million to subsidise the faltering trading activities of the Company and to keep up its dividend in London. By 1818 the Indian revenues in British hands amounted to some £22 million.[7] They were used to cover the large deficit on Britain's balance of trade with both India and China. First, there were large unreciprocated transfers of bullion and bills from India to Britain which were known as the Home Charges. This was the prime component of what the nationalist historians were to term the 'drain of wealth'. With the salaries and fortunes also transferred the total amounted by 1820 to £6 million annually. This 'political profit' must have dwarfed the profits made from the £15 million of import-export trade between Britain and India. The importance of the political element is even greater when we consider that the most valuable components of India's exports were themselves 'administrative' rather than 'free' trades. This was because indigo was often sold at a loss on the London market in order to transfer home the salaries and perquisites of British residents. Opium, the other great commodity, remained a government monopoly in India even after 1834 when the Company lost its monopoly of the China trade to the free-traders. Opium continued to provide up to 15 per cent of the Indian government's income and to account for up to 30 per cent of the value of India's trade up to 1856. Indian revenues were in fact remitted to Britain as a form of tribute – as contemporaries were readier to recognise than more recent historians. Arthur Wellesley argued that this was payment for the new security conferred by Britain on India. But the scale and implication of the transfers were hardly called into question.

Control of the land revenues brought large advantages to Britain in other sectors of the Indian economy. Besides financing the lucrative China trade, it helped to keep Government credit high. This attracted large inflows of investment into Company bonds to help fund war and expansion. Company 'paper' carried regular, safe yields of between

[7] E. T. Stokes, 'The rationale of British Indian Empire, 1828–56', unpub. seminar paper, School of Oriental and African Studies, London, 1977.

eight and twelve per cent per annum, a copper-bottomed investment for up-country magnates and merchants. A strong Company credit position in turn benefited private trading concerns based in the residencies since it increased the overall pool of capital and meant that interest rates could be kept lower. Finally, of course, land revenue funded the Company's large and expensive army which was deployed throughout Asia in campaigns which directly or indirectly protected Britain's commercial interests. The Bengal and Madras armies were used in Burma and south-east Asia; the Bombay marine was used to cow the Wahhabis of Arabia and the rulers of Mesopotamia. All this helped to open up Asia's trade to British goods. The conquest of Sindh and the Punjab pushed private trade to the north-west and led to the growth of the port of Karachi. The lucrative timber trade was forwarded by the defeats of Burma (1824–6 and 1852). Finally, in the 1850s, the intervention of the British and Indian armies in China widened the entrée of British trade into valuable Far Eastern markets. None of these campaigns was directly created by private merchants. The Company's strategic interests and desire for new sources of revenue were paramount, though such conquests did create economic benefits on the side.

Monetary policy, the policies of the courts in Calcutta and Bombay, the structure of internal tariffs – all these restricted the role of indigenous exporters and ship-owners in inter-Asian and inter-continental trade. Even humanitarian moves such as the Lascar Acts of 1820–4, which were designed to improve the conditions of Indian seamen, had the effect of reducing the competitiveness of indigenous participants in Britain's world trade. They were unable to capitalise on their one great advantage – cheap labour, since minimum wages and conditions were now enforced by law. Access to Britain's highly sophisticated insurance, credit and financial systems inevitably gave British merchants added advantages over European and Asian rivals.

Yet Britain's growing stranglehold over India's external economy failed to lead to the transformation which the free merchants and officials of the 1820s hoped for. India was now firmly tied into cycles of north European trade and production. Some inland merchants and some peasant farmers profited even in the early nineteenth-century from the fitful booms in the export trade to China and Europe. But much of the buoyancy which had characterised some indigenous regional economies, even in the eighteenth-century, disappeared.

In part this was because the Company's political and economic aims were in conflict; in part because the Indian economy, though subordinate, proved resilient to invasion by European control or European styles of management. The Company was able neither consistently to advance the interests of private trade nor to inject growth into the economy itself. Free trade was introduced into India in a patchy manner. By the 1830s British officials, it is true, had withdrawn from internal grain markets during times of famine, secure in the belief that these calamities represented the iron laws of economics. Charles Trevelyan abolished internal transit duties in 1836. But the Company's attitude to the rôle of state power in the economy remained ambivalent at best. Its agents in Gujarat and Central India continued to secure supplies of cotton and other goods by driving other purchasers out of the market through the payment of uneconomic prices. The transit duties which operated between 1806 and 1834 had already had the effect of strangling many internal trade routes in the interests of merchants who traded export goods to Calcutta, Madras or Bombay. Even after 1834 the Company retained many local monopolies, notably in high-value goods such as opium, salt and tobacco. Most of all, the weight of land revenue itself dampened investment in the internal economy and worsened the periodic crises which arose from India's involvement in unstable world markets.

The Company's involvement in the rural labour market was equally ambivalent. Some measures to free tied labour were introduced. Agrestic servitude was abolished in Malabar; domestic slavery was officially outlawed in north India. The customary prohibitions against low castes owning agricultural land which operated in some parts of India were discountenanced. Yet other British measures had the effect of tying labour. Where the market was against them, official authority was often used through caste headmen to extract customary labour payments for state projects. No move was made to limit the practice of bonded sharecropping which was common throughout eastern India. In fact, the government's demand for cash payments, combined with the periodic scarcities of silver, may have acted to deepen the dependence of share-cropping peasants on their masters. Administrative measures designed to curtail the 'spirit of migrancy' helped in the same way to reduce the bargaining power of agricultural labour. The British had apparently introduced a free land market to India. Yet this was in large part illusion. Heavy land-revenue demand meant that zamindari rights had only low market values before the 1840s. The perquisites of lordship which were sold at auctions under duress usually went to other members of the same locally dominant agricultural caste. In any event, the great volume of land sales had little or no effect on agricultural production. No holdings were consolidated; little capital was applied to improvement.

The Company's new India was not a fair field for British capitalists either. The dream of introducing into India a flourishing plantation economy which would spread wealth to the peasant hinterland and massively increase the demand for British manufactures was fading by 1830. First it is important to note that very little metropolitan capital was introduced into India before 1850. 'British' capital in India was overwhelmingly the capital of agency houses in the presidencies representing accumulation of official salaries and fortunes made in an earlier period of conquistador imperialism. Investment in internal trade and production remained as it had been in the eighteenth-century – a way of laundering profits and returning them to England. This was why European-controlled indigo production massively increased in north India after 1815 only to collapse in 1827 and again in 1847 when the delicate chains of credit which supported it could no longer take the strain of an uneconomic commerce. In fact, far from attracting external capital, nearly £20 million was withdrawn from the Indian money market in the 1830s and 40s. Indian-controlled commerce suffered in turn. The modernising Indian capitalists of Bombay and Calcutta encountered institutional barriers and lacked international expertise. Still, their problem at root was poor funding; this was compounded by the unstable nature of British business activity in India. Only in development of the tea and coffee estates did British entrepreneurs break with the lethargic traditions of the eighteenth-century agency houses.

The Company's political aims and financial structure deepened the problems for both British and Indian entrepreneurs. Officials were very hostile to the direct ownership of land by British citizens, fearing that the land revenues might be impaired by conflicts over labour and land between zamindars and European planters. Lack of good roads, secure routes and local information meant that the European enterprises of the years 1815–27 almost always relied on Indian peasant producers and middlemen. Attempts to set up cotton plantations on the model of the southern states of America were a failure, so that the expatriates became just another level of appropriators living on the Indian peasantry rather than the harbingers of a true capitalist agriculture. In its turn the failure of economic growth and the poverty of the infrastructure meant that the hoped for boom in British manufactured exports to India was aborted. It is true that sales of British twist and yarn increased ten-fold between 1815 and 1834. But finished cloths did not make rapid headway until the later 1840s so that British penetration of the Indian market was a disappointment compared with the heady advances made in most other parts of the world. Empire had brought few of the expected advantages to the British state or even to its entrepreneurs two decades after the completion of political dominion. It was against this background that the Court of Directors of the Company, worried by the spectre of debt and war, dispatched Lord William Bentinck to India as Governor-General in 1828.

## DILEMMAS OF THE COMPANY'S STATE

The year 1820 was traditionally represented as a watershed in Indian history. All the major Indian states with the exception of the Sikhs had been brought to heel. Pliant régimes had been fostered and the 'freebooting system' had been suppressed. However, the completion of conquest did not bring stability for the Company. On the contrary, its problems in the first half of the nineteenth-century were very much an extension of the basic financial dilemmas which had first pushed it along the road of conquest in the late eighteenth-century. Insecurity on its extended frontiers and the desire to seize new revenues encouraged expansion. Expansion in turn generated new financial commitments which could only be met by trying to ratchet up land revenue. But squeezing the Indian states for tribute and the dependent territories for land revenue merely gave a spur to internal revolt and impaired the ability of India's peasant economy to generate new resources itself. Between 1820 and 1857 therefore, Company government lurched from expansion to retrenchment and back and efforts at reform were implemented painfully slowly. Despite the fine words, the problems faced by Lord Dalhousie when he became Governor-General in 1848 were essentially those bequeathed by Wellesley in 1805.

The much-lauded Age of Reform associated with the administration of Lord William Bentinck (1828–35) implied for many contemporaries reform mainly in the sense of 'economical reform'. This meant cutting the wasteful expenditure of government, rolling back its corrupting influences and breaking down vested interests. It represented a retreat from the swollen interventionist administration of the Napoleonic years like that which had already begun in Britain. In India the immediate cause was the imminent bankruptcy of government brought about by profligate salaries and swollen military expenditure which had been boosted by the war of annexation against Burma (1824–6). As the Age of Reform began, Sir Charles Metcalfe, a senior administrator who served his apprenticeship in the Wellesley era, gloomily remarked that India 'has yielded no surplus revenue. It has not even paid its own expenses'.[8] The Company, he said, was probably going to loose its monopoly of the China trade – the only profitable activity – as the free trade lobby grew in strength in Britain. The army was under-funded and grossly inefficient so that 'a very little mismanagement might accomplish our expulsion' from India.[9] Bentinck's main aim and main achievement was to cut establishment costs by trimming the army's perquisites and engineering a long-term fall in the number and remuneration of civil servants. Between 1829 and 1835 he transformed a budget deficit of one and a half million pounds sterling into a surplus of half a million pounds. Bentinck sought to cure the Wellesley disease; in fact he merely alleviated it. The underlying problems actually worsened during his administration. India suffered a sharp price depression and a collapse of European-controlled investment. Sales of British goods to India rose only slowly. Worst of all British India found stability neither on its internal or external frontiers.

It is against this background that Bentinck's social and educational reforms must be set. The Governor-General was certainly influenced by the utilitarian philosophy of government urged by James Mill. He believed that good laws make good men. He sympathised with evangelical Christianity. He was attracted to Ricardo's theory of rent which held that landlords were parasites on productive resources and he patronised officials such as R. M. Bird who were responsible for the implementation of anti-landlord policies in the North-Western Provinces. Yet these enthusiasms were tempered by a spirit of gradualism – a fear of the consequences of sudden change – and an appreciation of

[8] Metcalfe to Bentinck, 19 May 1829, C. H. Philips (ed.), *The Correspondence of Lord William Cavendish Bentinck* (Oxford, 1977), i. 199.
[9] ibid.; cf. Ellenborough to Bentinck, 11 October 1829, ibid., 310.

the vulnerability of Britain's position in India which was almost as profound as that of the great conservatives, Malcolm and Munro.

Bentinck moved against the practice of ritual murder and robbery associated with the wandering religious cult of the Thugs and supported their arch-enemy William Sleeman. But this merely reinforced earlier policies directed towards the suppression of sects such as the Gosains and Sannyasis. Only the 'Thug scare' was new and this derived from an exaggerated British fear of all wandering people, sharpened by the disturbed conditions of the 1820s and 30s. In taking steps against infanticide and human sacrifice Bentinck was attempting to stamp out practices which had never had the sanction of Hindu scriptures and had been specifically denounced by Sikh and Muslim lawgivers. Even in the case of the outlawing of widow-burning (*sati*) in 1829 he was only extending the earlier interventions by British authorities in Hindu custom. Horrifying as sati was, it was more a symbolic issue than a major social problem and it must be remembered that fewer than 1,000 widows were burned each year during the 1820s according to official figures. The practice has all the hallmarks of a 'reinvented tradition' which spread among the newly respectable commercial people of the Calcutta region. The colonial authorities were much more circumspect in their policies against what they saw as obnoxious customs among the warrior peoples of north and central India. This is not to imply that such measures were unimportant as symbols of a new spirit for the British and their conservative Bengali opponents or even as humanitarian statements, simply that their impact on society was severely limited.

This was true also of the changes in the Indian educational system which concerned Victorian writers. The use of Persian was abolished in official correspondence (1835); the government's weight was thrown behind English-medium education and Thomas Babington Macaulay's Codes of Criminal and Civil Procedure (drafted 1841–2, but not completed until the 1860s) sought to impose a rational, Western legal system on the amalgam of Muslim, Hindu and English law which had been haphazardly administered in British courts. These fruits of the Bentinck era were significant. But they were only of general importance in so far as they went with the grain of social changes which were already gathering pace in India. The Bombay and Calcutta intelligentsia were taking to English education well before the Education Minute of 1836. Flowery Persian was already giving way in north India to the fluid and demotic Urdu. As for the changes in the legal system, they were only implemented after the Rebellion of 1857 when communications improved and more substantial sums of money were made available for education.

Bentinck and his successors were impeded in carrying out even those limited measures of reform of which they approved – road-building, irrigation and public works improvements – by the malaise of the colonial economy and the ideology of minimalist government. Government revenues were seriously diminished by the price depression which affected many parts of India during the first half of the century but which was particularly severe in the 1830s and 40s. The decline of the rupee value of agricultural produce was sharpest and most long lasting in Madras presidency which had been the milch cow of Indian finance in the eighteenth century and was to become so once again in the late nineteenth century. Here the index of prices taken as 100 in the decade 1816–25 had fluctuated greatly, declining at one point to 50.8 for the years 1840–5 and not recovering to base until 1855–60.[10] In Bombay there was a similar level of decline though at a slightly later date. In northern India the feverish commercial boom after the end of the Napoleonic wars continued until about 1827 when the coming turbulence in cotton, indigo and fine grain prices was heralded by the sudden failure of European indigo concerns. Here the depression was over in most areas by the early 1840s as cotton demand from China picked up sharply.

Use of the terms 'depression' and 'price depression' to describe these phenomena was made popular in the 1930s by two Madras economists, P. J. Thomas and B. Nataraja Pillai. They drew parallels with the world depression of their own era which can be a little misleading. It is true that the contraction of world silver supplies after the Latin American Revolutions affected price levels internationally, and was especially disruptive for silver-based economies such as India and China. But India in the 1830s was not closely enough integrated into the world economy for international developments to be the sole cause for her internal problems. India, too, was hardly a single national economy in the 1830s. There was much internal variation in price movements, even if governments were generally in poor financial circumstances.

[10] P. J. Thomas and B. Nataraja Pillai, *Economic Depression in the Madras Presidency* (Madras, 1934), pp. 4–11.

Three further general forces appear to have been at work in creating an impression of economic malaise. First, the very heavy revenue rates imposed by the incoming colonial power appear to have forced farmers to produce more crops for the market. Since difficulties in inter-regional and international transport remained, severe gluts developed. Secondly, the rapid disintegration of the high-spending Indian courtly élites and armies reduced demand for commodities such as fine grains, silks and spices. The colonial army was much smaller and was operating away from the main areas of production. It could not initially fill the gap. The economic policy of colonial government was also directed by 1828 to cost-cutting. Finally, the government itself imposed upon this developing set of problems a short-term crisis of liquidity by closing several regional mints which had played an important rôle in recycling gold and silver from rural hoards into general circulation.

Local conditions were also important, explaining the marked variation in response between one region and another. Madras suffered continuous bullion scarcities in the early nineteenth century. The Presidency had lost about 40 per cent of its export trade in cloths between the period 1824–34 and 1840–50. Much of the contraction was in south-east Asia where British manufactures ousted the Madras blue and red cloths which had previously been great silver earners. The particular problems of Madras were also exacerbated by the very rapid imposition of cash revenue and rents in place of grain rents in the period 1800–10, by heavy provincial expenditures on the wars in south-east Asia between 1820 and 1824, and also by chronic problems concerning the cashing of Company bills at Madras. In the Delhi–Agra region, by contrast, the sudden crash of the indigo concerns which had been debtors to local landholders and bankers caused great disruption. Central India in turn suffered from the sudden cessation of Company raw cotton purchases when its monopoly over the China trade was ended in 1834. These difficulties were deepened by famine in 1838 and persistent wars of 'pacification' against local Rajput chieftains.

Even where regions escaped lightly, supported perhaps by a better mix of crops or lucrative grain sales during the famines of 1833 and 1838, there was an air of economic stagnation which dampened the optimism of officials and merchants. The collapse of European indigo producers and associated agency houses between 1827 and 1838 reduced official optimism that European-controlled capital could vitalise India's agrarian economy. The Indian commercial classes, battered by entry into the world market on unfavourable terms, seemed unlikely to provide colonial rule with a sturdy range of allies. Modernising enterprises in ship-building, coal, and joint-stock forms such as those pioneered by Dwarkanath Tagore in Calcutta, fell early victim to trade cycles and the short-sighted exclusiveness of British financial interests. Most significant the long depression revealed the almost universal failure of the Company's raj to secure growing revenues from willing allies in the countryside – this was despite the Whig Permanent Settlement, the conservative ryotwari arrangements in the south and the first flush of utilitarian enthusiasm in western India. The fall in agricultural prices in Madras caused the magistrate of Cuddapah to conclude in 1843 that the 'universal complaint and request of the ryots [peasants] is to be allowed to reduce their farms, a convincing proof that cultivation is not profitable and that land has never been saleable.'[11] Even as late as 1856, Lord Harris, Governor of Madras, concluded that the area under cultivation was only 'one fifth' of the total cultivable acreage and similar cries of alarm had been common in Bombay during the previous decade.

All this would have been less serious if there had been hope of stability on the Company's internal and external frontiers. Bentinck's reforms had swung the deficit into a surplus of £½ million by 1835 but the improvement was paper thin and easily eroded by revolts in India and wars on the borders. Bentinck's cost-cutting presupposed a policy of non-intervention in the Indian States. Yet demilitarisation and depression there had created hardship which converged ominously with dislike of the British and their puppets. Indeed, some officials such as Meadows Taylor[12] saw a general pattern of imperial degeneration in the rash of revolts during the 1830s. The Lingayat peasantry of the Nagar Taluka of Mysore revolted in 1830 and the ham-handed response of the court embroiled the British in direct and costly administration of this once model state after 1831. In Hyderabad disturbances continued among dispossessed military factions and Hindu chieftains. British revenue agents were withdrawn from the state in 1830, but the situation scarcely became more settled. In 1839 the Nizam's brother Mubariz-ud-Daulah, was implicated in an abortive

[11] Magistrate to Board of Revenue, 25 July 1845 cited Thomas and Pillai, *Economic Depression*, pp. 18–19.
[12] Meadows Taylor, *The story of my life* (Edinburgh, 1878), p. 73.

coup d'état and there was an official panic because it was incorrectly assumed that radical Muslim divines were implicated. By 1832 the situation in Awadh had also degenerated as the court was squeezed between zamindar revolt and Company pressure. By far the most costly brushfire wars, however, were those associated with the pacification of tribal societies. In the 1820s the Burma wars had unleashed new pressures on tribal lands on the north-east frontier as the British army built roads and Hindu moneylenders moved into the forests in their wake. Revolts broke out among the Kasias and the Nagas. The pressure of pioneer peasant settlers and British interference also stirred the Kol and Bhil tribal peoples of central India to reaction.

Ultimately, however, it was events on the north-western frontier of British India that plunged the Company's authority and finances back into crisis again. The Bombay government and that city's private interests had always favoured commercial expansion up the river Indus. With the China trade out of the Company's hands, even Bentinck found it difficult to resist the lure of the area's supposed trading riches. He had concluded a commercial treaty with the Emirs of Sindh before he resigned. Whig notions of the balance of power to counteract Russian advances in central Asia with a strong British presence in north-west India also turned eyes to the tracts beyond the 'natural' boundary on the Jumna. But the most important consideration, which resulted in the outpouring of money and blood in Sindh, the Punjab and Afghanistan, was the gradual disintegration of Ranjit Singh's polity in the Punjab after his long-expected death in 1839. The Afghanistan adventure and occupation of Sindh (1838, completed 1843) was in large part a misconceived reinsurance against further instability on this crucial frontier.

The evolution of both Punjab and Sindh indicated the lines of change along which other eighteenth-century regional states might have proceeded had they not been regarded as more direct threats to British interests. Ranjit Singh had pursued a policy similar to that of Tipu Sultan or the Marathas a generation earlier. He had built up an infantry and cavalry army of about 40,000 men (80,000 with peasant militia) and 150 serviceable heavy guns to replace the old mounted Sikh war-bands and he had officered it with Europeans trained in the Napoleonic style like the Italian D'Avitabile. The army allowed him to increase his large revenue resources (estimated at Rs 100 lakhs at one time) overawing other Sikh magnates and extending his rule into the

THE EAST INDIA COMPANY'S STATE

Muslim north-west. The army itself, organised through networks of local communities and drawn from the peasant brotherhoods of the Rechna and Jullunder areas proved a useful counterweight to the Sikh aristocrats, descendants of the eighteenth-century irregular cavalry. Ranjit Singh had gathered around himself a generation of new men including Muslims and Sikh religious leaders from the villages. Such men balanced the power of the Sikh religious establishment based on the holy city of Amritsar and the military brotherhood of the Akalis. Like the Talpur Emirs of Sindh, Ranjit Singh was also a great monopolist, enhancing the economic strength of the central government through control of the grain and salt trades and the valuable commerce in Kashmir shawls.

Yet the stability of the Punjab depended on the astuteness of the old monarch himself. His death opened up the many fissures in society caused as much by the British diplomatic and economic presence on the periphery as by the conflicts following the creation of a new army and ruling élite. Peasant army and royal relatives were pitted against Sikh magnates of the eastern Punjab who had been suborned into connection by the British.

Further to the north something similar was happening in Afghanistan, though the foreign *éminence grise* in this case was thought to be the Russians. The Emir, Dost Mohammad was also modernising his army and trying to extend some semblance of central authority beyond the environs of the capital Kabul. This was regarded as peculiarly menacing in the contemporary 'domino theory' because Afghanistan was the technical overlord of Sindh whose own rulers controlled a rich vein of trade from Bombay presidency to the northwest. Again, the economic policies of Sindh were peculiarly obnoxious to the British, consisting as they did of close control through state granaries of the province's agricultural produce and swingeing taxes on trade down the river Indus. Sindhis were 'certainly the most bigoted, the most *self-sufficient*, and the most ignorant people on record.'[13]

Fortified by Whig self-confidence and the spirit of expanding commerce, Lord Auckland (1836–42) tried to solve India's problems of rickety finances and external instability with Wellesley's policy of annexation and conquest. Sindh was conquered by Sir Charles Napier

---

[13] Paper on Sindh by J. McMurdo communicated by J. Bird, *Journal of the Royal Asiatic Society*, i, 1834, 244 (my itals.).

between 1839 and 1842 thus cutting a path to Afghanistan. The Punjab was invaded and defeated in 1845 and a British-controlled council of regency was established to bring the peasant army and outlying chieftains to heel. Since it was Wellesley's policy it was predictable that the result would be Wellesley's indebtedness. The total cost of these expeditions was well over £15 million, so that the budget carefully balanced by Bentinck went soaring back into deficit in the late 1830s. But unlike Wellesley, Auckland did not have the benefit of the Duke of Wellington or the brilliant diplomats of the Malcolm and Munro school, so the military consequences varied between uncertain and disastrous. Sindh was pacified, but British intervention in the Punjab merely served to compound the instability. It succeeded in weakening the power of the Sikh aristocracy while enraging and frightening the peasant army. Worse still the Afghanistan episode ended in bloody humiliation for the British. The appearance of a foreign army at the heart of this pious Islamic society sparked resistance in and around Kabul while the British had dragged out their lines of communication across a terrain whose intricate tribal politics they barely understood. Thus 20,000 men perished in the two occupations of Kabul and the Company began to look with disfavour upon the eastern Indian sepoys who had served it so well since the 1760s.

## REFORMATION OF THE COMPANY'S STATE;
### 1845–57

Despite the Afghanistan débâcle Governors-General Ellenborough (1842–4), Hardinge (1844–8) and Dalhousie (1848–56) did not give up the policy of expanding Company power to its 'natural' frontiers within the subcontinent. The British could hardly draw back from the Punjab, while the other big dependent states were tempting prizes for authorities desperately seeking out new sources of cash. Yet revenue shortfalls emerging against a background of debt and foreign war did cause a more fundamental reappraisal of the colonial state's relationship with rural society. As the depression lifted and external trade improved, the lineaments of the late Victorian Raj began to emerge. The basic principles were to be a more realistic level of agrarian taxation which allowed some degree of development and helped create a peasantry exporting agricultural raw materials. They, it was hoped, would in turn buy the produce of Lancashire looms. Government's revenues and India's overall balance of trade with Asia would thus begin to recover. The technological advances of the 1850s – the scientific revenue survey, improved roads, railways and irrigation along with rapid transit to Europe, could be enlisted to give substance to the declarations of modernity heard in the 1830s.

Senior officials in the provinces had already initiated the change before Lord Dalhousie put his seal on it. The new order was signalled by the revenue conference held in 1847 by the three heads of the Bombay Revenue Survey, G. Wingate, H. Goldsmid and D. Davidson. Without challenging the concept of a ryotwari settlement, they had begun to operate since 1841 a new detailed mode of assessment which varied rates of revenue according to the different types of soil and took into account costs of production. Pressure from Manchester and other cotton consumers for cheaper, better-quality and more regular supplies played a part in setting the new trend, but persistent revenue shortfalls and peasant indebtedness provided the catalyst. While the rhetoric of the survey's leaders was sometimes indistinguishable from that of the 'utilitarians' of the 1830s, they were influenced by the ideas of the economist Richard Jones who argued against Ricardo and Mill that 'rent' (revenue) should not cut into the peasant's subsistence. This more sophisticated understanding of peasant economics went along with a clear statement that revenue rates would be secure for at least thirty years and that investments such as wells and groves put in over that period would not be taxed. Only occupied lands were to be taxed and generous arrangements for remissions in case of bad seasons were introduced. The effect was to reduce significantly tax on poorer lands and marginal holdings.

The new Bombay revenue rates came into operation when external circumstances also were beginning to be more favourable. The assessments were generally fixed against prices in the period 1835–45 when the depression was at its most severe, but prices had begun to edge up. The disappearance of the Company as a major purchaser in 1834 and the growth of demand from Europe and China initiated a period of prosperity for Bombay cotton exporters which was only temporarily interrupted by the slump at the end of the American Civil War. Government and the towns did well. Land-revenue receipts in Bombay which had remained static and even fallen in the first half of the century picked up from Rs. 21 lakhs in 1850 to Rs. 29 lakhs in 1870–1 and Rs. 34 lakhs in 1890. Price rises outstripped revenues in real terms so that land values began to lift and even peasants' occupancy rights became a valuable form of private property. The Parsi and Gujarati merchant communities of Bombay flourished despite Europeans' strengthening position in the export trade as the electric telegraph and iron ships gave them an edge. These were the years when Bombay saw a boom in the construction of neo-Gothic buildings.

In the countryside of southern Gujarat the British finally began to see what they had devoutly awaited since the time of Munro – a rich yeoman class which would provide a solid ballast for the Raj. The Pattidar community of Gujarat, long known as careful farmers and experts in the use of manure, gained disproportionately from the prosperity built upon good communications, a relatively low population density and competition between agents of Bombay-based European firms.[14] A small number of substantial Pattidars of districts such as Kaira and Ahmedabad liberated themselves from professional moneylenders and began to lend money themselves and cart their produce to market. The new direction in revenue management was less successful in the harsher conditions of the upland Deccan. An early expansion of the acreage under cotton between 1840 and 1860 rapidly came up against the limits of cultivable land. In 1838, 50 per cent of arable land in the Bombay Deccan was reckoned to be waste, but in 1871 the percentage was tiny. There were only limited possibilities for improvements through state-supported irrigation schemes in the north Deccan. Many cultivators remained heavily in debt to immigrant moneylenders so that rural conflicts intensified. Yet a small élite of substantial men does appear to have emerged in districts such as Poona and Sholapur with some minor stake in the stability of colonial government.

In the Madras Presidency there was a more piecemeal movement towards more 'scientific' and lower agrarian taxation. In all three of the major physical divisions – plains, river valleys and the upland Kongunad – high revenue rates, falling demand and poor transport had impeded development between 1810 and 1845. After 1845 some improvement was detected in Kongunad where the enterprising Vellala peasants displayed some of the characteristics typical of the Gujarat Pattidars. The Collector of Coimbatore remarked in 1851 that a large number of new wells had been built and collapsed old ones opened up

[14] Shri Prakash, 'The evolution of agrarian economy in Gujarat, 1830–1930', unpub. Cambridge University Ph.D. diss., 1984.

in the previous fifteen years. One good effect of the ad hoc lowering of rates on 'garden' cultivation was that lands were 'becoming saleable' and that discussions were now arising on 'old dormant claims to lands long since waste'.[15] In 1845 the Madras Department of Roads was formed, new construction was commenced and the rate of cart hire showed a steady decline. In the 'black soil' plain lands of Ramnad and Tinevelly cotton acreages advanced steadily and the port of Tuticorin served by enterprising Roman Catholic Paravas became a major south-coast exporter. A new level of substantial yeoman farmers began to show itself, different from the village headman of the past, though often also engrossing village offices.

Swifter changes were soon in evidence in the river valleys. Since 1800 rural poverty and government neglect had allowed many of the indigenous irrigation works to decline. This was particularly true in the districts along the Kavery, such as Trichinopoly and Tanjore and also on the delta of the rivers Krishna and Godaveri where constant zamindari disturbances and bankruptcies during the 1830s had damaged output. Between 1836 and 1860, however, a large-scale plan of irrigation improvement was initiated by Arthur Cotton, one of the greatest of the Anglo-Indian civil engineers. This had the effect of bringing nearly a million acres of new paddy land under cultivation in the valleys. Dense settlement and large networks of markets were to make the southern valleys among the most vibrant agrarian societies in India. While many of the technical details of the scheme were mis-handled and indigenous irrigation schemes were allowed to decay, there was a clear medium-term improvement in output. In the later nineteenth century the Indian government was to fund many of its projects from the regular and easily extracted surplus of the southern paddy farmers.

Even amidst the complexity of north India the later 1840s stand as a period of real rather than vaunted change. After a bad start the auth-orities in the newly conquered Punjab began to gratify the productive Sikh and Jat farmers of the riverine tracts with low revenue assess-ments. In Bengal the substantial farmers of the eastern delta began in the early 1850s to turn to jute, the cash-crop staple of the following century. In the north-western provinces during the 1830s and 40s utilitarian-inspired assault on large magnates and talukdars had rela-

[15] Cited in S. Saraswathi, 'The Kongu Vellalas of the nineteenth-century', unpub. M.Phil. diss., University of Madras, 1979, p. 36.

tively little economic (though considerably more moral) effect. The forfeited lands which poured on to the market in the 1830s were mainly those of the poor, joint-cultivating communities situated in badly irrigated and isolated areas. Buoyed up by sporadic demand from Europe for sugar and China for cotton the agrarian economy began to improve marginally in the 1840s. The population of all-India appears to have begun to move up significantly about the same date slowly fuelling an increase in consumption. About 1848, grain prices, which had oscillated around a stationary mean since the 1820s, began appreciably to move up. The value of zamindari rights, which had been estimated at no more than one and one-third years of the revenue as late as 1837, had risen to three and one-half years' revenue by 1848. The cultivated area itself began to leap forward from about 1845, partly stimulated by the rapid recovery of population from the famines of 1833 and 1838[16] Better seasons and slowly rising export prices and population lay behind this change. But government policy was not insignificant. In some parts of the north-western provinces revisions of revenue were quite indulgent after 1836, and under Dalhousie promised irrigation improvements began coming through with the full extension of the Jumna canal system and opening of the Ganges Canal in 1854. Here also, the foundations were laid for a relatively prosperous yeoman élite which could sustain government revenue and rural peace later in the century. Kurmi peasants in the east and Jat farmers in the west stepped forward to occupy the position left by the declining brotherhoods of Rajput village controllers who could not adapt to more productive cultivation because caste status forbade them from touching the plough. Ironically, the differentials opened up by this very uneven acceleration of agrarian production were to envenom the 1857 struggle in the Ganges–Jumna plains. The inequitable growth of the later nineteenth-century was already foreshadowed.

Dalhousie inherited in 1848 an agrarian economy which now had the capacity for slow but sustained expansion. The revenue shortfalls of the 1830s and 40s were now past. The seasons after 1838 were much better. Though the volatility of the external market was demonstrated by the recession of 1848 and the disruption in China during the Taiping rebellion, India's external markets were beginning to improve. Before the 1857 rebellion the acreage under tea and coffee in the Nilgiri

[16] E. Stokes, 'North and Central India', D. Kumar and M. Desai (eds.), *Cambridge Economic History of India*, ii (Cambridge, 1983), 55.

Hills and Assam was appreciable and jute and sugar had replaced ailing indigo as major export crops. In 1852 as the international economic situation began to improve and the Government's budget came into temporary surplus, the first considerable quantities of British metropolitan capital were invested in the subcontinent. Over the next decade more than £10 million was put into India's railway schemes by European investors looking for outlets for capital beyond continental railways and Egyptian loans. The Government set out to encourage these schemes by forming local railway committees, as much for military as for economic reasons. Dalhousie who inherited the modernising rhetoric of Bentinck along with the rigour of Peel's administration in Britain, pressed forward the development of the infrastructure and the rationalisation of bureaucracy. The electric telegraph was installed and presidency merchants were given access to it in 1853. The limited advances of railway lines (200 miles by 1856) and the telegraph began to bring together grain prices throughout India and to help export merchants in up-country towns.[17]

Yet Dalhousie was a Governor-General firmly in the tradition of Wellesley. Modernisation of the Indian economy and the use of 'native agency' were firmly subordinated to the needs of military and financial security. The most striking way in which he sought to nurture India's convalescent budget was not by improvement but by annexation. Like all the governors-general before him, Dalhousie was haunted by fear of Britain's strategic weakness in the subcontinent. The outbreak in 1849 of revolt in the still-untamed Punjab army as much as the revolt of the Santal tribesmen (1853–6), a resistance movement within a day's ride of Calcutta, emphasised the feeling of fragility. The displacing of 'sham kings' within troublesome Indian states and the extension of frontiers to India's 'natural boundaries' seemed to be the only ways of providing permanent stability. With the exception of the annexation (in 1852) of the Burmese delta kingdom of Pegu, where the men on the spot exceeded their orders, Dalhousie's expansion was not a manifestation of any jingoism of 'free trade imperialism'. Manchester cotton interests were, of course, pleased by the annexation in 1853 of the rich cotton-growing tracts of the Berars (designed to 'solve' Hyderabad's chronic fiscal haemorrhage). Central Asian trade and the Russians

[17] For Dalhousie's period a good recent treatment is D. J. Howlett, 'An end to expansion. Influences on British policy in India c. 1830–60', unpub. Ph.D. diss., Cambridge University, 1981.

were again introduced to justify the final annexation of the Punjab. Prudential concerns of strategy and revenue maximisation were, however, at the heart of policy making. Dalhousie's famous 'doctrine of lapse' by which kingdoms without a direct male heir escheated to the Company on the death of a ruling raja, secured three strategically placed territories in Satara (1848), Jhansi (1853) and Nagpur (1854) and added £5 million to revenues with very little expense. The annexation of Awadh (1856) was expected to bring in a further £5 million along with a rich agricultural tract and a commercial and financial community which had invested huge sums in Company loans over the past forty years.

It is the case of the Punjab, however, which most clearly reveals the direction of Dalhousie's policy. The turbulent frontier in the north which had worried the British since the death of Ranjit Singh in 1839 was finally settled by 1852. Ranjit Singh's powerful peasant army was disbanded but nearly half its soldiers were absorbed into the new Company force which was to be weaned away from its dependence on recruits from eastern Awadh and the Benares region. The agricultural communities of the Jullunder and Rechna Doabs which had provided a majority of the Punjab soldiery were to be placated by heavy investment in irrigation improvement and a revenue settlement which after several false starts took from them as little as 25 per cent of the value of produce, and did so after the crops had been harvested rather than before so that they could pay more easily. This was the famous Punjab system of Sir John Lawrence. Here then the India of the Crown was already in gestation. It was to be the India of a mercenary army whose career as an overseas 'fire-brigade' for the British Empire had already begun in earnest with the campaigns in China and south-east Asia. It was to be an India where the acquiescence of rural society was bought by a progressive fall in the weight of land revenue on the more prosperous, by a slow but clear expansion of agriculture in Madras, Gujarat and the Punjab and by intermittent attempts to associate powerful villagers with the alien government.

It is ironic that in the short term the birth of this new empire was to be aborted by a massive revolt in the heart of the Company's territories which finally destroyed its finances and blew it into oblivion after it had survived more than sixty years of assaults from free traders. For in the countryside of north India a generation of depression and grindingly high rates of revenue had been alleviated in a manner so piecemeal and inequitable that any spark could have set off rural revolt. The prudence with which the Regency diplomats like Wilks and Metcalfe had assuaged the bruised sensibilities of Indian princes and their courtiers had been thrown aside as 'sham kings' and 'drones on the soil' were deposed with the hard edge of early Victorian dogmatism. Cultural reaction converged furiously with an uprising of landlord and peasant. And the occasion of revolt was to be the Company's attempt to discipline the haughty Bengal army, perhaps the only part of the reform programme to be pursued with vigour.

The East India Company had penetrated the subcontinent by making use of its buoyant markets in produce and land revenue. But the needs of its financial and military machine had tended to snuff out that buoyant entrepreneurship of revenue farmers, merchants and soldiers which had kept the indigenous system functioning. Only by the 1850s was this lesson beginning to be learnt. The government was boxed in by its inability to reconcile financial stability with economic growth. However, the period was certainly not one of social stagnation or the simple continuity of pre-colonial political forms. The next chapter turns to social and ideological change in early-nineteenth-century India.

# CHAPTER 5

# PEASANT AND BRAHMIN: CONSOLIDATING 'TRADITIONAL' SOCIETY

The East India Company inherited on a greatly magnified scale the conflict between state entrepreneurship – the desire to squeeze up land revenue or create monopolies – and the entrepreneurship of merchant and peasant which had bedevilled many eighteenth-century Indian kingdoms. The result for the British was a long period of economic lethargy which was barely obscured by the slow introduction of the panoply of the modern state. Yet this should not be taken to imply that the early nineteenth century was an era devoid of significant social change. On the contrary, as this chapter will show, these years were critical in the creation of the modern Indian peasantry, its patterns of social divisions and its beliefs.

Many early Victorian writers were convinced that India was on the brink of a rapid transformation. Hinduism was fading in the face of evangelical Christianity; 'caste disabilities' suffered by the lower orders would disappear in the face of good laws; the 'isolation' of the Indian village would be blown apart by the impact of industrialisation. Writers in the second half of the twentieth century have dissented. Some have argued that the subcontinent was condemned to stagnation by its subjection to colonial interests – that society was frozen into caricatures of its feudal past by British land-revenue systems and the destruction of its artisan producers. Others have argued that colonial rule was peripheral to most of Indian society: it could effect changes neither for good nor ill because the new export trades were fitful and the waves of reform and regeneration were merely paper debates conducted in the corridors of Government House, Calcutta.

Neither of these formulations is entirely satisfactory. The deep changes expected by the early Victorians evidently never occurred – or at least not until better means of communication, the railways and the printing press came into their own after 1860. Yet there is no doubt either that society was different in important respects on the eve of the rebellion of 1857 from what it had been one hundred years earlier.

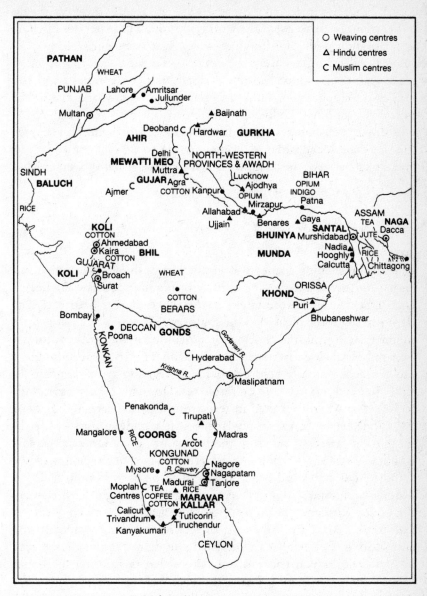

○ Weaving centres
△ Hindu centres
C Muslim centres

PATHAN
WHEAT
PUNJAB    Lahore  Amritsar
                  Jullunder
Multan ◉

SINDH
BALUCH

RICE

                          △ Baijnath
                  Deoband C
                          Hardwar   GURKHA
        AHIR
                  Delhi
MEWATTI MEO
        Muttra △   NORTH-WESTERN
GUJAR Agra        PROVINCES & AWADH
Ajmer C  COTTON Kanpur   Lucknow
                          Ajodhya △   BIHAR
KOLI                      OPIUM       OPIUM
COTTON                    Mirzapur    INDIGO
◉ Ahmedabad       Allahabad △ Benares  Patna
◉ Kaira           Ujjain  △      △ Gaya   ASSAM
    BHIL  COTTON          Benares  SANTAL  TEA  NAGA
GUJARAT                   BHUINYA  Murshidabad ◉  Dacca
KOLI ◉ Broach                      Nadia        JUTE
    Surat  WHEAT          MUNDA    Hooghly ◉   RICE
                 COTTON            Calcutta    Chittagong
Bombay ●         BERARS   KHOND  ORISSA
        ● DECCAN                  Puri △
          Poona  GONDS            Bhubaneshwar △
              Godavari R.
              C Hyderabad
        Krishna R.
                 ◉ Maslipatnam

        Penakonda C
                 △ Tirupati
Mangalore ● RICE COORGS  ● Madras
                 C Arcot
        KONGUNAD
        COTTON   Nagore
Mysore ● R. Cauvery  ◉ Nagapatam
        Madurai ● Tanjore ◉
Moplah C TEA △ RICE
Centres  COFFEE MARAVAR
Calicut ● COTTON KALLAR
Trivandrum ● Tuticorin
Kanyakumari ● Tiruchendur

        CEYLON

5  British India: economic and social

Dominant lineages, patterns of local power and religious institutions showed remarkable resilience to the effects of colonial rule, but the context within which they operated was significantly different. Some of the changes represented the working through of processes of commercialisation and state building which had been initiated by pre-colonial rulers; others were the result of the slow incorporation of regional Indian economies into a single unified economy, and the further development of links between this economy and the world capitalist economy. Colonial government operated to speed up or slow down such changes more often than to initiate them. This chapter considers the social order and religious and social ideas and seeks to find links between developments which have usually been treated separately.

## THE CONSOLIDATION OF THE INDIAN PEASANTRY

One area of striking change was in the relationship between man and his natural environment. The century beginning 1780 saw the beginnings of extensive deforestation in the subcontinent. Before 1860 it was the trees of the plains and the southern hills which fell. Large scale commercial logging and clearing for agriculture in the northern forests were only in their early stages. Yet the denudation of peninsular India had proceeded rapidly before population began to grow significantly after 1845 and put pressure on resources. During the early nineteenth century denudation resulted instead from the pacification policies of the colonial state, from the movement – often under duress – of pioneer peasant farmers, and from the beginnings of commercial exploitation. Climate and social patterns were already changing in response.

Indigenous states had begun the denudation of the countryside for reasons of military security. According to the eighteenth-century chronicler Kirmani, the Mysore Sultans cleared off much forest in their wars against the tribesmen of Coorg and the Nayars.[1] In the north, Sikhs and Afghans completed the deforestation of the area around Delhi which had probably proceeded fast during the boom of the Mughal economy. The Sikhs again levelled the forests of the

[1] W. Miles (trans. ed.), *History of the reign of Tipu Sultan: Mir Husein Ali Khan Kirmani's 'Neshani Hyduri'* (London, 1844), p. 79; for the Marathas in Rajasthan, E. Thornton, *A Gazetteer of the territories under the government of the East India Company* (London, 1854), i. 61.

Peshawar valley to deny their Muslim enemy natural cover as they acquired a shaky dominance over it in the 1820s.[2] But the British who could draw on their experience of 'clearings' in Scotland and Ireland took ecological warfare to a new level. Arthur Wellesley drove roads through the forests of Malabar and cleared trees to a mile on either side in his campaigns against the Pyche Raja (1800–2). The territories of the conquered poligars and even the Company's allies were also speedily cleared to deny them to Pindaris and tribesmen as hiding places. Sir Thomas Munro remarked to the young Raja of Pudukottai in 1826 that the forest had been dense when he had travelled this way as a young officer in the 1780s, but now 'the woods had been almost cut down and cultivation was going on, some thin wood remaining in places'.[3] The policy of settlement and deforestation had been suggested by the British resident.

Movement of peasant cultivators had also pushed forward the degradation of the forests in many areas. Under the pressure of the heavy land revenue levied on the better soils, farmers moved up into the hills or on to poorer soils and cleared the forest as they went. Others sought to escape from the diseases of the river valleys which were particularly ferocious in the 1820s and 30s. The consequence was an acceleration of felling on the higher lands. Even though aggregate population growth was slow, there had been a significant expansion of the cultivated acreage, and especially the acreage under exhausting crops such as cotton. There was also a rapid expansion of the demand for fire wood and wood for river boats. The British disliked slash-and-burn agriculture even when it was conducted by tribals and had little long-term effect on the evironment. Official statements must therefore be treated with scepticism. Still, there is evidence of an acceleration of permanent felling during this period. Most of the Deccan was now completely treeless by 1840, while Dr Gibson, a botanist, warned in 1846 of 'the rapid destruction which is going on amongst the forests along the whole length of the district [of Kanara] by the process of Cooneri [felling and burning] cultivation',[4] and there were similar complaints from the whole of the western mountain range and Mysore.

[2] Shahamat Ali, *The Sikhs and Afghans in connection with India and Persia* (London, 1847), p. 263.
[3] R. Aiyar, *History of Puddukotai*, i, 366.
[4] Extract from Report of Dr Gibson, 9 March 1846, *Selections from the Old Records of the Trichinopoly District* (Madras, 1931), p. 104.

A more serious threat to the forests was commercial logging. Indian régimes had sought to tax and monopolise valuable timbers. Raja Martanda Varma, for instance, had drawn a large revenue from the teak forests of Travancore. The impact on forests probably varied greatly between areas. A Muslim traveller, Shahamat Ali's, observations on the Himalayas in 1839–40 suggest that much timber was still procured from trees which were uprooted by winter storms and brought down the mountain rivers rather than by felling.[5] But the demands of the European entrepreneurs and the colonial state were more extensive. Massive quantities of teak were felled in the western forests by contractors for the Bombay marine between 1800 and 1830. Reserves were so far threatened that in 1810 the local government appointed a special officer for forest preservation.[6] Meanwhile Palmer and Co., the notorious agency house based in Hyderabad, had begun logging in the Berars. The destruction gathered speed after 1840 when coffee plantations sprang up in some numbers in the south and tea began to expand rapidly in Assam and the Bengal hills.

The wider effects of the felling and degradation of forest are still in need of research. But the cries of alarm spread by botanist officials throughout the Empire in the 1840s – almost an ecological panic – probably did have some independent factual basis.[7] In the 1830s one observer attributed a supposed increase in the intensity of the hot winds of the northern plains to felling in Awadh. It was reported that deforestation in Mysore had diminished the supply of water travelling down the crucial Kavery watercourse and had raised the summer temperatures in Tanjore and Trichinopoly in 1842. Combined with the widespread decay of indigenous village irrigation systems, this sense of decline encouraged the government of Madras to more active water-development policies in the 1850s. Yet the main consequence of felling at this stage was probably the invasion of tribal lands and the increased penetration of money into the tribal economies. This presaged the further incorporation of tribal peoples into patterns of agrarian wage labour in the plains.

The expansion or migration of the plains population of Hindu India at the expense of local cultures and of economic systems which were not geared to the production of an agrarian surplus had proceeded

[5] Shahamat Ali, *Sikhs and Afghans*, p. 111.
[6] Thornton, *Gazetteer*, i, 74.
[7] Richard Grove, 'Ecological change and Imperial policy, 1800–1860', unpub. Ph.D., diss. Cambridge University, 1987.

steadily before colonial rule. For instance, the adoption of Islam among tribal people in east Bengal was indirectly connected with the expansion of rice cultivation into mixed and forested areas. Low caste Bhuinyas in the hills of south Bihar appear to have been descendants of tribal groups which were incorporated into the Hindu system as rice agriculture also expanded into this area between 1400 and 1800.[8] By the eighteenth century money payments had already become part of systems of dependence which had previously been more like ritualised patron–client relationships in which the Hindu warrior masters had played an important part in the religious practice of their servants. The economic changes introduced alongside colonial rule in the early nineteenth century expanded the labour-for-money element in the relationship and tied it to the creation of surplus for export markets.

In some parts of Central India the colonial authorities had deliberately sought to wean or coerce hillmen away from their traditional slash-and-burn or hunter-gatherer life-style to solve a perceived problem of policing. The Bhil tribes of the Khandesh hills, adjoining valuable cotton-growing lands, were first subjected to a series of pacification wars in the 1820s, then settled. So 'The Bheels were registered and waste lands were allotted to all those who were willing to form themselves under certain restrictions into colonies.'[9] By 1826, 300 ploughs were in use among the hillmen of this district and settled agriculture proceeded fast over the next generation. Among the Munda of southern Andhra, punitive expeditions against recalcitrant tribals were justified by British abhorrence of human sacrifice. Such invasions allowed the British to set up raja landholders as mediators and gradually extend both private landed property and a system of reserved forest areas into the hills. In the longer term the resources and mobility of the tribal populations were severely curtailed.

In most areas, however, the slow penetration of Hindu and Jain capital and styles of consumption into the forests and grazing lands was the most significant change. The partnership between the Company and the moneylender-trader which had facilitated the subjugation of India now proceeded in the conquest of India's internal frontiers. Monied settlers from the plains trickled into the central Indian tribal zone secured by types of landlordism and forms of debt

[8] Gyan Prakash, 'Production and the reproduction of bondage. Kamias and maliks in south Bihar. *c.* 1300 to the 1930s', unpub. Ph.D. diss., University of Pennsylvania, 1984.
[9] Thornton, *Gazetteer*, iii, 260.

recovery alien to the domestic economy of the tribal people. Colonial administrators, solicitous for the stability of revenue, conferred on them proprietary rights and legitimised their bonds through the colonial courts. Unequal economic relations between hill and forest dwellers and caste Hindus, including slavery, had existed before colonial rule. But debt bondage and agrarian servitude now become more widespread as the economy recovered from the setbacks of the 1830s and 40s. In 1847, for instance, L. Michael noted that the Kader tribe of the Annamalai Hills were in 'an abject state of slavery worse than anything on the western Ghats'.[10] Traders from the plains bartered rice, salt and coarse cloth for tribal supplies of wood honey, wax and ginger. The indigent tribals only received a tiny proportion of the real value of these commodities from the Hindu traders, and consequently fell into debt. Previously the unequal relations between plains-dwellers and forest or hill men had been periodically adjusted through the looting and plunder by the tribals of settled farmers. Pax Britannica increasingly precluded this type of adjustment. By the time the export economy began to have a significant impact on inland India in the 1850s, tribal people were beginning to resort in much larger numbers to areas of settled agriculture such as the Gujarat cotton zone or the central India wheat zone where they acted as seasonal migrant labourers.[11]

There was also a sharp decline in the fortunes of the extensive nomadic and pastoral economy of the plains in the first half of the nineteenth century. In the eighteenth century, cattle-grazing people had provided an important part of the diet of this, the only populous Asian society which was lactose tolerant. Horse-breeding and trading was also of vital importance to a military aristocracy which marked itself off from the commonalty by the possession of horses. Elephant-catching and trade in the animals was a source of income, as elephants signified royalty. Sheep were suprisingly widely reared as woollen clothes and blankets were vital for winter wear in the colder north of the subcontinent. Though historians have unduly neglected it the importance of the grazing, nomadic lifestyle of many Indians before 1800 is clear from countless legends and rituals. Lord Krishna, modern India's favourite deity was a cowherd. The city of Lucknow was

[10] Actg Secretary Board of Revenue to Collector Trichi, 15 November 1847, *Trichi Old Records*, p. 104.
[11] Crispin Bates, 'Regional dependence and rural development in Central India, 1820–1930', unpub. Ph.D. diss., Cambridge, 1984.

supposedly established by cattle-keeping rajas; a piece of deer-hide still played a part in the initiation ritual of the most orthodox Brahmins. Nor were the hunters and their lords a world apart. At the end of the eighteenth century nomads still plundered the settled agriculturalist, but at the same time they provided them with milk and took their goods to distant markets. The Banjara carriers gave logistical and military support to the rulers of the settled tracts who rewarded them with titles and concessions.

All this changed rapidly in the early nineteenth century. Large nomadic and pastoral populations still persisted in the plains of Haryana, the central Deccan or the north Punjab as late as 1860. However, the British were not enamoured of the nomad. Everywhere they sought to settle and discipline groups such as the Gujars, Bhattis, Rangar Rajputs and Mewatis who moved their herds around, extracting 'protection rent' as they went. The assessment of waste land and creation of more rigid property rights enforceable by court order restricted the nomads' mobility. Many of the herdsmen carrier-peoples of the Deccan for instance, had already become sedentary and subordinate agricultural castes before 1870. The imposition of 'peace' was also significant. In the eighteenth century India had been a world centre of horse breeding and whole communities drew their livelihoods from horses. The Marathas and Sikhs had owed much of their military success to tough breeds of indigenous horse. However, as Balfour wrote in the 1850s 'native breeds of horses declined under British rule'.[12] The Multani, Kutchi and south Deccan varieties of Indian horse were all but extinct and the large communities which had bred them were broken up and had taken to agriculture. Cultivation had spread over the old grazing lands. More important, British success against indigenous régimes had cut off the demand, while Arab and south African horses had largely supplanted the indigenous breeds. The Indian horse stock itself declined because those which served with the British armies were worked all round the year. Previously Indian armies had operated seasonally and mares were able to foal in the slack season.

Changes also overtook cattle breeders and hersdmen. The great bands of pack bullock owners which had roamed the plains in the late eighteenth century, spreading both plunder and trade, were broken up into small groups. The huge Indian armies they once serviced had

[12] E. Balfour, *Cyclopaedia of India and of eastern and southern Asia* (Madras, 1857), ii. 64: 'horse'.

melted away. Cattle disease had struck in the north in the 1830s and many of the great herds had been decimated. In addition bullock carts owned and operated by merchants with hired labourers gradually ousted the freelance pack-bullock merchants of the earlier era. The great contractor Tori Mull could still assemble as many as 160,000 head of cattle for service during the second Sikh war, but such concentrations were hardly seen again after 1850. More important, the remaining herds were broken up smaller and smaller while there seems also to have been a gradual deterioration of stock. In part this seems to have been because grazing land was coming under the plough with the growth of population; but elsewhere the allotment of large areas of grazing ground to speculators, as in the districts south of the Himalayas, seems to have pushed the nomadic cattle which invigorated the settled herds on to poorer and poorer grass.

In terms of the relationship between man and his environment the early nineteenth century was a formative phase. India as it is commonly conceived, a land of settled arable farming, of caste Hindus and of specialist agricultural produce, was very much a creation of this period. The stranger, older India of forest and nomad where the agricultural frontier was as often in retreat as on the advance, began to disappear. The more homogeneous society of peasants and petty moneylenders which emerged in the later nineteenth century was a more appropriate basis for a semi-European colonial state. It also held out better hopes of profit to the importers of Lancashire cottons than the fragmented consumption of nomads and tribals. Still, in the destruction and degradation of forest, forest produce and herds, the people of India had lost some of their resources with which to guard against bad seasons or the intrusion of the larger society from outside. A hundred years later forests and grazing grounds, along with the cultures they supported, have virtually disappeared.

The other side of this story was, of course, the advance of the settled agriculture and peasant petty commodity production. Technological change on the family farm itself seems to have been slow in the early nineteenth century. The Persian wheel type of irrigation system which had spread under the Mughals made further headway, as did the iron-shod plough. But the most significant changes were probably in the external context of farming. Before 1850 there were some significant beginnings in irrigation. The Kavery schemes of Sir Arthur Cotton and the East and West Jumna canals were underway. Some of the new British canals differed from the Mughal canals, moreover, in that they were dug – canals in inhospitable terrain rather than extensions of existing river systems. The massive expansion of production of cotton, indigo and sugar in northern and western India after 1800 also greatly changed the subcontinent's ecology. New varieties of seed, such as American cotton and improved varieties of fodder grass introduced by the colonial authorities were not generally successful. But the balance between existing varieties changed markedly to high-value cash crops. There were some innovations. Jute production expanded rapidly from the early 1850s in East Bengal as demand for sacking grew with the expansion of world trade. Tea and coffee plantations were already established in the Nilgiris by 1830. The foundation of the Assam Tea Company at Darjeeling in 1839 heralded the complete transformation of the ecology of the northern hills and the creation of enhanced demands for agricultural labour.

This spread of crops designed for distribution to Indian and foreign markets was one of the main forces which created a more homogeneous agrarian society in the early nineteenth century. Not only were tribal people and nomads being settled and subordinated to the discipline of producing an exportable surplus but many of the gradations in status and function between people of the settled agricultural tracts which had existed in the Indian states were disappearing and giving way to simpler distinctions based on wealth and landholding. 'Subjects', 'children' and 'dependants' (designated by terms such as *raiyat* and *praja* and *peon*) were becoming peasants in the common Western sociological sense: that is smallholders working on individual plots, deriving sustenance almost entirely from agrarian occupations and distant from the sources of power located in towns. So the colonial impact split the old warrior peasant communities. Their most eminent lineages were separated off as a domesticated aristocracy, or eliminated by war. Inferior families of warrior land-controllers still retained great reserves of power and status in many parts of the countryside. Yet their authority was perceptibly eroded and many families were absorbed into the upper reaches of the peasantry.

In the lower reaches of agrarian society distinctions based on personal status were also breaking down. Domestic and field serfdom for untouchable groups, a status which had been infused with ideas of religion and magic, was falling into disuse. The colonial authorities had abolished the condition which they called 'slavery' on the south coast and moved against the most obvious cases of domestic serfdom in the north by 1850. The British peace also suppressed the practice of taking serfs during war which had remained quite common at the end of the eighteenth century. But more important was the spread of cash crops, of money use and the growth of population which eroded tied, patronal relations such as this. Though the overall population growth rate appears to have been slow in the period 1800–50 (probably under 0.5 per cent per annum), there was a modest doubling of population in areas such as the Deccan and Haryana which had notably low population density at the end of the eighteenth century. Slow population growth combined with more general access to land provided a tied peasantry quite adequate to the purposes of the colonial state and Indian entrepreneurs. Deeper and socially more complex forms of servitude became redundant.

As late as 1840 it was labour rather than land which was the scarce factor of production in much of India. The changing colonial economy did not necessarily increase the proportion of landless labourers. For if the pressures of the land revenue and of agricultural depression forced some poor peasants from the land, there is evidence that persons of very low caste who had previously been debarred from holding land were themselves becoming poor peasants. In eastern Hindustan Buchanan noted that the abolition after 1812 of interdicts against the holding of land by low castes had the effect of increasing the demand for labour, since this customary prohibition had been a way of maintaining a labour pool. In Chhatisgarh in central India, Chamars (a low leather-making and scavenging caste) were building up landholdings.[13] In the south, Paraiyans were becoming tenant farmers[14]; while in the hills of Bihar low-caste farmers were taking on tribal dependants as tied labour, a right which had previously been restricted to high-caste warriors.[15] The settlement of armed retainers of the southern warrior chiefs (*peons*) between 1790 and 1820 and the general abolition of military tenures in favour of cash-revenue and cash-rent forced greater reliance on agricultural income. The weight of qualitative evidence and several new quantitative studies suggest that there was a significant decline of specialist weaving communities in the early nineteenth century. This was especially concentrated in the great

[13] Balfour, *Cyclopaedia*, ii, 145, 'Chamar'.
[14] Ramappa Kamic, 'Memoirs on the origin of slaves' c.1819, published in J. Shortt (ed.), *The Hill Ranges of south India*, iv (Madras 1874), p. 36.
[15] G. Prakash, 'Production and the reproduction of bondage', op. cit.

artisan towns of the pre-colonial period such as Dacca, Murshidabad and Mau in Awadh. Rural weavers in areas such as Tamilnadu, where weaving had been less specialist, survived better. The decline of specialist weaving and spinning drove artisan families to more intense exploitation of their landholdings. Consequently, the proportion of field labourers holding no land rights to the landholding and tenant population may have remained fairly constant at about 20 per cent in the early nineteenth century.

Both the landholding peasantry and the rural labouring class appear to have become more homogeneous during this period. Certainly, the long distance migration of villagers to work as labourers as 'protection seekers' on distant farms appears less common. The colonial government and population growth restricted internal migration and deprived agricultural labourers of much of their bargaining power. At the same time the decline of indigenous states and certain types of village service community amalgamated the great range of subtly differentiated dependants of the pre-colonial period into a recognisable class of cash-earning field labourers. An overall growth of the percentage of cultivating peasants and agricultural workers in the general population is consistent with the view taken by several contemporaries that the agricultural price depression of 1820–50 was in part the result of local overproduction in a situation where sales of grains and pulses were limited by poor transport.

The relationship of this process of social levelling to standards of living and the question of the subcontinent's inheritance of rural poverty is a very complex question, and adequate data does not yet exist. The loss of by-incomes (soldiering, herding, etc.) and the effects of high revenues, famine and the price depressions must have gone a long way to eliminate any gains from the suppression of warfare and the expansion of export cash cropping. The relative bargaining power of rural wage labour must also have been reduced by the colonial state's dislike of migration and the rebound of population in Bengal and the wet south from the travails of the famines and disturbances of 1769–90. It may well be that there was no decisive trend upwards or downwards in rural standards of living in the early nineteenth century, though some peasants, cultivating opium or cotton, may have achieved prosperity amongst this stagnation.

Distinctions of function and status in the higher reaches of the agrarian hierarchy were also being eroded. In the south and west, village élites had been clustered around village office – particularly the office of patel or headman. The headman had been a little king in the village and his control over waste land and revenue management made of him and his kinsmen much more than peasant 'bosses'. The status of headman had already been modified in the later eighteenth century as Maratha and Mysorean officials had sought to limit his privileges. Headman's right had also been monetised and sold to élites which sought shares in village management. Under colonial rule the pressures on the headman lineages greatly increased. In parts of the Central Deccan by mid-century there had been general 'abrogation of the rights of the Patel and his degradation to the level of the other cultivators'.[16] British officials had sometimes tried to purloin the rights of the headmen and had generally attempted to wrest from them control of village waste lands. But agricultural depression and population growth had similar effects. Patels' remuneration was divided up generation by generation so that the receipt to the individual sharer in 33 villages in the Central Maratha Deccan was the paltry sum of Rs.15 per head. Other ancient 'liberties' given for the performance of caste or religious functions in the village and beyond had also been sudivided or eroded by time and the disinterest of European government. So while the total amount of land exempted from taxation on the grounds of 'service' may have been great enough to attract the attention of jealous administrations throughout India in the 1840s, these perquisites were so widely scattered and so fragmented that they no longer provided the basis for a distinct rural service élite in many parts of the country. Even if there was some physical continuity of the families of the village magnates of 1800 through to the small group of 'rich peasants' of the second half of the nineteenth century, the nature and context of their power had changed.

Other classes of village élite had also declined in status. It will be remembered that in parts of south India and throughout north India village élites based not on office-holding but on joint village proprietorship had existed in the pre-colonial period. In the south these statuses were termed mirasi and in the north they were represented by the village-controlling brotherhoods of Brahmins and Rajputs (*pattidari* or *bhaiachara* systems of landholding). While the political struggles of the eighteenth century had sometimes reinforced these associations for

---

[16] Neil Charlesworth, *Peasants and Imperial Rule. Agriculture and agrarian society in the Bombay Presidency, 1850–1935* (Cambridge, 1985), p. 27.

local security, especially in the north, strong states had tried to break them down. There is evidence that mirasi was already on the wane in Mysore under the sultans, while Mughal régimes in the north preferred to deal with individual rajas and revenue-farmers rather than 'hornet's nests' of armed village leaders. Nevertheless, at the end of the eighteenth century what the British saw as joint-village proprietors held great power throughout India. Their power derived as much from their status as lords, warriors and protectors of the village shrines as from any simple notion of proprietorship. And in the same way their livelihood derived from military service and their rights over local service and artisan communities.

The influence of these communities also tended to decline in the early nineteenth century and many of them were absorbed into the wider peasant body. The operation of the market was important here. In the south mirasi seems to have disappeared fastest in areas of expanding cash-crop production or in the environs of the great towns where such rights were marketed, split up and in time became simple free-hold types of property.[17] In the north, the depression of the 1830s and 40s combined with British land-revenue policy to throw the rights of many of the village brotherhood communities on to the market. These communities were squeezed hard when prices fell, and now that their rights in the villages had been welded by the British to their capacity to produce land revenue, arrears inevitably led to auction sales. Some of these rights found their way back into the hands of new purchasers of the same broad caste group. Yet thousands of families of old proprietors still suffered a decline both of income and, more important, of status as they battled against the new landlords from outside the village or village group.

Three other important influences on the position of the eighteenth-century village-controllers are relevant. First the effects of population pressure were felt very strongly. As the Hindu system of inheritance divided and subdivided proprietary rights and income, large sections of these communities had to fall back on their small plots of personal cultivation. In many cases, indeed, they were forced to cultivate with their own hands, something which they felt to be acutely derogatory to their dignity. Secondly, the decline of openings for military service with the advance of the British peace had a significant impact. In both

---

[17] See, e.g., Madras District Revenue Volumes, 1021–22 of 1817, extracted in *Guide to the Records of Madras District from 1719–1835* (Madras, 1836).

south and north India, British rule had severed power in the villages from military service in the armies of overlords or of the distant Mughals. Groups such as the Bais Rajputs of Awadh or the Muslim Rohillas of the lands north of Delhi had served in Muslim armies from at least the fourteenth century, redirecting the profits of their service to the villages. It was this loss of status and political rights at village level, the experience of gradually being reduced to the status of the ordinary peasant castes of the village, which was to be such a powerful incentive to revolt in 1857.

## THE TRANSFORMATION OF ÉLITES

British legal measures did not 'create' the Indian peasantry in a simple sense. They speeded and generalised changes which had gathered pace over centuries. Demand on foreign markets for Indian agricultural produce was an important stimulus to peasant commodity production and settled agriculture. So also was internal demand generated by slow population growth and the emergence of landlord and merchant groups since before colonial rule. Even amongst these landed élites, British social engineering was effective mainly where it went with the grain of indigenous social change. The British did, it is true, create a new type of property right in land by welding together existing forms of proprietary dominion with the obligation to pay the land revenue. Previously failure to remit the state's revenue might attract severe punishment but it had not led to the sale of the right of dominion on the open market as it did in the British revenue courts in Bengal and north India after the Permanent Settlement of 1793. In law the proprietor was now also armed with a more exclusive right which he could employ in a strong land market against non-occupancy and even occupancy tenants whose rights in the pre-colonial period had existed alongside with his own. Yet it remained the balance of local political power, the historical status, influence and resources of different lineages which still basically determined the outcome of the ensuing legal battles. On its own the possession of a piece of paper from a collector or revenue court did little more than swell many local battles to a frenzy.

Much scholarship has been directed over the last generation to showing that the creation of a wider market in land did not, in fact, bring about the far-reaching changes which British optimists or pessi-

mistic nationalists thought they saw. In north India where powerful
and well-entrenched bodies of peasant landholders existed, land rights
sold to moneylenders and outside speculators usually found their way
back into the hands of the same caste and clan groups. While individual
families might have suffered the loss of income and status, the great
bodies of Jats, Rajputs or Brahmins who controlled the villages still
clung on tenaciously even in the mid-nineteenth century. In Bengal,
where the Permanent Settlement and subsequent land sales were
thought to have decimated the zamindars, there was a proliferation of
smaller estates owned by literate men or indigo magnates. However,
the most powerful of the eighteenth-century agrarian superiors had
recouped their losses and emerged as an élite of *rentier* landlords in
Calcutta or Dacca by the 1840s. In the south, communal forms of
agrarian management tended to decline as the individual peasant proprietor was recognised in law under the ryotwari system. But there
had already been a vigorous market in shares in village management
before British rule and the tougher agricultural communities were
*physically* much the same in 1750 as in 1850.

In the same way the losers in the early nineteenth century were
those with fewer means to control agricultural production through
force or kin connections, and their position had been as vulnerable in
the pre-colonial kingdoms. In north and central India Muslim and
Islamised Hindu writer or service communities were sometimes dispossessed by land sales because their links to the new colonial state
were weak. Holt Mackenzie in one of the most over-quoted remarks
in the colonial record spoke of the 'melancholy revolution' in landed
property under colonial rule. He was perhaps thinking of small
Muslim landed proprietors near Delhi who had flourished on the service of the Mughal and post-Mughal régimes but had little access to
the new white raj. Otherwise, it was the old intermediary magnates –
the *mamlatdars* or agrarian managers in western India or the more
intractable warrior chieftains from among the poligars of the south
who failed to adjust to the new imperial dispensation. There had been
much attrition among such groups in the eighteenth century also.

A more subtle and pervasive change was in the spirit of the colonial
administration and the definition of Indian aristocracy. Though even
here it is possible to underestimate the degree of movement towards
commercial and pragmatic land management in the eighteenth century, and to overestimate its progress in the nineteenth. Still, the

capacity to mobilise followers through the politics of the camp and court, the importance of parochial alliance and faction, of fortune, gesture, nuance and slight was diminished. Kingliness and the distribution of honours became less important and less practicable, while 'economy' and 'good management' were the measure of success for the dependent princes and the landlords of the British territories.[18] Eighteenth-century magnates (such as the rajas of Bharatpur) had sometimes sought to create armies and scribal classes from foreigners at the expense of overmighty kinsmen. In the nineteenth century zamindars tried more and more often to expel from privileged land-holdings kinsmen and caste fellows, who would previously have formed the core of their political influence, in order to substitute more amenable and 'productive' cultivators from lower castes. Royalty, royal arbitration and royal sacrifice had come to play a less creative part in the organisation of the Indian social order, a change which was abruptly reinforced when the Rebellion of 1857 revealed the moral and ideological bankruptcy of the old leadership. The physical – almost biological – continuity of the old order into the colonial period should not obscure the new sources of power which colonial landlords commanded and the radically changed context in which they used it. The pressures of colonial administration and the world market had fractured the unity of the local kin-based land-controlling corporations (such as the north Indian *pargana*).

As rural magnates were subtly transformed into 'mere' landholders, the rôle of the literate specialist and merchant also changed. Administrative families had continued their surreptitious accumulations of power throughout the eighteenth century, though many were overturned in political storms. Persian-knowing gentry from the small towns and cities of north India found service under the new dynasts of the eighteenth century in the environs of Murshidabad, the Muslim towns of the Deccan and Vellore, Arcot or Madras. Further from the Muslim heartlands of the north even self-consciously Muslim monarchs were forced to rely on members of the Hindu literate castes. Tamil administrative Brahmins served in the Mysore of Haider Ali and Tipu Sultan, as well as in the Hindu state of Travancore. Chitpavan, Nagar and Saraswat Brahmins in western India secured an important

---

[18] See e.g., Pamela Price, 'Resources and rule in zamindari south India, 1802–1903: Sivaganga and Ramnad as kingdoms under the Raj', unpub. Ph.D. diss., University of Wisconsin, Madison, 1979.

share in the power and perquisites of the Maratha kingdoms. Sometimes such clerical and administrative families were rewarded with grants of land or purchased rights in village management or revenue farms. Sometimes they went further to convert such rights into hereditary zamindaris as they had done around the small towns of the north. But many famous families found the going rough in the conditions of political flux. The famous Bara Sayyid families of the districts north of Delhi were largely dispossessed of their land rights after 1730. In the south the Muslim Navaiyit clan which had once served in the Deccan kingdoms and controlled the Nawabi of Arcot, were reduced in influence by the rise of Mahomed Ali Wallajah and the Hyderabad state in the second half of the eighteenth century.

British rule also induced much change among the service communities. For those which survived the rewards were great. Since British rule expanded out from commercial Calcutta and it was Hindu entrepreneurial families who served the British as banians, it was they who cashed in on British expansion. Higher caste Bengalis were already entrenched in up-river cities such as Patna, Benares, Agra and Delhi before 1850, serving the colonial administration as mint-masters, commissaries and subordinate officials in the courts. By contrast the predominantly Muslim service families of Murshidabad or Dacca tended to lose influence and slowly forfeit their land-rights. In the south Tamil and Telugu Brahmins moved into British service with alacrity. They accompanied British armies and administrators to Ceylon (after 1796) and Malaya and Singapore (after 1819), while maintaining their rôle in the administration of the Deccan states. In several parts of India, notably Bengal and the North-Western Provinces, government servants seized the opportunity of the disorganised and harsh British land-revenue settlements of the years 1793 to 1830 to buy their way into *rentier* landholding, stabilising a social position which had been dangerously exposed under the indigenous régimes.

Yet once again the spirit of Western administration wrought subtle changes. Large areas of moral and religious adjudication which had once fallen to the lot of the literate service people were now severed from the utilitarian colonial administration. Muslim *shariat* law and Hindu customary jurisdiction were formalised in codes and pushed to the edge of the legal and administrative system. Notions of largesse and gifts for service succumbed to European concerns for financial rectitude and educational qualification. Rational systems of legal and administrative thought and the commercialisation of government were, of course, features of the immediate pre-colonial realms. However, under the British, 'training' of civil servants became a concern. After the abolition of Persian in 1835 and its replacement with English in the higher reaches of government business the mystique of the old scribal order was slowly undermined.

On the face of it, the indigenous merchant community were the great beneficiaries of the Western impact. In the early days of the conquest Indian moneylenders consolidated the hold over state and military finance which they had gained during the previous era. Bankers stepped in to finance the heavy demand for revenue in the North-Western Provinces (1800–1818), in the Central Provinces and Maharashtra (1818–30) and notably in Baroda (1805–20). The great flows of merchant people to new centres of trade intensified. Marwaris from Rajasthan drifted into north India and Bengal. Gujaratis continued to move to the growing metropolis of Bombay. Tamil Muslims, Hindu Chetties and Christian Paravas financed south-east Asian trade and the pearl fisheries of the Ceylon coast. At the same time, the heavy bias in English law and the revised 'Hindoo' Law in favour of contract and private property in land favoured commercial men who were released from the fear of forced levy which hung over many during indigenous régimes. Some acquired large bundles of land rights, especially in north India during the depression of the 1830s. A symbiosis developed between *rentier* landlordship and usury capital which possibly impeded the emergence of true capitalism in the villages.

While monied men achieved new influence in the countryside colonial rule acted as a straitjacket on many commercial operations. Indian capital was slowly squeezed out of ship-owning and ship-building and restricted in all export trade by the inaccessiblity of technology, world-market information, finance and insurance. The European agency houses maintained a strong hold over the commanding heights of the colonial economy in the great coastal centres of Bombay, Calcutta and Madras. Even before 1860 merchants in Ahmedabad, where European influence was less constricting, had made a start in the development of cotton manufacturing. But against this success was set the failure of the modernising attempts of Calcutta merchants such as Dwarkanath Tagore who fought the Europeans with their own weapons but found themselves unable to enter the club of the creditworthy. The early-nineteenth-century 'Age of the Bania' did not signal the birth of modern Indian capitalism because ultimately it was difficult for entrepreneurs to flourish against the background of an economy in which growth was so fragile.

## COLONIAL RULE AND THE CREATION OF 'TRADITIONAL INDIA'

The richness and variety of Indian social and religious life makes it difficult to generalise about change under colonial rule. It is seductively easy to reduce complex matters of faith and interpretation to simple reflections of social and economic change, or intellectual 'modernisation'. Yet the broad social trends which have been discussed in this chapter did hold implications for the definition and operation of caste and for the practice of the Hindu, Muslim, Christian and Jain religions as they evolved during the nineteenth century. The consolidation of peasant society and its epochal defeat of the India of the nomad, the soldier and the tribesman set the scene for the emergence of a more stratified and more rigid system of castes and more homogenous religious practice within all the main communities. The literate and monied townsmen whose security was greatly strengthened in the first generation of colonial rule found much to attract them in the rationalistic type of spiritual teaching which was already established within all the main religious traditions. It was in the context of well-developed indigenous movements of reform and practical reconstitution of religious organisation that some Indians felt the influence of Christianity and Western rationalist and positivist thought.

Neither Victorian writers on empire nor contemporary historical anthropologists have given sufficient weight to these material and moral transformations of pre-colonial society. For the evangelicals and utilitarians of the 1820s and 30s the rigid, traditional caste system and superstitious or bigoted Indian religions were on the point of dissolution, buffeted as they were thought to be by the winds of individual conscience and scientific thought. Marx and the first generation of socialists saw the same process but made it a material one. For them the basis of caste was the cellular and hereditary nature of the village economy which would soon be blown apart by the railways and Lancashire exports. But the picture was essentially the same, for they also considered that Indian society had undergone no significant social change before British rule.

Some modern writers have almost seemed to turn this argument on its head. Pre-colonial caste and religious practice for them was fluid, eclectic and uncodified. Families could change their caste ranking in quite short periods of time; degraded liquor distillers might serve armies, become revenue managers and even landlords, elevating their caste status in the meantime. Traditional India was not a rigid society. It was British rule which made it so, codifying many localised and pragmatic customs into a unified and Brahminised 'Hindoo Law' and classing people into immutable castes through the operation of the courts and ethnographical surveys. Colonial society was seeing a mirror image of itself when it understood Indian society as rigid and stultified.

A more realistic picture than either of these would give weight to deep-rooted social changes and conflicts of interpretation within Indian society itself. Hierarchical application of caste which stressed the great gulf between the pure and the polluted and the immutability of caste boundaries and lifestyles were long established at the ancient centres of Hindu scholarship in India where Brahmins clustered in numbers and a constant process of textual recension and interpretation went on. Tanjore, Benares and the newer centre of Nadia in central Bengal were all places where the high philosophical traditions of Hinduism prevailed and notions of purity and pollution were expected to define social life. Indian normative codes and the descriptions of travellers suggest that life in the ancient agricultural areas dominated by these religious centres was, in fact, conducted according to principles of purity, pollution, endogamy and hierarchy. In the last centuries before colonial rule the growing power of Brahmins and scribal people and the desire of new dynasties to legitimate themselves in terms of orthodoxy ensured that this was a powerful tradition in the process of constant reinvention. And it was from the adepts of this tradition at Nadia in particular that H. T. Colebrooke derived the material and the ideology which was to form the basis of his Hindu law code prepared for the use of Warren Hastings's neo-traditional administration in Bengal.

Yet while most areas of the subcontinent, including the tribal fringes, were aware of the hierarchical and Brahminical interpretation of the universe and responded to it in their own rituals and daily life, there were still in the eighteenth century powerful ideologies working against hierarchy and rigid caste boundaries. Where such ideologies were fused with expanding movements of peasant colonisation or supported by the sharing and decentralised styles of life of tribal people and nomads, Brahmins were peripheral and the social system extremely malleable and inclusive. Here notions of pollution and purity were at a discount. The ideology and social organisation of settled Hindu society was powerful and adaptable. But a precondition for its expansion to encompass the whole subcontinent was the defeat by the state and the peasant economy of alternative styles of living which were still powerful, and in places still expansive in 1800.

The hierarchies of kings and priests were not very influential where Hindu devotional religion (*bhakti*) had spread among egalitarian rural brotherhoods. Devotion to the deity (sometimes a form of Shiva but more often Vishnu in the form of Krishna) did not necessarily imply equality in this life. In their second and third generations bhakti movements often became temple- and ritual-centred. But where they suffused a society composed of groups of warrior landholders who made wide-ranging marriage alliances among rural castes of roughly equal esteem, Brahminical ritual and rigidity were marginal or inappropriate. The Sikhs were a good example of such a group, though their faith was formally distinct from Hinduism. The Sikhs believed that the line of their gurus preaching service of god had ended in the seventeenth century. Religious authority inhered in the sacred scriptures, the guru Granth Sahib. There was less room for the development of a formal hierarchy equivalent to Brahminism, though Brahmins were sometimes enlisted on the fringes of Sikh society to confer blessing in the ritual of everyday life. Similar attitudes prevailed among the Kunbi peasants of western India who filled the Maratha war bands. Even after 1720, when Chitpavan Brahmins enhanced their power within the Maratha states, the Maratha warriors and peasantry clung to many tribal features. Women were freer in their camps; Kunbis continued to marry other closely related peasant castes, and Shaiva bhakti devotion transcended the divisions of social life.

In the early nineteenth century, however, the spirit of hierarchy and ritual distinction became more pervasive. The British peace speeded the rise of high Hindu kingship, Brahminism and the advance of principles of purity and pollution in the countryside. Writer and administrative communities such as the Kayasths of north and central India now served in British and not Muslim administrations and began to aspire to a more Brahminical style of life, throwing off what were now seen as degrading Muslim and lower-caste habits such as the drinking of 'wine' and extravagant marriage customs. Pastoralist and tribal communities lost status, as we have seen, becoming amalgamated with low-caste village service communities as the market for agricultural labour developed. The great agriculturalist castes also appear to have become less permeable and more internally divided themselves. The Jats around Delhi began to prohibit the practice of taking concubines from women of other similar agricultural castes; following their rajas, many senior families began to seclude their women and adopt complex rules for marriage. Rural Rajput clans who had been exogamous or even in some cases had married with lower-caste military people (such as the Pasis in Awadh) to enhance their power had become endogamous by the mid-nineteenth century. Princely lineage replaced the war-band as the focus for Rajput loyalty or pride.

So hierarchy and the Brahmin interpretation of Hindu society which was theoretical rather than actual over much of India as late as 1750 was firmly ensconced a century later. The reasons for this were complex. Population growth emphasised the need to control land by the exclusion of rivals rather than control of people by incorporating them from many different backgrounds. The expansion after 1800 of pre-colonial cities and merchant people encouraged the search for status and security which often took the form of a nice emphasis on caste distinction. The British indirectly stimulated such changes. Early officials began the process of ranking and grading the Indian social order in an attempt to understand and control it. So James Tod's neo-Gothic extravaganza, *The Annals and Antiquities of Rajasthan* (1829–32) itself became a reference book for the princes of that region in history and marriage customs. In the same way British law began to dispense to all castes and communities the high Brahminical and scholarly traditions derived from the seminaries of Nadia or Tanjore. Yet the colonialists did not create this interpretation of India; rather they speeded up and transformed social and ideological changes which were already in train.

Much has been written to show how Christian, deistic and rational ideas transformed the interpretation of Hindu religion in the early nineteenth century. Reform movements such as the Brahmo Samaj and its opponents, or later the Arya Samaj, were no doubt an important influence in the creation of 'secular', rationalistic, modern India. But the missionary and utilitarian critique of Hinduism, which became more bitter after 1813, had the effect of concealing here also the vitality of developments which arose from within the three main categories of Hindu religious activity – ritual, devotion to god, and the recension of knowledge – and which were often only lightly influenced by the West.

Centres of knowledge continued to flourish throughout India and their texts and ideologies were adapted by the colonial courts and codifiers. Ritual, the way to salvation through acts of piety and worship, benefited from the expansion of pilgrimage along with travel and trade in the nineteenth century. Pilgrimage to Benares, Gaya or Tirupati had remained strong in the eighteenth century, but the British abolition of 'pilgrim taxes' and easier transport redoubled the flow. Brahmins and high Brahminical ritual introduced by eighteenth-century rulers such as the rajas of Travancore or the poligars, spread in the protected states of the nineteenth century for whom conspicuous piety replaced warfare as the chief charge on state revenues. New men who built up their fortunes through the service of the British invested in elaborate death anniversary ceremonies (*shraddhas*) in rural Bengal, while many of the great temples of Madras were renovated and expanded in the vivid styles of the early nineteenth century.

Movements of ecstatic devotion, especially those connected with the worship of Lord Vishnu and his avatars (secondary manifestations), also proliferated, softening these tendencies to more hierarchical religious practice. The great age of devotional movements had been the central years of the Mughal empire. These were the years when rural Bengal had been entranced by the teaching of Chaitanya who disparaged caste and ritual, stressing the need for individual absorption in god. Comparable movements centred on Krishna's fabled homelands around Muttra and Ajodhya in north India and flourished in the Tanjore delta. During the eighteenth century such movements passed from an expansive, preaching phase to a period of consolidation. Those which had created corporate monastic-style institutions were well placed to ride the disturbances of the period. Bodies of Shaivite and Vaishnavite ascetics, loosely known as Bairagis or Gosains, contributed powerfully to the survival of inter-regional trade since they also functioned as armed mercenaries. At the turn of the nineteenth century, fortified with corporate wealth and properties in fast-expanding urban land markets, they were strongly entrenched in the Hindu life of the colonial towns.

One important sect of this sort were the Ramanandis, followers of Rama (Vishnu) who apparently came to prominence in Nepal and Rajasthan during the seventeenth century. In the following century they secured considerable patronage from local rulers including the Muslim nawabs of Awadh, at whose court they operated as 'skilful courtiers' according to Buchanan.[19] Firmly based at Ajodhya and Muttra, they expanded their influence in the early colonial period among the pious mercantile and service élites of the towns, whose spiritual guides they became. Ramanandis spread the use of the Hindi translation of the great epic the Ramayana of the poet Tulsi Das. They emphasised frugality and moderation. They rejected caste distinctions sufficiently to spread their faith amongst the poor and low caste; and 'many of the heads of the minor sections are drawn from the class of menials'.[20] Overall their influence tended to spread the polite, unostentatious Hinduism of the merchant and literate classes rather than to accomplish an egalitarian revival. Well-suited to the colonial milieu, Ramanandis received the approval of their British rulers and indirectly supported them in return. From the earliest period members of the merchant castes and respectable artisans had supported movements of spiritual discipline which emphasised sobriety of conduct and equality in spiritual matters. Their ambivalence about rank and caste in this world made it possible for them to make their peace with the society around them and function as quiet, productive communities. Despite wide differences in theology, Buddhists, Jains, Nanakshahi Sikhs, Charan Dasis and Ramanandis always had this in common. Sectarian life styles like this developed readily in the context of the slow urbanisation and growth of the commercial economy which was taking place under the Mughals. Their tenets of sobriety, orderly householding and commercial rectitude flourished in colonial India too, making as significant a contribution to the way the modern Indian middle classes think as did the more spectacular borrowings from Western rationalism and positivism.

Many other representatives of the devotional tradition within Hinduism, and movements distantly associated with Sikhism such as the Nanakshahis, quietly developed and consolidated themselves during the transition to colonial rule. Yet the classic case of the flowering of

[19] Buchanan, in Montgomery Martin (ed.), *The History ... and Statistics of Eastern India* (London, 1838), ii, 485.
[20] W. Crooke, *The North-Western Provinces of India* (1897, new. edn. Karachi, 1972), p. 255.

indigenous movements of religious revitalisation in the colonial context is probably that of the Satya Narayanis of Gujarat (*c.* 1780–1830). Swami Narayan, the founder, rejected many aspects of Brahminism and ritual, preaching an austere form of Vaishnavite devotion which had earned the displeasure of the then Maratha rulers. In the early years of colonial rule Swami Narayan became connected with a number of educated men of the towns of Bombay and Surat who formalised his teachings into a few simple principles and circulated them in printed form throughout the Bombay Presidency. The Swami Narayan sect dismissed caste as irrelevant to the soul's status before God. In practice caste distinctions remained visible among them though reduced in complexity. Most interesting, though, was the sect's role in helping to suppress tribal and low-caste forms of religion which persisted on the warrior and nomadic fringes of the society of Gujarat. Swami Narayan condemned animal sacrifice, feasting and fire-walking ceremonies. His reclamation for a purified Vaishnavism of warriors and plunderers attracted the approval of the British who applauded 'the recovery of thousands of these unfortunate men to be found throughout Gujarat, whose means of subsistence were equally lawless and precarious'.[21] The Satya Narayanis attempted to settle new converts in standard agricultural communities around their temples. They were thus acting as an integral part of the process of creating colonial India, but they derived their inspiration from social and religious forms prior to and outside the colonial milieu.

At an even lower point in the Hindu ritual scale, the Chamars of Central India (perhaps 12 per cent of the population in several districts) were becoming cultivators by clearing jungle. Their transformation from village menial and scavenger to peasant was accompanied by a spiritual transformation by the Satnami or Raidasi sect. The teachers of this devotional religion forbade ritual and images and emphasised monotheism and frugality. The Satnamis were 'no longer weighed down by a sense of inferiority ... the Satnami holds together and resists all attempts from other castes to reassert their traditional domination over them'.[22]

None of the developments mentioned here was a simple process of change. In the same local society new priestly hierarchies and ritual centres could grow concurrently with devotional sects. Magical cults

---

[21] H. G. Briggs, *The cities of Gujarashtra* (Bombay, 1849), p. 238.
[22] Balfour, *Cyclopaedia*, ii, 145, 'Chamar'.

of blood sacrifice might persist in the midst of communities devoted to pious vegetarianism. Incorporation and accommodation rather than the annihilation of one set of practices by another was the method of change within Hinduism, so that paradoxes abounded. In the south the devotional worship of the great gods of the Hindu pantheon continued to gain adherents by merging with the cults of local blood-drinking goddesses in a symbolic form of marriage. In Bengal worship of the Mother Goddess in her aspect of dangerous power (*shakti*) actually expanded in the eighteenth century. Fierce debates took place with the quietist Vaishnavites of the countryside who disliked ritual and blood sacrifice. Against this shifting background most families managed some kind of accommodation. In one *shakta* subcaste the fierce goddess continued to receive her annual sacrifice, but it was severed cucumbers and not goats which were offered up to her in deference to Vaishnavite devotionalism. The proper context for the Christian and rationalistic impact of the early nineteenth century was therefore the vitality and not the decadence of Hindu (and Muslim) religion in India.

Yet while Western rationalism had only a limited impact on Hindu thought and practice before 1850, its importance for the future should not be underestimated. Here Calcutta was the crucible of change, though Bombay and Madras also had societies for religious reform before 1850. Warren Hastings's desire to master India through an understanding of her languages and scriptures was accompanied by the publication of Halhed's *Grammar of the Bengalee Language* in 1778. In 1781 the Calcutta Madrassa was founded. Wellesley's Fort William College, designed for the education of civil servants, published Hindu works of mythology and scripture as did the Hindu Sanskrit College (founded 1821). This encouraged their teachers such as Mritanjay Vidyalankar to refine and question their own view of India's past. The need for a written redefinition of the nature of Hinduism became pressing after 1800 when a Baptist missionary complex was founded at the Danish Settlement of Serampore under the forceful leadership of William Carey. Evangelical missions of the Church of England and other denominations became more active after 1813 when the revision of the East India Company's charter allowed missionaries to gain freer access to its territories. The arrival of Bentinck in 1828, openly committed to humanitarian reform, seemed to confirm the arrival of the millennium of conversion.

Indian reaction to these changes was complex. Some, like the icono-clastic Michael Derozio and his followers, abused and mocked Hindu and Muslim religion. Derozio himself later became a nominal Chris-tian. More important is what might be called the neo-orthodox school, represented by men such as Vidyalankar who criticised both the missionaries and Indian reformers who attacked Hindu customs. Collecting and publishing Hindu texts and justifying a purified form of caste on the basis of the divine nature of the Vedas and Puranas, such men were an important influence on the future form of Hindu orthodoxy. This anti-reformist school, for instance, collected nearly 50,000 signatures and assembled in the Dharma Sabha (Divine Society) to oppose Bentinck's ordinance of 1829 in which widow-burning was finally declared illegal.

Between these poles were the moderate reformers exemplified above all by Ram Mohun Roy who founded the Brahmo Samaj (Society for the Transcendent Deity) in 1818. Alongside him must be set Deben-dranath Tagore, scion of one of Bengal's most important commercial families, who fostered the Samaj until it became a critical influence on the life of Calcutta's emerging intelligentsia. Indigenous influences were not lacking in the beliefs of the Samaj. Apart from the influence of the monastic philosophy of the seventh-century Hindu sage Shank-aracharya, Ram Mohun's first published work echoed the rationalistic style of argument of contemporary Muslim thinkers on the excellence of monotheism. Amongst later Brahmo Samajists the tolerant de-votional traditions of Bengal bhakti were evident, particularly after 1850 when the movement began to spread to country towns. Again, many Bengali Brahmos failed to abandon caste and traditional mar-riage practices as its founder stipulated, especially in the second and third generation as the movement became something more like a tra-ditional Bengali sect.

All the same there is no doubting the critical importance of Western notions in the practice and belief of the Brahmos and like-minded Bengalis. The responsibility of the individual soul, the imminence of God (a train of thought which owed much to English Deism), the irrelevance of caste and the possibility of achieving salvation through rational knowledge of the divine were all themes taken up and devel-oped. Comte's positivism, Mill's emphasis on political as well as social liberation, the ethics of Christ – these revelations powerfully shaped the mind of Calcutta's reformers.

Similar developments took place in Bombay and Madras. Radical reformers gathered around the Elphinstone Institution in Bombay (1827) and a number of clubs devoted to religious reform were convened especially within the consciously modern Parsi community. Even in orthodox Poona pamphlets were written denouncing the abuse of the caste system in terms which were reminiscent of the assault on privilege during the French revolution.[23] Orthodox counter-reaction was also fierce. In Madras there were riots against missionary conversions by the Church of Scotland in 1843. More seriously, the Government's decision in the same year to withdraw from protection of Hindu temples on the ground that this was fostering 'heathenism' was taken as a direct sign of missionary success. There were riots and demonstrations throughout the Presidency associated with a self-protection association known as the Sacred Ash Society (after the sacred ash smeared on devotees of the god Shiva).

A balanced view of the Indian reformers of the early nineteenth century would need to take account of their adaptation of Western methods of argument and education, the creation of an educated public and of a historical interpretation of India's past – and future. Yet it is striking how limited was the social vision and social impact of these stirrings. Partly, no doubt, this was because the reformers hailed from an embattled élite whose dynamism, economic and moral, was constricted by the colonial situation. It was the British who controlled schools, banks and public offices. At the same time religious rationalism and freemasonry, debated often in Sanskrit and English, was unlikely to find echoes in a society which saw its moral future either in the spread of hierarchy and ancient righteousness, or in movements of simple devotion to godhead.

Actually, the most successful social reformers of the 1830s and 40s were Muslims, for they were able to elaborate a rationalistic system of religious education and take advantage of the consolidation of a stratified peasantry and a colonial urban élite. Before 1860 the influence of Western thought was quite limited. Some teachers at the Delhi College taught European literature and science. By 1840 they had trained up several dozen young Muslims, and had influenced scores of others who spoke English and took positions in government service. But the Muslim public was indifferent or hostile to them. For a time a social

<hr />

[23] O'Hanlon, *Caste, conflict and ideology*, chapter 3.

boycott was enforced against the pupils who attended the Delhi English College for Boys which was an associate of the College.[24] There were also small groups of modernist Muslims who applied the methods of textual criticism to the Koran developed at the Calcutta Madrassa. In Madras Edward Balfour, surgeon general and an eminent orientalist, founded the Mahomedan Literary Association in 1852.[25]

Of much greater importance in shaping Muslim attitudes was the flowering of a range of purist movements which had emerged during the eighteenth century in north India, reflecting a much wider spirit of godly reform throughout the Islamic world. Three strands were important here. First there were the teachers belonging to the Chishti Sufi order who preached their message of submission to God to the Muslims of the Punjab countryside. Secondly, there was the stream of reform associated with teachers of the Naqshbandiya order in Delhi, notably Shah Walliullah and his son Shah Abdul Aziz; these men opposed unorthodox religious practice and the revivified Shia sect. Third, the philosophical and learned tradition of the Lucknow seminary, Firangi Mahal, was incorporated into a new educational syllabus (the Darz-i-Nizamiya) which was propagated throughout India during the eighteenth and nineteenth centuries.

These movements varied to such an extent that it is dangerous to see them as a single stream of revitalisation. Much of the success of the Chishtis in the Punjab, for instance, derived from their more accommodating stance towards the worship of saints,[26] which was a feature of rural society. By comparison some Delhi teachers denounced saint worship, propagating a strict monotheism. Yet there were common features. All these movements reacted both against the eclecticism of the Mughal ruling class and the loss of Muslim political power in the eighteenth century. Shah Waliullah and his followers wished to purge Muslim practice of lax habits which he thought had become more common as Hindus and Shias (always regarded as more latitudinarian by Sunnis) achieved power at the declining Mughal court. All these traditions also had indirect links with the schools of the central Islamic

---

[24] Shahamat Ali, *Sikhs and Afghans*, preface, p. ix.

[25] S. N. Khalandar (Suhrawady), 'The development of Urdu Language and Literature in Tamil Nad from 1745 to 1960', unpub. M.Litt. diss., University of Madras, 1960, pp. 59-seq.

[26] M. Zameeruddin Siddiqui, 'The resurgence of the Chishti Silislah in the Punjab during the eighteenth century', *Proceedings of the Indian Historical Congress, 1970* (Delhi, 1971), pp. 408-20.

lands in Mecca, Medina and Cairo where a thoroughgoing reinterpretation of law and tradition was in progress. A spiritual and social self-strengthening was called for. Shah Abdul Aziz in particular emphasised that political regeneration could only follow a regeneration of Islam in society.

This regeneration sought to find a new balance between different aspects of Muslim belief and knowledge. An attempt was made to bring together mosque- and school-centred religion with the esoteric knowledge of the Sufi sects. The practice of multiple ordination of learned men into Sufi orders had already grown in popularity in eighteenth-century Delhi. This bringing together of the two idioms would make it easier to purge sufism of its saint worship, reform the Shia festival of Muhurram and discountenance other festivals and dancing which displayed polytheistical features. The emphasis was on purging, for the Muslim reformers (often called the Tariq-i-Muhammadiya) did not wish wholly to extirpate Sufi belief as did their contemporaries the Wahhabis of Arabia with whom they were erroneously compared. Finally, much of the new teaching and literature sought to hold up the life of the Prophet Muhammad as an exemplar to all Muslims. Around this symbol of spiritual power the faithful could draw together.

In propagating these themes the Islamic reformers reached out beyond the learned and élite in a manner impossible for the *bhadralog* intelligentsia of Hindu Calcutta. They found a ready audience among common people seeking dignity and righteousness in a period of social dislocation. The charismatic teaching of Abdul Aziz's confrére, Sayyid Ahmed of Rai Bareilly, attracted Muslims of artisan caste in declining weaving towns such as Allahabad, Mau, and Patna. Fortified by a strong sense of corporate identity weavers in the towns of the Deccan and even weaving centres such as Melapalaiyam in the Tamil country gave support to local variants of the reformist message. Muslim preachers were particularly successful in taking the offensive where a sense of social unease was compounded by the appearance of Christian missionaries and Western schools, as in Agra during the 1850s.

Rural people also turned to Muslim revitalisation and reform movements. On the North-East Frontier hill tribesmen, disturbed by the simultaneous appearance of plains Hindu moneylenders and the British army, sought a millennial Muslim kingdom in the 1820s. More orthodox reformist messages were taken up in east Bengal during the Faraizi movement of the following decade, which emphasised the fundamental importance of the Koran. While this and similar movements in Bengal attracted support from rural religious teachers, artisans and petty landlords, the substantial Muslim yeoman farmer (the jotedar) seems to have been heavily represented in them. Jotedar conflicts with Hindu landlords during the 1830s and 40s introduced a sense of social rivalry into religious debate, and the rhetoric of spiritual reform was sometimes accompanied by denunciation of the rent and revenue system.

Yet these strands never fused into anything like popular revolt against landlords or the colonial rulers. The emphasis was on sobriety and respectability and many subordinate government servants who were to play a loyalist rôle during the 1857 revolt were influenced by notions of an inward cleansing. Thus though Shah Abdul Aziz of Delhi issued religious pronouncements in which he castigated Christians and unbelievers, the general tendency of his teaching was to encourage Muslims to behave as if India were still a society in which Islam could be freely practiced. The more militant Sayyid Ahmed who fought the Sikhs in religious war between 1829 and 1831 declared that his movement was 'never meant simply to be a revolt', and his attitude to the colonial authorities was ambiguous. In fact where the British did uncover 'Wahhabi' conspiracies as in the Pathan State of Kurnool in the Carnatic or in Patna in the 1850s, this seems usually to have been a rationalisation of their own suspicions of reformed Islam and provided little evidence of political purpose.

The international aspect of pan-Islamic reform and its literacy has obscured the importance of other indigenous traditions within Indian Islam. In fact, the Islam of saints, of regional languages and of syncretic practices was equally vital during this period. The purist reformers viewed it with some suspicion, yet its influence on the beliefs and worship of most Indian Muslims was even more profound than theirs. The boundary between the reformers and expansive local cults is difficult to draw. The Chishti teachers of the Punjab, for instance, wished to reform the practice of eighteenth-century Punjabis to prepare them for struggle with Sikhs and other infidels. Yet their preference for the doctrine of the immanence of God encouraged the development of saint worship at their tombs. The manner in which the great Jat landed clans encouraged commonality across the boundaries of religion meant that many Hindus worshipped at these festivals and fairs. In the 1850s the incoming British continued the policy of Maharaja Ranjit Singh who had sought to attach powerful Muslim shrines to the Sikh kingdom through grants of land and immunities. Far from falling back in the face of purist onslaughts the fame of many Sufi saints throughout India flowered with the development of communications and settled agricultural society. The greatest of the shrines, that of Sheikh Muin-uddin Chishti of Ajmer received large donations from the Marathas as well as the eighteenth-century Muslim kingdoms. Later the Company stabilised the trade routes through Ajmer on which the shrine thrived. The religion here propagated was prayer for the intercession of the saint to relieve men from their sins and disease, women from barrenness. The method was ecstatic possession by the saint, the use of talismans and amulets.[27] In south India the nawabs of Arcot patronised the notably syncretic shrines of Shah Nattarwali at Trichinopoly and Shah Hamid Sahib at the seaport town of Nagore – and this at the same time as they extended patronage to reforming theologians from north India and the Deccan. In Bengal and Tamilnadu the devotional hymns in praise of the saints, propagated in the regional languages and greatly appealing to ordinary people, were converted into literary forms and later disseminated through the printing press. In general the relations between reforming Islam and the saint cults and great festivals had to be flexible despite surface conflict. For both traditions were dynamic, and both sought converts from among tribal and marginal groups whose special deities seemed vulnerable as settled government and settled agriculture converted jungle and hill-land into India.

[27] Thornton, *Gazetteer*, i, 55.

CHAPTER 6

# REBELLION AND RECONSTRUCTION

Three basic forces moulded the nature of Indian society in the early colonial period. First, social relations and modes of thought and belief which had consolidated themselves in the later years of Mughal India continued to develop under British rule. These were distorted or modified by the second range of influences which derived from the military and financial needs of the colonial state and from sporadic and uneven developments in the European world economy. In turn, armed and unarmed resistance from within India itself blunted and deflected these influences. So pressure and rebellion operating at all levels of political power within the subcontinent, provided the third determinant of the nature of colonial Indian society. Revolts and armed rebellions were not hopeless causes as the old District Gazetteers tended to suggest. On the contrary, they frequently forced the British to modify their system. In some cases the colonial authorities were constrained to deploy expensive armies to utterly uproot centres of resistance. This had been the case with some of the poligars of the far south or the Pindari raiders. More often collectors were forced to come to an accommodation with the powerful social groups who retained control of resources in the villages and small towns. Thus resisting village leaderships such as the mirasidars of parts of the wet South were afforded preferential treatment. Tribal magnates were selected out and given the rights of rajas. Recalcitrant princes retained some share of power within the system of native states. None of the rebellions and uprisings with which this chapter deals 'succeeded' in the sense that they were able to exclude the influences of the world market or the Company's state. Yet many of them forced reassessments of policy and practice which partly disarmed these influences.

## RESISTANCE IN EARLY COLONIAL INDIA

Among the myths which became current in the wake of the rebellion of 1857-8 was the idea that it was a unique event, something that had to be explained in terms of the peculiar folly of the revenue policy of the government of the North-Western Provinces or the foolhardiness of the annexation of Awadh in 1856. In fact armed revolt was endemic in all parts of early colonial India. What distinguished the events of 1857 was their scale and the fact that for a short time they posed a military threat to British dominance in the Ganges Plains. Another contention, perpetuated by some recent historians, is that the Revolt was not essentially an anti-colonial movement so much as a mêlée of local factional conflicts: 'the arbitrary adjustment by the sword of the ancient disputes of the land'. This is correct in the sense that many of the participants in the warfare and plunder of 1857 were not motivated by any definite animus against the distant white rulers. Yet it is also superficial. The conflicts which occurred throughout the early nineteenth century and climaxed in 1857 were all related to the policies and conditions of colonial India. Many of these policies and conditions created tensions similar to those once released by Mughal attempts at centralisation. However, the British pursued their aims more rigorously within the context of a world empire and a developing capitalist economy which provided them with considerable new resources.

The study of revolt as a thing in itself goes some way to correct the picture of stability under the Raj which comes out of much earlier history. But it is more useful in elucidating the policies and impact of colonial rule than the mind of colonial Indians. The boundary between 'revolt' and 'collaboration' was often very faint, defined more by the prejudices of individual officials or by the internal factional politics of Indian states and villages than by any clear predisposition towards anti-colonial resistance. Many of those who apparently collaborated, the Calcutta intelligentsia for instance, regarded their British with contempt at some level, or like the Sufi saints of Delhi withdrew into an internal spiritual exile to contemplate the travails of the Prophet. Many also, from clerks in offices to Rajput princes, used conformity to British orders as a way of building their empires of patronage and havens of self-respect within the colonial system itself.

With this in mind, several broad types of dissidence can be isolated from the great range of revolts between 1800 and 1860. Most notable were the periodic revolts of zamindars and other superior landholders fighting off demands for higher revenue or invasions of their status as 'little kings' in the countryside. Then there were conflicts between landlords and groups of tenants or under-tenants objecting to the transformation of customary dues into landlord rights or to some violation of the obligations between agrarian lord and dependant. Next there was a range of conflicts arising from tension between wandering or tribal people and settled peasant farmers which usually centred on the control of forests, grazing grounds or other communally exploited resources. Finally, there were frequent revolts in cities and towns. These had many causes: some were riots over market control and taxation. Some involved bloodshed between religious or caste groups or the protests of embattled artisan communities. All these types of conflict were widespread but they surfaced in exaggerated form in the course of the Mutiny and Rebellion of 1857.

To the Mughals all failures to pay revenue were tantamount to declarations of rebellion. The great eighteenth-century revolts of Sikhs, Jats and Marathas were revolts of the countryside – of petty gentry, peasant landholders as well as tenants – against their revenue machinery and demands for tribute. The British were at once more relaxed and harsher in their policies. They were more relaxed because once the countryside was largely pacified, withholding revenue was seen as a civil misdemeanour actionable by the sale of zamindari land in a revenue court and not necessarily as rebellion which merited torture or death. They were harsher since a family's zamindari land could be forfeit forever simply because an individual failed to pay revenue. Under colonial rule revenue rates were higher, exactions more rigorous and relief and compromise was less common. For this was a system of close cost-accounting in which collectors achieved advancement in their careers by raising the yield of their districts. Provincial Boards of Revenue were very reluctant to allow the accumulation of 'balances' (deficits) or sanction relief for drought- or flood-ravaged areas.

The British encountered prolonged resistance from zamindars and their followers on two main counts. The first was when they attempted to impose their own nominees on the thrones of princely states in violation of the sense of the neighbourhood and the dominant alliances in local polities. Thus British interference in the succession among the Marathas in the 1770s, in Awadh in 1797, and in several Rajput states in the 1820s and 30s, provoked serious opposition from the supporters of the spurned claimants. Trouble in smaller kingdoms or within individual zamindari estates often arose from similar causes. In the Hathwa Raj of north Bihar, for instance, the British had expelled the incumbent Raja in the 1780s and imposed his cousin's line on the unwilling populace. Zamindar supporters of the deposed branch kept up a series of local revolts through to the 1840s and this division coloured rural politics well into the later nineteenth century.[1]

The most widespread dissidence was encountered when the British attempted to control and tax territories which had never really come under the direct rule of their eighteenth-century predecessors. In the south, for instance, the Madras government continued the policy of the Nawabs of Arcot of trying to bend to their will the Hindu chiefs of the far south, the poligars. In the model of Mughal hegemony adopted by the southern Muslims, these chiefs were no more than zamindars who owed service and allegiance to their Muslim overlords. The British eagerly took up this notion and designated the poligars 'auxiliary forces' – magnates who, it was implied, held their lands on a kind of military service tenure from the Company whose own rights were ultimately granted by the Mughal emperor. In fact the poligars should be regarded as inheritors of shares in the sovereignty of pre-Muslim Vijayanagar rulers. They were seen as sovereigns in their own right – even aspects of the living deity – by the local people, as became clear during the Sivaganga Revolt of 1799–1801 when the poligars put up fierce resistance to the Company's forces and were supported by massed levies from within their villages. Several poligar leaders became local heroes whose renown and magical powers are celebrated in Tamil folk ballads which are still recited in the countryside.

Conflicts over the Company's claim to total dominance continued to occur across the country up to two generations after conquest. The British consistently saw any form of resistance as the work of 'contumacious' zamindars or rebel chieftains. For they were seeking not simply an increase of their revenues but a monopoly of all sources of political authority throughout Indian society. Only the arbitrarily designed category of 'native princes' was to be allowed any degree of sovereignty under their paramountcy. If other chiefs resisted they were rebels, or plunderers, or bandits, defined out of existence by a power which perceived itself to be unitary and unchallenged as no other had done before it. Revolt was inevitable in areas where more fluid, segmented forms of polities had been preserved by climate or terrain from the weaker pressures of Mughal centralisation. Wellesley and Munro for instance encountered fierce resistance from the Nayar and Maratha chieftains notably Daundia Waugh, the Cotiote Raja and

[1] Anand Yang, 'Hathwa Raj in the early nineteenth century', unpub. Ms.

the Pyche Raja between 1799 and 1806 for here 'the natural state of the country and the violence of the monsoon secured them [the rebels] for some months of the year against all military operations'.[2] Riots and disturbances followed all the attempts to tax this area and in 1836 there was another major rebellion led by the chief Puttabasapah.[3] The southern Maratha country provides another example. Since the British regarded the Maratha polities as 'an empire' with the Peshwa as its head, and since the Peshwa was first their ally and later their pensioner, they were not prepared to view the local chiefs here as anything but dependants. In the countryside towards Goa in 1844–6 there was a 'long, continued and obstinate rebellion',[4] which was put down by James Outram, later conqueror of Awadh. In this revolt as in those in Tamilnadu and Kerala, village headmen willingly provided recruits and resources for the rebels, which throws doubt on the British claim that these were simply attempts by local tyrants to avoid the payment of revenue.

Company raj also encountered resistance in those parts of the northern plains where the Mughals and the eighteenth-century successor states had never really imposed their authority. The northern and southern fringes of Awadh caused continuous trouble for the Lucknow authorities and for adjacent British collectors, particularly during the tense 1830s. On the southern fringes of the plains the rajas and clansmen of the central Indian hills opposed both the British and the attempts of the local states of Gwalior and Rewah to coerce and tax them on a regular basis. In 1842 there was a serious revolt among the Bundela Rajput chieftains which disrupted trade and agriculture in the region for some years. In many instances these were to be areas which again threw up prolonged resistance in 1857.

We have already seen how rebellions of this sort damaged the Company's finances and reputation, eroding the possibilities for positive military or economic reform. At the same time the need to find allies against such rebels forced agents of the Company to concede privileges to those poligars or Rajput chieftains who did not offer direct resist-

---

[2] Munro to Madras Board of Revenue, 18 June 1800, *Letters of Sir Thomas Munro relating to the early administration of Canara. Selections from the Records of South Canara* (Mangalore, 1879).

[3] *Lewin's report on the insurrection raised by Puttabasapah and others, 1837*, ibid. (Mangalore, 1913).

[4] Actg Magistrate to Government, 30 December 1844, *Correspondence on the Sawuntwaree Disturbances in the Province of Canara in 1845* (Mangalore, 1912)

ance. From such groups emerged the princes and landlords of later colonial rule.

Resistance by village leaderships was also common. In the course of the British revenue 'squeeze' of the early nineteenth century peasant landholders on coparcenary tenures and village headman families in the west and south suffered as badly and sometimes worse than the superior zamindars who held whole groups of villages. But lacking local leadership, acquiescence, migration or desertion were usually their only possible response. There were some exceptions, though. During the Goldsmid–Wingate settlement of the Deccan in the 1850s and early 60s (which was ultimately to bring down rates of land revenue) inferior tenure-holders and village officers put up fierce resistance in some districts. There were serious riots against the revenue survey in the Deccan district of Khandesh in 1852. While some leaders of this outbreak seem to have been substantial farmers who had benefited from a buoyant cotton market, Wingate thought that 'the hereditary and stipendiary officers have evidently been at the bottom of the movement'.[5] Between 1857 and 1859 the *kothi* landholders of the Konkan withheld cooperation from the revenue officials in a form of passive resistance. Before the 1870s the British had evidently failed to secure the cooperation of significant sections even of the peasant élite, but they had learned to be wary of their local influence. Many officials already warned against the uncontrolled expansion of commercial forces into the Indian countryside. These voices became stronger in the second half of the century.

The fragile expansion of cash-cropping in the early nineteenth century also set the scene for conflict within the ranks of rural society, between tenant and landholder and between arable farmer and nomad or herdsman. All these forms of tension were also to play a part in the 1857 revolt. Revolts by tribal peoples occurred on several occasions – among the Bhils in the 1820s and the Kols (1829–33) and Santal (1855–6) tribesmen on the Bengal borders, for instance; the invasion of their lands by pioneer peasants and logging agents was a common grievance.[6] But many affrays between agriculturalists and marginal groups were entered in British police reports as criminal offences. Some districts had long traditions of such conflict. The Haryana region near

---

[5] Charlesworth, *Peasants and Imperial Rule*, p. 52; J. F. M. Jhirad, 'The Khandesh Survey riot of 1852', *Journal of the Royal Asiatic Society*, 1968, 3 and 4.
[6] See E. F. Dalton, *Descriptive Ethnology of Bengal* (Calcutta, 1872).

Delhi was the scene of perpetual small-scale rioting as nomadic and wandering groups seized the cattle and silver of nearby farmers. The Kallar and Maravar districts of the south were notoriously unsettled. Despite its severe revenue assessments, the Company state generally favoured arable farmers at the expense of nomads or pastoralists. Wandering people of any sort were suspect as carriers of dissidence. Just as British officials had helped weld rather diverse sects into generic groups like Thugs or Pindaris, so herdsmen like the Gujars, Rangars and Bhattis of north India were beginning to be regarded as 'criminal tribes', a concept which was enshrined in punitive legislation after 1870. Yet even if tribals and wandering peoples were forced on the defensive, the colonial state had to pay a price. Special administrative and political arrangements were developed to shield these groups against too rapid change; the social separation of tribals from India began at the very time when the India of the peasant farmer and the merchant was inflicting a decisive defeat on the tribal economies.

Agrarian conflicts between landlords and their dependants in areas of settled agriculture were also common between 1780 and 1860. The most usual response to high rents or excessive lordship levies by rural magnates was desertion or migration. Sometimes, as in the Chingleput District of Madras in the 1790s, temporary desertion by agrarian dependants was an almost ritual form of bargaining between superior and inferior. Yet as the population on the land grew after about 1840, this option became less attractive, for landlords could always secure new tenants or share-croppers. Far better known, however, are the cases where agrarian conflict took on a religious character as a result of the teachings of reformed Islam. Notable here was the Faraizi movement of eastern Bengal which lasted from the 1820s to the 1850s. Haji Shariatullah (1781–1840) and his son Dudu Miyan (1819–62) were teachers of a reformed Koran-based Islam. But the movement also had a strong social message. Shariatullah was known as 'the spiritual guide of the weavers' while his son declared 'no man has the right to levy tax on God's earth'.[7] Both men were associated with attacks on Hindu trader money-lenders and European indigo estates. Sporadic violence continued in parts of east Bengal until 1860 when the colonial authorities imprisoned Dudu Miyan.

The Moplah revolts of the central Malabar coast also combined the features of religious devotion with social protest. The Moplahs in

[7] Qeyammudin Ahmed, *The Wahhabi Movement in India* (Calcutta, 1966), p. 95.

question were not the merchants of the towns but an inland cultivating group of putative Arab descent. They had been favoured under the rule of Tipu Sultan who had attacked their Hindu landlords (known as *janmis*). The onset of British rule and the restoration of the landholders set the scene for a series of outbreaks in which individuals or groups of Moplahs attacked and murdered Hindu landlords or British officials. The most violent of these disturbances took place in 1802, the late 1830s and again in 1849–52. Elsewhere there were periodic outbreaks of revolutionary messianism particularly among Muslim communities suffering rapid social dislocation. In 1808, for example, Abdul Rahman of Mandvi in Gujarat declared himself chosen leader (Imam Mahdi) and led a movement of weavers and Muslim agriculturalists against Hindu landlords and British personnel.[8] Again on the north-east borders of Bengal a Muslim millenarian movement led by one Tipu Sahib converged with a reaction by tribal hillmen against the demands of incoming Hindu landlords and the British military presence during the Burmese war of 1824 to give a generation of unrest. Tipu Sahib is reported to have declared that 'The Government was drawing to its close, that he was become king of the Sherpur pargannah [sub-district] and that the zamindars would be no more.' People consequently refused to offer labour services to the landholders.[9]

In all these movements there was conflict between landholder and tenants, agrarian labourer or tribal. The pressures of the British army or the colonial export economy also fuelled the feeling that some novel and illegitimate assault on custom was taking place. Still, it would be wrong to portray them as simple class conflicts or unanimous reactions to colonial oppression. In those cases where the ideologies of revolt can be reconstructed it seems that the abolition of taxation was seen as contingent on the extirpation of infidel rule, an event in some golden age rather than an immediate political programme. The enemy was often not the landlord as such but the infidel outsider; the solidarity of rural classes was fractured by religion, status and factional conflict. The indigo riots in Bengal between 1857 and 1859 perhaps stand as an exception to this generalisation. Here indigo cultivators felt the weight of the oppression of European planters and the neglect of the colonial state which had begun to discourage indigo and favour

---

[8] H. G. Briggs, *Cities of Gujarashtra*, Appendix B.
[9] B. B. Chaudhuri, 'Millenarian elements in the tribal and agrarian movements in eastern India in the nineteenth century', unpub. paper, p. 10.

more valuable crops like jute. The radical intelligentsia of Calcutta also played a part in developing peasant organisation through the propaganda of the newspaper *Nil Darpan*. However, even in this case, local landlords struggling with indigo planters for scarce labour supplies provided much of the impetus for rural agitation. The fragmented opposition of local communities to specific injustices rather than class consciousness was the dominant ideology.

These events nevertheless gave the British a heightened awareness of the role of religious revitalisation in popular protest. The willingness of the colonial power to grant special privileges to 'Sikhs', 'Muslims' and even 'non-Brahmins' in the later part of the century was in part a response to their painful loss of blood and treasure to such movements in the period of consolidation.

Urban revolts were an important though shadowy feature of the events of 1857. These also had many precedents in the previous three generations. As repositories of wealth, cities had always received the attentions of rural plunderers and impoverished labourers. In some areas the Sikh and Maratha movements had begun as assaults on the town-dwelling Mughal élites, and chroniclers portray several instances of town riots against Mughal officials and wealthy people. New tensions, however, were introduced by colonial rule. The precipitous decline of urban weavers after 1815 produced no social explosion. However, artisans were prominent in the riots in Rohilkhand and Benares between 1809 and 1818, and more ambiguously in the Hindu–Muslim conflicts of the 1830s. They also engaged in attacks on rich Hindus in Calcutta in 1789 and Surat in the 1790s and 1800s. The teaching of Sayyid Ahmed of Bareilly among weavers in the towns of the North-Western Provinces and Bihar was supposed by officials to have contributed to their mood of defiance. Of course, the links between economic tension and pious religious expression were quite indirect. Muslim weavers formed closely knit communities in most Indian cities. A sense of piety and worth as Muslims strengthened guild-like organisations which had often staged strikes and agitations against local officials and merchants.

Grain riots and protests against the monopolistic activities of grain dealers and interventions by British officials were also very common. Outbreaks in western Hindustan and Delhi in 1833–8 were particularly violent, but even a supposedly peaceable city such as Madras suffered from regular affrays. Here there were riots about alleged threats to Islam in 1806 at the time of the mutiny in the military station of Vellore; rice riots in 1806, 1833 and 1854 and serious demonstrations against Christian conversion between 1844 and 1858.[10] Yet the most common form of disturbance throughout the early nineteenth century in the towns was led by men of status in the quarters of the cities and directed against taxation by the colonial authorities. This was not simply an issue of material deprivation. Urban populations felt that their domestic custom was invaded by attempts to levy house taxation on them. Moreover, the decline of the law officers of the old Mughal cities (the kotwal, kazi and mufti) as they were replaced by brusque and faceless colonial officials created a sense of unease. A common cry of the 1857 rebels was for the restitution of the old system, for the bringing together again of civil and moral law.

Events of this sort may appear feeble and unimportant by comparison with the great rural rebellions. Yet they were significant nevertheless. The British willingness to protect merchant communities and their concern to associate urban magnates and leaders with their administration through 'local self-government' had already become apparent before mid-century.

This discussion of dissidence in early colonial India suggests several conclusions. First, the Indian rebellion of 1857 was unique in scale but not in content. Secondly, dissidence and disturbance was widespread throughout the whole of India and not simply a speciality of Hindustan. Thirdly there was almost always a revolt somewhere in the subcontinent, though particular periods, such as the height of the Wellesley conquests and the 1830s, may have been even more disturbed. Certainly, it is not easy to classify, revolts into 'post-pacification' revolts and 'traditional resistance' movements as some have done. One wave merged with the next without any obvious changes in style or content. Finally, though, the fragmented and uncoordinated nature of these revolts must be noted. Almost everywhere the British could rely on some part of a local population – the lowly and the poor as often as the zamindar or raja – to support them. There may have been a common dislike of the white ruler, as realists such as Sir Charles Metcalfe acknowledged, though common dislike was far removed from common action.

[10] J. Talboys Wheeler, *Chronological Annals of the British Government at Madras from the earliest days* (Madras, 1862), pp. xxiii–xxviii.

## THE ARMY AND THE COURSE OF REVOLT

Common action did not arise out of any inexorable trend to agrarian crisis. The 1830s saw widespread distress and much worry among officials about how varied forms of revolt might coalesce ominously. But the 1840s and 50s were years of better prices and harvests. As the last chapter showed, provincial governments even began to reduce the rate of revenue and grope towards a more realistic system of agrarian taxation. An external cataclysm was needed to release the pent-up tensions. The mutiny of the Bengal army in May 1857 was the trigger for the legitimist and agrarian uprisings which were to follow it. British victory partly resulted from the failure of the Bombay and Madras armies to follow the lead of the north Indian sepoys. Ironically, though, it was the Madras army which had the most striking history of disturbance. Large contingents of it had mutinied in the early 1780s because of arrears of pay and resentment at the Company's intrusion into the privileges of the Nawab of Arcot. A more serious revolt took place in June 1806 when the garrison at Vellore turned on its officers and was only subdued after a pitched battle in which several hundred men died. The Vellore mutiny had interesting parallels with the events of 1857. The mutineers apparently feared some assault on their religion as the result of the introduction of European headgear. There was an undercurrent of millenarian expectation as there was again in 1857. Muslim holy men were spreading rumours of an imminent end to British rule as the French and the followers of the now-sanctified Tipu Sultan combined to drive the infidel from the land. Hindu and Lingayat grievances centred on the rapid destruction of the poligar states of the far south.[11]

The Bengal army also wavered on a number of occasions. A company had mutinied in Java in 1815 and Gwalior in 1834. There was trouble during the Afghan campaign of 1839–42 when the deficiencies of white leadership were only too clearly exposed. Bengal sepoys in their home territories had customarily displayed a 'haughty' attitude to visiting British officials and Sir Charles Metcalfe put it on record as early as 1832 that 'a very little mismanagement' could result in the British losing India as its army and Indian servants were merely 'fol-

[11] P. Chinnian, *The Vellore Mutiny, 1806* (Madras, 1892).

lowers of fortune'.[12] However, the sepoys' real grievances began to mount in the 1850s. The General Service Enlistment Act of 1856 which demanded that sepoys should affirm their readiness to serve abroad, potentially exposing them to the risk of pollution, was an attempt to make the army more flexible in the aftermath of the disasters of the Afghan War. It went along with policies designed to introduce a wider range of caste and regional groups which naturally alarmed the Hindi-speaking rural Rajputs and Brahmins from Benares and Awadh who had hitherto dominated its service. These men or their relatives had other troubles too. The invasion of Awadh in 1856 had reduced the sepoys' pay (as they lost their benefit from service 'abroad') and diminished their status in the eyes of other enlisted men. It also looked set to deepen the economic problems of the high-caste village land-holding brotherhoods who provided many of the recruits. The spectre of higher revenue distressed petty landholders whose gentry status was already at risk from generations of subdivision of property. The rumours that the cartridges for the new Lee Enfield rifle would pollute their caste and force them to become Christians was only the final spark. The gulf between a complacent officer corps and an embittered soldiery had already become wide.

Why did the revolt spread so rapidly in its initial stages? Yet why were the British then able to confine it roughly within the bounds of the present-day state of Uttar Pradesh with a few outbreaks in Bihar and central India? The initial crucial link in the chain of revolt was the march of the rebellious troopers of the XI Native Cavalry from Meerut to Delhi on the night of 10–11 May 1857. Once the ageing Emperor Bahadur Shah was persuaded to lend his authority to the revolt, a number of discontented servants of the vanishing Mughal régime, notably Nawab Walidad Khan in the Bulandshahr District, came over to the rebellion. Mutinous contingents of sepoys in other stations also saw in the Emperor a legitimate authority with which to replace their white officers. British forces did not pursue and destroy these first Meerut mutineers, it appears, because the local commander feared for the safety of European residents of the civil station. Urban mobs, composed of artisans, dissident police and day-labourers, had appeared on the streets almost immediately. So from its inception the civilian rebellion and the mutinies reinforced each other. After a brief lull further mutinies and urban revolts occurred in the garrison towns

---

[12] Metcalfe to Bentinck, 11 October 1829, Philips (ed.), *Bentinck Correspondence*, i, 311.

north and west of Delhi in June and July 1857, effectively severing the British forces in the eastern provinces from those in the Punjab.

Yet it was crucial that even in this, the heart of revolt around Delhi, British power was not eliminated. In several of the western districts magistrates and collectors put together scratch forces, protected treasuries and attacked and burnt out villages which had risen in revolt. The need to guard their rear from the small parties of British troops still scattered across the countryside was one reason why the mutineers were unable to concentrate for a determined attack on the British forces from the Punjab who quickly assembled to march on Delhi, or to attack the garrison in Kanpur. From the first, then, rebellion failed to create a liberated area in which support for the rebel régime could become safe as well as legitimate. Local groups tended instead to consult their own interests and prosecute their ancient feuds. More momentously, the gathering struggle over Delhi itself quickly became the moral centre of the whole anti-British movement. Contingents of mutineers from the south and east as well as magnate leaders tended to converge on the capital. This had the effect of limiting and concentrating revolt rather than allowing it to spread outwards towards new areas. Delhi was thus the greatest victory and ultimate undoing of the revolt.

The second major centre of revolt was Awadh. Discontent here had been growing since the British occupation of the summer of 1856. Martin Gubbins's summary settlement of the Awadh revenues managed to antagonise both the great Talukdar magnates and the village proprietors whom British policy was supposedly favouring. In the city of Lucknow the ex-Queen Mother and a variety of military leaders, incensed by the Company's dismissal of more than 50,000 troops, concerted with Muslim religious leaders. When the news from Delhi was received in early June revolt spread quickly with very wide support from the nobility and urban populace. British public opinion and nationalist myth has often concentrated on the war in Awadh, and in particular on the relief by Henry Havelock of the small British garrison imprisoned in the Residency in September 1857, followed by Colin Campbell's second relief of the new contingent in November. Certainly, the revolt was nearest to a popular movement here. Even as the British armies fought their way towards Lucknow further talukdar magnates joined the rebellion, driven to despair by the new assault on their status as local kings which British policy represented. In the southern marchers of Awadh British troops sustained heavy losses well into the summer of 1858, fighting village by village as they encountered stiff resistance from those very high-caste village brotherhoods which had provided the best recruits for their army.

Yet from very early on it was clear that the Awadh revolt was an heroic sideshow. The kingdom had already been pushed to the margins by half a century of social and economic change. Crucially, the impetus to revolt failed to carry to the banks of the Ganges and Jumna and thus sever British communications between Delhi and Calcutta. There were a very few days when the river and Grand Trunk route was cut, but in general the Company was able to supply its garrisons up-river and move its gunboats and grain boats with impunity. There were two main reasons for this. First, many of the talukdar magnates of southern Awadh hedged their bets in the contest. Some were too aware of British strength; others had a history of conflict with the Awadh centre in Lucknow and were distinctly unimpressed by the prospect of the revival of the Shia kingdom. Secondly, the British districts lying along the Ganges–Jumna had already thrown up a group of new magnates dependent on if not actually committed to British rule. The Bhumihar rulers of Benares and their kinsmen straddling the river in Mirzapur and Allahabad districts had risen by defeating and subordinating precisely those tenacious Rajput brotherhoods which were now in revolt. Their dominance in the region had pre-dated but was ultimately strengthened by British rule. In some districts commercial men had moved out from the major colonial cities to acquire land-rights in the hinterland. These were now surprisingly active in the British cause. Ultimately, the failure of revolt to gain a strong foothold in the riverine districts meant that the three subsidiary centres, Awadh, central India and Bihar, were split from each other and the British could deal with them one by one.

Revolt in the south suffered from similar fragmentation. In the Maratha states of central India (Gwalior and Jhansi) an ancient dislike of British rule which went back to the days of the Maratha hegemony was sharpened by colonial intrusion into the states' affairs, notably Lord Dalhousie's decision to annex Jhansi in 1853 on the pretext that there was no legitimate heir. Further south in Hyderabad there was much dry tinder also. The residents' meddling had tended to favour the group of Hindu financiers and northeners surrounding the diwan at the expense of the old Hyderabad Muslim nobility and the fiercely independent Hindu chiefs of the hinterland. Islamic revivalist movements had also taken root around the capital; as early as 1838 the British had expected a Muslim rising. Holy war was indeed declared in 1857, and on 17 July a body of Rohilla soldiers and bazaar people led by a local Muslim religious leader attacked the Residency. Revolts and mutinies at other centres followed, though unlike the situation at Meerut these were immediately countered by Company troops. What was critical was the fact that even discontented chieftains had held back from revolt because it was initially perceived in the south as a Maratha movement and Marathas had been the fierce enemies of Hyderabad during the conflicts of the previous century.[13] The failure of rebellion in Hyderabad released troops of the British Madras army who were deployed in the Benares region during the crucial months of August and September.

Similar combinations of military chance and Indian disunity played into British hands in other parts of India. In Gujarat an ancient suspicion of the old Maratha hegemony along with a new, more lenient, régime of agrarian taxation fragmented opposition to colonial rule. The Bhil tribes and their leaders had been successfully conciliated through the creation of the Bhil Corps which was in turn used against other more recalcitrant groups. Critically also, the British were very well entrenched in both the Holkar and Baroda courts. Precisely because these old Maratha states had been suspected of intrigue and fierce anglophobia, successive British political agents had worked hard to build up personal links with the leaders and their 'feudatories'.[14]

The Punjab, of course, was decisive for it was from here that the British thrust east against the Delhi revolutionaries. Punjab had been recently conquered and so there were large numbers of British troops on the spot to suppress the several mutinies which broke out in Punjab garrison towns and amongst Muslim pastoralists in the dry west of the province. But everything depended on the stance of the Sikh magnates and village brotherhoods. Luckily for their future in India, the British had played their cards here much better than they did in Awadh. At least 16,000 of the defeated Sikh army had been taken into Company service with generous pay and allowances. An initially severe revenue

[13] H. Briggs, *The Nizam. His history and relations with the British government* (London, 1861), ii, 76 ff.
[14] Shri Prakash, '1857 in Gujarat', unpub. MS in author's possession.

assessment was made more lenient after 1852 and British irrigation plans in the central Punjab had proceeded at a cracking pace compared with the lethargy of the North-Western Provinces; the Punjab civilians had soon come to appreciate the merits of the Sikh Jat peasant brotherhoods. At the same time there was little love in the Punjab for the Hindustani soldiers who had taken such a forward part in the conquest of their territory. Punjab remained a solid base for the British throughout the revolt and emerged afterward as the main beneficiary of military expenditure and recruitment.

In Bengal, finally, neither military nor social conditions favoured revolt. The British had retained four battalions in the immediate vicinity of Calcutta whereas they had stripped the North-Western Provinces in order to police the Punjab. New British troops were arriving in Bengal by the beginning of November 1857, diverted from an expeditionary force to China which was conveniently passing through the Indian Ocean. Most important, however, was the fact that the people of Bengal had a much more realistic and sophisticated understanding of the power of their rulers. There could be no sense here as there was in Awadh that British manpower had already been exhausted and that England was stripped of able-bodied men. Few leaders of the old pre-colonial military aristocracy survived comparable with the Rajput kings of upper India to lead the countryside in revolt. Indeed, the zamindars of the Premanent Settlement had conspicuously benefited from the rising value of agricultural produce while village-level controllers like the jotedars of north and east Bengal had been able to strengthen their grip on the ordinary peasantry. Created by, yet restricted and humiliated by, colonial rule, the new professional classes of Calcutta and the district towns were still little inclined to support a movement which they saw as a typical zamindar revolt in a backward area of the country.

### IDEOLOGY AND COHESION

The failure of the rebels in 1857 goes beyond the question of inter-regional suspicion and military chance. The underlying deficiency was the inability of its leaders to throw up a series of creative goals and strategies for the defeat of the Company. Sepoys showed themselves astonishingly brave in individual manoeuvres and encounters. The bloody war around the walls of Delhi threw up desperate guerrilla heroism. Yet without their British officers the sepoys often found it impossible to mount the final bayonet charge which could rout their enemy head-on. Instead, fighting tended to degenerate into sharp-shooting and a desperate defence by zamindars and bodies of sepoys of their own villages.

Something similar happened to the political leadership of the revolt. Many leaders, Hindu and Muslim, had vague notions of the Indian-style political order which they wished to reinstate. However, it proved very difficult for them to create new institutions or coherent plans with which to confront the social crisis. One noteworthy feature was the fragmentation of the Muslim response compared with its dominant role in the 1820s revolts in Java or later events in the Indian subcontinent, such as the Khilafat movement of 1918–21.

Undercurrents of Islamic millenarianism were not lacking. The mobilisation of Persian forces against the Company in 1856 was seen in Delhi as the percursor to a great Islamic war which would drive the 'nazarenes' from India.[15] In Lucknow the mood of unease which preceded and followed the annexation of Awadh was reflected in the activities of Muslim millenarian preachers who proclaimed the end of Company rule precisely one hundred years after its inception at the battle of Plassey. A Sunni divine had marched with his followers on Lucknow in 1855 to protest against the insolence of the British and Hindus.

Once revolt had begun several strands to the Islamic movement can be isolated. First, there was the appearance at Delhi of several thousand militant *ghazis* (warriors of the Faith) who sacrificed themselves in fruitless frontal assaults against British troops. These men appear to have come from places such as Bhopal and Tonk (former centres of the Pindaris and of Muslim state-building) and they may have been associated with the fringes of the militant Naqshbandi sufi movement which the British called 'Wahhabis'. Others were men of the Chishti Sabri order from the Delhi region and East Punjab where there was a long tradition of militant opposition to the Sikhs. Secondly, the war in the Saharanpur and Muzaffarnagar districts, north of Delhi, took on a distinctly Islamic flavour. Here was a strong concentration of Muslim service gentry who had been associated with the Delhi empire and

---

[15] Translation of petition of Muhammad Darwesh; copy of evidence taken before the court appointed for the trial of the king of Delhi, *Parliamentary Papers*, 1859, First Session, xviii, 69.

here, also, teachers of the school of Shah Abdul Aziz who had declared India 'land of war' in 1802, wielded much influence. Several proclamations of the learned (*fatwas*) declaring holy war were issued, especially from the towns of Deoband and Thana Bhawan which later became centres of a major religious movement. Further, there was a good deal of Muslim response to the revolt in the small rural towns of Awadh and eastern U.P. Here again teachers of the more militant wing of the Naqshbandi order had been active among weavers and bazaar men. In Awadh popular Islamic leaders such as the maulvis of Fyzabad and Allahabad organised fierce resistance to the British.

Yet for all this the Islamic response lacked cohesion. There were several reasons. First, the Muslim community was itself split socially and theologically. The distinction between Sunnis and Shias surfaced in some areas. Thus in Allahabad a Shia divine argued that revolt could not be holy war without the leadership of a Shia Imam, while in Lucknow tension between the Shia court and the Sunni leadership of the popular movement led to the Maulvi of Fyzabad arguing that he himself should become 'king'. Many Sunnis also argued that the key conditions for a declaration of holy war had not been met. For some the British state had not made the continuation of Muslim worship impossible. For others there was little likelihood of success in revolt, and this had been a key condition for holy war (*jihad*) urged on the community by the caution of the Prophet.

Again, tensions which appear to be more social than theological split the Muslim community. It is true that British resumption of revenue-free grants given by previous rulers had damaged some Islamic institutions (though more so in Bengal than in upper India). Still, the landed Muslim establishment had survived the first half-century of colonial rule relatively well. Muslims had lost land rights in total but no more so than other representatives of the old order. There was a natural reluctance among well-placed members of the landed gentry to endanger their livelihoods and property by joining in the revolt. So even in pious Saharanpur there were a number of social and religious leaders prepared to issue statements to the effect that this was no religious war. Many government servants also remained committed to the British – out of fear, out of deep-seated loyalty, or out of a canny judgement that Islam must reform internally before it could face down the West. Among these latter was Sayyid Ahmed Khan, later founder of the Aligarh movement and harbinger of Islamic modernism in India.

Apart from their internal differences Indian Muslims were also inhibited from raising a more full-blooded call to Islam by their relations with Hindus. As soon as Delhi was liberated the Mughals banned the Muslim sacrificial practice of cow-slaughter and dissuaded their officers from seeking a declaration of holy war on the grounds that it might offend the 'eastern [i.e. Hindu Brahmin and Rajput] soldiers'. Later rebel proclamations such as that of the Queen Mother of Awadh and the Maulvi of Fyzabad scrupulously sought to link Hindus and Muslims by arguing that the 'Firingees [foreigners] have sought to destroy both the Hindu and Mahomedan faiths'. Elsewhere attempts to reinstate Islamic forms of urban government through kazis and kotwals were tempered by the need to avoid offending the Hindu population. That this was a necessary caution was illustrated by events in the small towns of Rohilkhand where raising of the 'Muhammadi flag' sometimes signalled conflicts between Muslim weavers and artisans and their Hindu moneylenders, or between older Hindu zamindars and the lately come Rohilla Afghans. Locally at least, the tensions released by revolt sometimes caused the 'tree of Hindu–Muslim aversion' to grow deeper roots, as Sayyid Ahmed later put it.

Hindu themes of millenarian regeneration proved an even more fragile basis on which to build a true revolutionary movement. Many of the great leaders of revolt – men such as Kuar Singh in Bihar or Tantia Topi and the Rani of Jhansi in central India – became cult figures, the subjects of heroic ballads and festival images in later times. Doubtless many Hindus saw in 1857 the grim harvest of the final age of the Goddess Kali. Rebel proclamations similarly emphasised the need to re-establish the old social order, to give service to artisans and zamindars and beat back the tide of low men of base caste origins. But the fragmented and localised nature of Hindu kingship in the region, hammered to pieces by both Mughal and British rule, provided little in the way of a commonalty of interests. And for the Hindu kings the Mughal centre was at best an ambiguous focus of loyalty. The Jat king of Ballabgarh, south east of Delhi, held a number of Mughal titles of honour; in 1857 he pledged himself to Bahadur Shah in the name of the ancient loyalty of his house. However, the Jats – once 'bandit plunderers' to the Mughals – must have viewed the re-emergence of a power in Delhi with mixed feelings. It is not surprising that these same princes soon opened up correspondence with the British forces besieging the city.[16]

[16] Petitions of the Chief of Ballabgarh, *Parliamentary Papers*, 1859, First Session, xviii, 33–8.

Ultimately no coherent ideology or programme existed to channel the aspirations of the rebels. Peasant millenarianism could not provide a common platform even to the extent that it did in the first stages of the contemporary Taiping Revolt in China. There were too many representatives of the old order involved from the start. Nor did nationalism provide a basis since it was from the marginal or declining areas of Indian society that the most prolonged resistance generally came.

## THE ECONOMIC ORIGINS OF REVOLT

Over the last generation the conviction of the Bengal military that the Mutiny was in large part a civil rebellion has been borne out by detailed research. It was once considered that the inroads of the hated bania moneylender into the countryside as a result of the forced sales for arrears of the British revenue courts was the mainspring of revolt. More recently, the weight of government land revenue, only marginally eased from high points of the 1830s depression, is now considered the culprit. Both explanations may appear to smack of economic reductionism. Did Indians only revolt when they were hit in their pockets or stomachs? This is a misperception, for questions of land and rupees simply summarised a whole range of grievances which resulted from the clash of an imperial centre, now galvanised with new managerial and technological power, with the self-regard of many local communities.

This theme can be illustrated by reference to communities at every level within Indian society. On the fringes of settled cultivation and Hindu society alike were a range of wandering and pastoralist groups who played a key rôle in violence in most areas – but visited it on both 'sides' in the national struggle. There was a great difference in status between the lordly Rangar or Bhatti Rajput chiefs of cattle keepers, the bullock-pack Banjaras, and the humble pig-keeping Pasis who acted as watchmen and thieves throughout the plains. But all were alike the victims of the expansion of the arable, of the pioneer peasant and of the colonial revenue system. In the Delhi Territory and Haryana, for instance, huge areas of former grazing grounds had been assigned to the Jat peasantry at the expense of the nomadic Gujars and Bhattis in the decade before the Mutiny. Not surprisingly, the Mutiny in this region seemed very much like an assault of the marginal communities of the dry areas against the more prosperous peasant villages and the symbols of imperial rapacity which had spelled the end of their old dominance. As in the Great Fear of the French Revolution, the collapse of British authority was sometimes signalled by rumours that roaming and plundering peoples who symbolised the untamed forces of the jungles were on the move. Elsewhere, as in the small bazaar town of Shikokabad guards and wage labourers from the semi-settled 'criminal' tribes living in peripheral villages were prominent in plundering. Groups like these were among the first to attack the British civil lines. But resentment against towns, wealth and trade was by no means confined to those where British rule and its allies survived. The Mughal emperor's lines of communication were also plundered by 'vagabonds and wretches' in the summer of 1857.

Much to the horror and surprise of the British, however, many standard peasant communities also revolted in 1857. These do not often appear to have been conscious revolts against the landlord system. Usually, they were uprisings of whole local communities, landlord and tenant alike against outsiders, for where a substantial body of people joined the rebellion the British had to fight village by village. There were three great arcs of revolt amongst independent peasant farmers. To the chagrin of revenue officials the careful Jat farmers who lived north and west of Delhi, particularly in the villages of Meerut District, were widely involved in direct anti-British activity. These men had fought the armies of the Mughal in the eighteenth century, but in 1857 substantial numbers of them found their interests and sympathies were at one with the last of the Mughals. Then again, revolt was fierce among the coparcenary petty landlords of the villages which lay in the dry ravine-ridden lands of the tract along the length of the rivers Ganges and Jumna as they pass east from the city of Agra through Allahabad, to Benares. Finally, the British noted that revolt spread very rapidly among the high-caste peasant communities of Awadh even where Martin Gubbins's summary settlement of 1856 had apparently helped them by making them petty landholders, responsible for the payment of land revenue. All these forms of revolt worried the colonial rulers and threw doubt on the picture of the sturdy peasant as the main pillar of the Raj. Why did they occur?

Those Jats who revolted in 1857 were relatively prosperous by the standards of the Rajput petty proprietors of the east. They were predominantly owner-occupier holders in an area where there was still 25–30 per cent of good, cultivable land to take under the plough. But the rebellious Jats in western Meerut, Saharanpur and Muzaffarnagar districts appear to have been distinguished from those who did not revolt in a number of ways. For instance, there were social distinctions which derived from different waves of Jat expansion into the region and persisted in the form of conflicts between multi-caste factions led by Jats. Then again, existing hostility was deepened by the resentment of the 'dry tracts' – lands which had not profited from the expansion of the irrigated acreage after the extension of the East Jumna Canal and the opening of the Ganges Canal in 1854, and yet were still subject to a very high land-revenue demand which led to the auction sale of their lands. In such dry villages Jats sometimes joined their caste inferiors, the Gujars, who had taken to settled agriculture more recently, in attacks on British positions or in pouring supplies into rebel Delhi.

However, it was not always as straightforward as this. Some of the Jat farmers of the south-west part of Saharanpur District, living in well-irrigated and beautifully cultivated countryside, also exploded into resistance. Here very severe revenue assessments in the 1830s and 1840s – an ironic recognition of the Jats' excellence as farmers – appears to have been a cause of long-standing resentment. It worked particularly inequitably, depressing the relative status of these farmers in comparison with their old social connections and marriage partners in other parts of the district. Two important points emerge from the detailed studies done by Eric Stokes in this region. First, that caste categories are only very crude guidelines to the complex distinctions between 'rebel' and 'loyalist'; Jat farmers fought on both sides. Secondly, material deprivation or the inroads of the moneylender were not in themselves enough to cause revolt: a conviction of the decline of status and honour in relation to other communities was a more powerful and subtle incitement against the status quo.

The force of these points is redoubled if one looks to the centres of main-line peasant revolt further to the east. Along the rivers Ganges and Jumna the British had to fight village by village through the poor lands which lay to the north and south of the Grand Trunk Road. These were not the rich areas which had done well out of the river trade in cash crops, but they bore a very heavy weight of land revenue nevertheless. The proud but indigent Rajput communities of these areas had few sources of credit and no rich produce to sell. Their strong clan-like social organisation, at or below the *pargana* level, had survived precisely because commerce and land legislation had little effect here. The British and their rich hangers-on among the money-lenders and Bengali administrators of the major towns seemed natural enemies.

The situation was different in Awadh. Here bodies of gentry with small jointly administered rental holdings were scattered in among the huge estates of the area magnates – the talukdars who often preferred to have low-caste men as tenants rather than troublesome relations and caste-fellows. The British, following the anti-landlords policy which had come into vogue in the 1830s, sought to deal with village-level powerholders (often called *mokkadams*) when they made the summary settlement of 1856. The idea was that if the 'parasitical' magnates could be pensioned off on 10 per cent or thereabouts of their old take from the villages, it would be politic to make a land-revenue settlement with the true rural élite – the sturdy yeoman – who would provide the underpinnings of a more stable and prosperous British India as was apparently already happening in the Punjab. But as the British were to learn in what appeared to be the cardinal lesson of nineteenth-century agrarian policy, the new village proprietors did not support them and throughout much of the countryside went over to support the dispossessed talukdars and members of the Lucknow court.

Why this occurred still remains obscure. One of the features of revolt was, of course, that the government had very little idea what was happening in the rebel-held areas and where information was available it generally concerned the activities of the great magnates. Where magnates took an active part for or against the revolt it was difficult for the village communities to oppose them. Yet this is not to say that small zamindars and peasants simply waited for the initiative of their superiors. For instance, when the Raja of Balrampur remained 'loyal' to the British only 3,000 of his men were prepared to side with him, 'the sympathies of the rest and of all about him are with the rebels'.[17] Elsewhere small zamindars and sepoys who had returned to their villages were found forcing their talukdar leaders to declare for the Lucknow dynasty. The very widespread hostility to British rule

[17] Wingfield's memo., 17 May 1858, Bahraich, cited, T. R. Metcalf, *Land, landlords and the British Raj* (Berkeley, 1979), p. 176.

among the land-owning cultivators of Awadh is perhaps not as surprising as it first seems. There were, first, the grievances of the sepoys themselves, quickly transmitted to the villages by the returning mutineers. There was also the incalculable factor of loyalty to the Awadh court and dislike of the intrusion of strangers into the village communities. Yet it should not be assumed either that the peasant landholders actually felt that they would prosper under British rule. Their long-term history was of rapid population rise, subdivision of holdings into fractions of rupees and loss of outside earnings. The actual details of the summary settlement often left them with government revenue to pay without adequate resources of credit, and with the looming figure of the dispossessed talukdar on the social horizon. Whatever tensions may have existed between landholder and tenant, many of the great magnates were still seen as representations of Lord Shiva, as founts of patronage and honour in their localities, not lightly to be cast aside. Still, even if we accept the wider, popular character of the revolt in many parts of Awadh the men who fought staunchly against Colin Campbell's invading army were not the militant tenants of later nationalist history. They were village landholders, often not cultivators themselves, falling back on their status and the possession of a few rough-cast cannons.

The response of the larger rural magnates was vital in the hinterland districts. They alone could muster the forces to chastise recalcitrant villages, or alternatively provide a core of rebel organisation for dissident villagers. Many magnates were oppressed and insulted by the new overbearing manner of the officials of the 1830s and 40s. They resented the loss of local political honours and may have identified with the plight of the Mughal Emperor, whose pensionary status was by now fully revealed. Yet local values and local interests appear to have been paramount in their calculations.

Some of the great magnates of the North-Western Provinces had adjusted well to the high British land-revenue demand, introducing severer forms of land management and gaining from the advance of cash-cropping in the riverine districts. But others did not. The rajas of Etah and Mainpuri in the rather poverty-stricken heart of the Ganges–Jumna Doab both joined the rebels. Neither 'Awadh influence' nor loyalty to the Mughals can really explain their revolt. Instead it seems that the revenue settlements of the 1830s had reduced the rajas' income irretrievably, and being unable to profit from the growth of valuable cash-crops because of the poverty of their territories, they followed the rebellion as the last hope of maintaining the ancient prestige of their houses. Elsewhere, quarrels within families seem to have been a major cause of revolt. The British had made the fluid system of Indian inheritance more rigid. In cases of doubt their desire to favour amenable candidates had sometimes set up fierce struggles between rival parties of claimants to titles. In some cases the disgraced candidates themselves plunged quickly into revolt against the colonial rulers. Elsewhere men who had lost out in the immediate aftermath of the annexation saw a chance to reinstate themselves in British eyes when their favoured relations joined the revolt. So Ajit Singh of Taroul in Partabgarh District, Awadh, after a long blood feud with his kinsman Gulab Singh, came over to the British side when his relation was on the defensive and later claimed the reward of the Taroul estates for his 'loyalty'. In some cases the rationale behind different stances taken in the rebellion related to ancient feuds not within families but within whole sets of rival clans. In Rohilkhand enmities between the Rohilla Afghan ruling class of the eighteenth century and the Rajput clan leaders of Kutheir who had possessed the country before them were sometimes transformed into struggles between the rebels and 'loyalists' when some Afghans expressed their loyalty to Delhi; this, of course, had very little to do with any real attachment to British rule.

Perhaps the most significant general line of distinction between those who joined the revolt and those who hedged their bets or acquiesced in colonial rule has already been alluded to. This was the distinction between the magnates who had broadly survived the onset of colonial trade and administration and those who had been steadily losing land rights since the cession of 1801. Eric Stokes called the former 'new magnates'. Yet their newness did not consist in any innovation in agricultural management. Instead bodies of magnates like the Bhumihar rulers and landholders of the Benares region had slowly been accumulating economic power since the later eighteenth century, playing the land-market, moneylending and the British revenue courts with more success than their ancient bucolic rivals amongst the Rajputs of the interior. Along with the majority of men of commerce and a large proportion of civil servants, these magnates ensured that the British administration survived in the most important centres of north India and that the revolt was a phenomenon of the backwoods.

It is true that some features of the Great Rebellion were echoed at later stages in India's history of anti-colonial revolt. After a prudent interval the men of 1857 came to occupy an important rôle in the hagiography of Indian nationalism and peasant discontent. The high-caste village yeomen of Awadh who had been so hot against British rule in the Red Year, took some part in the later peasant movements of the 1920s and 30s. But the disjunction was very great both in ideology and in the social origins of resistance. By the 1860s and 70s rebellion in the countryside had a predominantly anti-landlord character, a feature which was rare or at least suppressed during 1857. This is not surprising, for 1857 was at the end of the last period before significant new differentials began to open up within the peasant society of north India. Inflation, population growth and new land legislation had transformed the society of the great plains within a generation of the last shots of the Mutiny.

## CONSOLIDATING THE NEW RAJ

The most dramatic and immediate consequences of the revolt were felt, of course, by the sepoy army itself and its rural allies. No quarter was given by the British, enraged at the atrocities committed against their women and children. Tens of thousands of soldiers and village guerrillas were hanged, shot, or blown from guns. Though the loss of life was small by comparison with other great historical revolts, many parts of the Doab, southern Awadh and western Bihar showed a significant drop in population between the censuses of 1853 and 1871. At a stroke Benares and Awadh ceased to be recruiting grounds for the British army and were speeded on their way to poverty and agrarian stagnation. The Punjab, notably 'loyal' during the revolt became the new favoured area, and the ancient traditions of imperial recruitment which went back to the time of Emperor Sher Shah in the sixteenth century were ruptured. By 1875, half of the British Indian Army was recruited from the Punjab, while Gurkhas from Nepal now replaced the Brahmin 'lions' from Benares as the shock troops of the British Empire. Hereafter, the British carefully fostered a sense of caste and tribe within their army – Punjabi Muslims, Dogras and Jats were kept in separate units, and a more professional officer corps was encouraged to 'know their men', and regularly visit the recruiting villages.

The Indian sepoy was at no time to outnumber European troops in the subcontinent by more than two to one and Europeans were placed in charge of artillery in well-fortified and segregated army cantonments. The new military expenditure had some economic effects. It brought about an increase of government expenditure, larger imports of bullion and a more rapid circulation of money in the interior. It also speeded the construction of railways for strategic routes and encouraged the extension of the Punjab canal colonies to favour the most important areas of military recruitment.

The Rebellion of 1857 also greatly changed the governance of India. Parliamentary and ministerial control which had been gradually creeping up on the Company since the India Act of 1784 was now fully revealed. The Company itself, which had long fought off the pressures of free traders, succumbed to its own military failure and was abolished. India was now to be governed from London by a Secretary of State for India assisted by a Council with fifteen members under the Act for the Better Government of India (1858). The Governor-General was constituted Viceroy and under the Indian Councils' Act of 1861 the Viceroy's Council and also the councils at Bombay and Madras were increased by the addition, for legislative purposes only, of non-official European and Indian members. These tiny advances in the practice of representative government were intended to provide safety valves for the expression of public opinion which had been so badly misjudged before the rebellion. Parliamentary intervention became more frequent and India affairs were drawn into British political debates to a greater extent than at any time since the later eighteenth century.

Changes in Indian finance pointed in the same direction. The rebellion cost the huge sum of £50 million (Rs. 50 crores) to suppress, and besides, there was a significant short-term loss of land and opium revenues. James Wilson, Finance Minister in the new Viceroy's Council drew up a reformed plan of taxation which included a licence tax, a revamped system of customs duties and India's first direct income tax. In time this evolved into a new pattern of provincial finance (1870–2). In Bombay and Madras the rate of land tax per acre had already begun to decline and these new measures generalised the trend across the country. Gradually land revenue diminished as a proportion of government income. But it is rather ironic that the colonial state, fearful for social order, had begun to lose the nerve to tax the countryside at the very point when rising agricultural incomes were creating the lineaments of a small class of independent peasants and affluent yeomen farmers in some parts of the country. This switch to direct taxation on incomes and trades in the towns carried important implications. Opportunities for sustained conflict between government and the professional or trading people of the large towns was increased. Also the need to assess and collect non-agricultural taxes combined with a desire for urban improvement to nudge the British cautiously into the beginnings of local self-government during the early 1870s. In time the municipal boards and the corporations of Bombay, Calcutta and Madras were to provide formal arenas where the conflicts between colonial government and its subjects would be dramatised by a new generation of public leaders.

It is important to avoid a 'Whiggish' interpretation here. Too many histories seem to assume a simple transition after 1857 from traditional resistance to modern nationalism and political organisation. Neither part of this equation is so simply drawn. There is no reason to apply the term traditional to the reaction of tribal peoples, peasants or zamindars against the invasion of their sphere by the colonial state, moneylenders and petty commodity production. Revolts of the types which occurred in the early nineteenth century persisted to 1947 (and indeed beyond). On the other hand, the early nineteenth century had witnessed agitation by urban and professional people as coherently articulated as that which is subsumed under the term 'nationalism' after 1880. The theory of the 'drain of wealth' from India by Britain was in wide circulation in the upper Indian cities during the series of taxation riots which occurred between 1809 and 1818. In 1806 Indian traders and scribal people in Madras had combined with the non-official European community to petition for the retention of a Welsh judge who had fallen foul of the Madras government. Much of the cultural activity of Calcutta in the 1820s and 30s was an implied critique of colonial rule. What was lacking in the early nineteenth century was only all-India organisation, and this lack largely reflected the absence of much overall cohesion in the British government of India itself. Historians of the future will begin to define the content of nationalism more widely and to date its origins much earlier.

Yet in 1860 the restiveness of traders and professional men was still a minor irritant. Instead government was concerned to soothe and cajole the great magnates of the countryside and the princes who had wavered during the crisis of 1857. In this they were largely successful. Though it is almost impossible to measure its impact, the new rôle created for the British Crown in the Indian polity appears to have been a stabilising influence. The destruction of Delhi and the show trial of the last Mughal finally released the British from their theoretical submission to the authority of the house of Timur. Charters and proclamations issued in the last days of the rebellion, including Victoria's famous declaration of religious toleration, were in the Queen's name. Hereafter the British gradually elaborated the royal cult and the language of feudal loyalty in India, particularly among the princes. This trend culminated in the Delhi Durbar of 1877 when Victoria was proclaimed Queen–Empress and princes and people were ranked and honoured by the principles of a peculiar amalgamation of Anglo–Norman and Mughal conceptions of race and royalty. If Hindu kingship flourished in the localities the rhetoric of public life in the major centres was transformed. The Indian National Congress, meeting in 1885 to criticise the shortcomings of British rule, was obliged to proclaim that 'loyalty is part of our constitution'.

Practical measures also helped to confirm the position of the great magnates and renew their acquiescence. The British abandoned their policy of sequestrating Indian states if their own conception of right succession was not fulfilled. There was some trouble over the influence of residents, especially in the Maratha state of Baroda, but in general British residents were able indirectly to foster 'modernising' diwans in the important native states. A succession of English-educated rajas and diwans in Travancore and Hyderabad's diwan, Sir Salar Jang, more effectively promoted British interests in their respective states than any number of interfering early-nineteenth-century residents.

Those revenue officials who before 1857 had called for a more cautious approach to the territorial magnates of northern India were, as they saw it, triumphantly justified by the events of 1857. Canning (Governor-General, later Viceroy, 1856–62) brought the war in Awadh to an end by buying off the Talukdars with the promise that they would regain control of their villages and secure a much lighter land-revenue settlement. Some great estates were seized by Government as punishment for rebellion, but officers made sure that these later came under control of the most important of the great rural connections. The yeoman proprietor, supposed beneficiary of the Summary Settlement of 1856, was given short shrift and a pedigree and ideology was elaborated for the 'Barons of Oudh' which resembled nothing so much as eighteenth-century rural Scotland. Worried by the thought that transfers of land to moneylenders had helped precipitate rebellion, divisional commissioners sought to give protection to the lands of spendthrift aristocrats through the institution of the Court of Wards which took over their estates in cases of incompetence or minority. The Talukdars' Encumbered Estates Act of 1870 which put brakes on the sale of land for debt was echoed in Central India where the British opted for a landlord solution and in the Punjab where the few great magnates who had survived the terminal crisis of the Sikh state were protected.

However, the 'tilt towards the landlords' was only possible in areas where large magnates existed to receive the benefits of Western education and instruction in land management. Elsewhere the British sought to improve their relations with the vast body of cultivators. In Bengal the indigo riots of 1859 resulted in the Bengal Tenancy Act of 1861 which gave occupancy tenants a limited degree of protection in their holdings. In western and southern India the rate of revenue levied on the owner-occupier peasants had already begun to come down before 1857. Even in the North-Western Provinces and Oudh an outbreak of disturbances between tenant and landlord in the early 1860s prompted legislation which marginally favoured more substantial peasants. British land policy after 1857 was in fact riven with contradiction. It was designed to mean all things to all men. Zamindars were to be capitalist farmers; but the state gave no aid in this unlikely transition. Improvement was supposed to be the order of the day, but the penetration of urban capital into the rural areas was inhibited by debt legislation for fear that it might give rise to further unrest. Peasant farmers were given a little protection against summary ejectment from their plots. Yet all the while the ancient inequalities of rural society were maintained by population growth and official inertia.

That the British were able to carry on this balancing act throughout the rest of the century was a result of developments largely unrelated to their post-Mutiny policies. In the first place the years 1860 to 1880 saw a quite rapid expansion of the communications network. In 1857 there were a mere 570 miles of railway line in India. By 1880 the figure had reached 4,300. In 1862 the Suez Canal was opened. Between 1856 and 1864 demand for Indian cotton almost trebled as a result of the

Civil War in America which reduced production in that quarter. These three developments made it much easier to sell India's agricultural products on the world market and enriched some farmers and merchant entrepreneurs. A slow depreciation of India's silver-based coinage against European gold-based coinages also continued to give a boost to the international competitiveness of the subcontinent's goods. Even the weather played fair so that the later 1860s and 1870s saw few bad harvests like those which had plagued the 1830s. Finally population began its secular movement upwards about the middle of the century. The annual growth rate accelerated between 1840 and 1870 from under 1 per cent per annum to about 1.5 per cent.

The growth of India's economy in the years 1860 to 1890 was to make only a small dent in its inheritance of rural poverty. In many parts of the country inflation merely opened up income differentials in the peasant economy. But it did at least give the new Raj a relief from the chronic agrarian problems of the first half of the century. The land-owning, commercial and urban élites were more stable. For the time being they at least continued to acquiesce in the distant rule of foreigners.

# CONCLUSION

## THE FIRST AGE OF COLONIALISM IN INDIA

By 1860 India was locked into a pattern of imperial subordination which was to be essentially maintained, despite formal constitutional changes, until 1935. The Indian Army had rid itself of the troublesome Hindi-speaking villagers of the Gangetic plains. The post-Mutiny army, furnished with a steady supply of Punjabi recruits, now carefully segregated on grounds of caste and religion, was forged into a reliable mercenary force for internal security or protection of the North-West Frontier against the supposed Russian threat. Indian troops were also dispatched with more confidence to East and South Africa, South-East Asia and ultimately, in 1914, to Europe itself. Detachments of troops from quiescent native states added to the paper strength of this large land army. Most pleasing of all to the new India Office in London and to the British Treasury, Indian taxation, which had been reorganised after 1857, continued to bear the cost of this expensively re-equipped force.

A more satisfactory imperial economic relationship – from the British point of view – had also emerged after the 1840s, though this was somewhat obscured by the bloody drama of 1857. Exports of British-manufactured textiles picked up sharply, despite a lull in the 1860s. Indian merchants created an excellent inland retailing system for Lancashire goods in eastern and southern India and they were now linked to the sea-ports by railway lines. It was calculated that one-third of the demand for moderate and finer cloth in Bengal and Bihar was met by British imports by 1860. Raw material exports to the developed world had also achieved a more stable trend. Railways and the penetration of the buying agents of large European firms into smaller markets helped supply. Demand for cotton was boosted by the American Civil War and grain by the opening of the Suez Canal. Opium exports from India which continued to supply more than ten per cent of the income of the Indian government maintained their insidious grip on the markets of China. Specialist plantation crops – notably tea and coffee – were firmly established, while the rapid growth in the volume of world shipping after 1860 increased the demand for jute from Bengal. All the while, large numbers of Indian indentured labourers were shipped to Ceylon, Malaysia, the Caribbean and southern Africa, replacing earlier slave populations.

If the orotund pronouncements of Sir John Strachey and Sir Henry Maine on empire and human evolution began to impart a certain *fin de siècle* air to Indian government, the traumas of consolidation were now passed. Small groups of 'partners in empire' had been teased out of Indian society. In the north the sons of talukdars attended chiefs' colleges to learn about crop varieties and agricultural improvement. In the west some peasant farmers shod the wheels of their carts with silver to celebrate their profits from the cotton boom. The fractious Hindu intelligentsia produced complaisant recruits for collectors' offices and district courts, while a policy for coopting conservative Muslims to imperial rule had already been foreshadowed with the publication of (later Sir) Sayyid Ahmed's, *An account of the loyal Mohammedans of India* (1860).

The British middle class gloried in the glamour of darbars and their status as a *Herrenvolk* in the east. Yet there were, as always, more sober commentators who understood that the hard benefits of the Indian Empire to Britain and the British economy, as opposed to small groups of entrepreneurs and officials, were more illusory. There was no reason to believe that British manufactures, textiles and machinery needed formal empire to penetrate Indian markets. After all, they had commanded markets throughout Asia, Europe and Latin America without benefit of collectors and judges. In fact, modern economic historians speculate that without easy colonial markets British industries might have modernised more rapidly in the later nineteenth century to face growing European and American competition. India would have sold raw materials on the world market regardless of her formal colonial status. Even the Indian army was used largely to patrol and contain dissidence within India. For this reason wise men at the supposed height of empire in the days of Victoria's coronation as Queen-Empress continued to reiterate doubts and questions which had persisted since the days of Edmund Burke.

For some the British Indian Empire had gone from adolescence to early senility without passing through an age of maturity. The reason for pessimism among Indian officials as much as Westminster politicians becomes clearer when they acknowledge how many false starts the Indian Empire had made on the road towards economic success and political stability by 1870. For the ambitions of colonial planners from Clive and Hastings through Wilberforce, Bentinck and Dalhousie had been disappointed again and again.

For one thing India had not become a rich colony of plantation and conversion, an Asian Brazil, as some had thought possible in the 1820s. British capitalism in India was a relative failure. Little money was put into the economy, except through copper-bottomed schemes like railway loans. Fear of an uncertain trading environment and the lack of commitment to the local economy of expatriates in Calcutta and Bombay ensured that profits would be returned to England not ploughed back into the Indian economy. Cape Town, Sydney, even Buenos Aires, saw the development of much more dynamic British expatriate economies. The feeble showing of Protestant Christianity in India meant that there was no force for assimilation to breach the racial boundaries between Europeans and Indians which were now widened by the hauteur of the post-Mutiny generation of officials and businessmen. The flourishing, if dubious Anglo-Indian partnerships of the eighteenth century were discouraged in the new age of Victorian probity. Moreover, Indian government retained its hostility to plantations and European ownership of land. There were too many opportunities for conflict with indigenous landowners to please officialdom.

Again, India had been written off as an indigenous plantation economy in which peasants produced crops under state control for flourishing export markets. This, J. B. Money proclaimed in 1860, when he unfavourably compared British India with Dutch Indonesia in *Java, or how to manage a colony*. The Dutch, through their Cultivation System, had forced Javanese peasants to produce crops for them as a form of tribute in kind, and this had bailed Holland's weak economy out of the depressions of the early nineteenth century. India, despite its size, was a relatively inefficient producer of agricultural raw materials with only a weak hold in foreign markets. Apart from opium valuable export crops made relatively little contribution to government finances over much of the country. The British never gained sufficient control over peasant producers to extract cash crops as a form of tribute, even in areas such as 'wet' South India where tribute had once been exacted as a proportion of the crop. The rigid *laissez faire* economy of free market which had become dominant in official thinking by 1815 was a significant discouragement to state control over the economy. In fact the so-called Age of Reform of the 1830s coincided with a withdrawl of government from many areas of economic management.

Finally what of the creation of a free peasant economy which was the proclaimed aim of many of the theorists of the 1830s and 40s from economists such as John Stuart Mill and Richard Jones to administrators such as Bentinck and John Lawrence? Several conditions, discussed in previous chapters, ensured that this aim was only imperfectly accomplished in a few regions such as Gujarat and the Punjab. The 'revenue squeeze' which accompanied the consolidation of British rule undoubtedly damaged peasant investment in new wells, bullocks and carts while the depression of the 1830s conspired to depress peasant income also. Yet there were deeper reasons. The structure of landholding in India as it had emerged from the pre-colonial period and had been consolidated by British administrators and revenue courts made it likely that profits from a period of slow expansion (such as occurred between 1860 and 1890, for instance) were monopolised by the rural moneylenders and landlords or by urban commercial people. Again, the social conservatism of colonial administration was confirmed by the rural resistance of the early nineteenth century which culminated in the Rebellion of 1857. The Indian authorities approached matters of agrarian reform with the greatest of caution. They were reluctant to tax the rich peasant and moneylender or to protect the poor occupancy tenant or day labourer. The limited gains from the cash-crop boom of the mid-Victorian years were soon swallowed up therefore by the gathering pace of population growth and land fragmentation.

It is with thoughts like this that the authors of the 1929 *Cambridge History of India* might have approached their sixth volume *The Indian Empire, 1858–1918* if they had yet been imbued with the pessimism of the post-imperial age. However, the failure of 'progress' as defined by an earlier age is no more an adequate paradigm than the supposed successes in the field of education, modernisation and local self-government which gave heart to the founders of the British Commonwealth in 1931. A more enduring perspective is to see the late pre-colonial and the early colonial periods as a critical era in the formation of the social order of modern India, and one in which indigenous forces of change continued to flow strongly even after the fuller incorporation of the subcontinent into the capitalist world system. India's resurgence since 1947 as a great Asian power and its re-emergence as a major centre of autonomous growth and of a certain type of Asian capitalism, though within a Western-dominated world system, suggests that such a perspective is more valid than the older imperial construction of Indian history.

One theme emphasised here has been the attraction and conflict between indigenous Indian forms of capitalism and forces generated by the European world economy. Contacts between Indian financiers, fiscal lords and merchants predated the coming of colonialism. Much of the amazing dynamism of early British penetration and conquest of the subcontinent was due to the underlying tides of petty commodity production, marketing and financial speculation within Indian society. By acting as an Indian merchant, fiscal entrepreneur and mercenary band leader writ large, the Company was able to suborn and conquer India. Relying on the support of Indian literati and financial expertise, the British were able to push forward the processes of peasantisation and create a sporadically productive export economy. Yet by the same token, the very form of this indigenous capitalism helped to frustrate their more grandiose economic plans. Zamindar entrepreneurs denied labour to planters; European business houses rarely penetrated beneath the intricately layered networks of Indian merchants and financiers; village magnates fought off the colonial state's attempts to extract the wealth of the rural élites in the style of Meiji Japan.

The early nineteenth century seen by officials such as William Sleeman as the 'Age of the bania', was a poor period for Indian merchants and by no means a success for the rural moneylender. Yet the vitality of the bazaar economy did survive the shocks of depression and the lineaments of a national market continued to develop above the tenacious patterns of regionalism. Despite the assaults of expatriate Britons, Indian traders in Calcutta (although Marwaris from north India) and merchant groups in Bombay kept a hold on some parts of their regional economies. From these groups were to emerge the first generation of India's industrialists, a transformation that was already in train in the freer atmosphere of Ahmedabad in Gujarat and even in a military station such as Kanpur in the north. Rural industries such as sugar-making and rice-husking which were equally significant for modern India's economy survived and consolidated themselves alongside these more spectacular developments. Service industries, notably

those connected with literacy and the law, often seen as purely para-
sitic, developed quite rapidly in the early nineteenth century. They
drew heavily on indigenous traditions of learning but also represented
a creative response to Western methods of organisation. India's stock
of educated expertise, one of its few great advantages in the present
century, emerged strongly out of this first colonial age.

This book has argued that the first half of the nineteenth century
was a critical period of the formation, by hammer blows from the outside, of the Indian peasantry. But ultimately, the resilience of country
people is what must be emphasised. Despite the pressures of war and
social conflict in the eighteenth century, heavy tax and commodity
extraction in the nineteenth, and the periodic toll of revolt and re-
pression, peasants continued to adapt in a creative way to their environment. The eighteenth-century village magnates and warrior
people found their dominance challenged and their privileges eroded
throughout the subcontinent, but their influence remained tenacious.
The British had fractured the unity of the land-controlling kin groups
at the *pargana* level, but had not swept them away. In the later nineteenth and twentieth centuries Rajputs and Bhumihar Brahmins in the
north, Kamma and Reddi cultivators in the Deccan and the south continued to play an important intermediary rôle in politics and social organisation between townsmen and the countryside. However,
beneath them and their like, groups of farmers less closely associated
with the warrior life-styles of the past had begun to assert their economic and social importance. Such were the Pattidars of Gujarat whose
descendants filled the ranks of rural capitalists in western India and
East Africa and later recruited themselves in some numbers into
Gandhi's political following. In the south a group such as the Vellalas
of Kongunad who had fertilised the upland plains of Tipu Sultan's
Mysore solidified into a recognisable rural interest. In Bengal the
Mahishya farmers of Midnapur profited from the expansion of jute
and rice cultivation, but also began to assert a higher social status and
push their children into the attenuated rural school system.

These developments, of course, should not be seen as an Indianised
form of a naive doctrine of national progress. This would be a mere
substitute for the historiography of modernisation and of triumphal
Westernisation propagated by the old writers. Pioneer peasants and
moneylenders prospered in part because they were able to break down
the resistance of tribal and nomadic societies, to annex the labour of

backward regions and often to subordinate more completely their low-caste underlings. Resistance movements throughout the nineteenth century were directed against more privileged groups of Indians as often as the British. In their turn, even the tribal, the low-caste farmer or the poor Muslim weaver created political strategies to protect their livelihood and communities though their existence is often obscured by the extant source material.

These privileged groups have been seen as a 'rich peasantry', whether because they genuinely improved their economic status, or simply because others all around them were more rapidly impoverished by land fragmentation, expropriation and lack of investment. However, what is more important is that groups of rural people of this sort continued to play a creative rôle in the formation of regional cultures and economies. Some took up and moulded to their values the devotional religious movements which continued to develop powerfully in the countryside. Others, such as the Jat farmers of the Punjab, or the Pattidars of Gujarat were to annex aspects of the faith of reformist religious movements such as the Arya Samaj to their own lives and their own patterns of worship and community organisation. More commonly, movements of social reform in marriage customs, movements to develop basic education and demands for self-respect amongst once-lowly people appealed to and were forwarded by well-placed and relatively prosperous farmers whose activities only became visible once the infant vernacular press began to report them.

The implications and directions of these stirrings were complex, even contradictory. In some cases they pointed towards the assertions of regional culture and political autonomy which became known in the later nineteenth century as non-Brahminism. Other comparable movements have been bundled by historians into categories such as Hindu or Muslim revivalism. Still others began quite early to contribute a rural and popular base to what is inadequately called Indian nationalism. All attested to the vitality of the societies of the Indian subcontinent which survived, adapted and consolidated through the great changes which accompanied the twilight of the Indian state and the onset of colonialism.

# GLOSSARY OF INDIAN TERMS

*Note*: Indian words which have only been used once or twice have been trans-
lated in the text. The renderings below are, of course, approximate and
incomplete:

| | |
|---|---|
| Arya Samaj | a movement of Hindu religious reform which sought to return to the pristine beliefs of the Vedas, or first Hindu scriptures. Active in the Punjab and North-Western Provinces. |
| *bania* | a Hindu grain trader; used more generally for members of the Hindu mercantile castes; mildly derogatory when applied to a substantial merchant. |
| *banian* | an Indian manager or factotum for a European merchant or East India Company servant; usually Bengal. |
| Banjara | the community of nomadic pack-bullock carriers. |
| Bedar | a hunting tribe of the Deccan, often employed in eighteenth-century armies as guerrillas. |
| *bhakti* | 'devotion'; used of the Hindu religious path which emphasises loving devotion to the will of the deity. |
| Bhatti | a Hindu nomadic, cattle-keeping community found south of Delhi. |
| Bhil | a tribal group of central and western India. |
| Bhumihar Brahmin | 'landholding' brahmin caste which had adopted the agrarian life style of the Rajput (q.v.); common in the Benares region. |
| Brahmin | the Hindu priestly order, though widely involved in 'secular' occupations by the eighteenth century. |
| Brahmo Samaj | a Hindu reform movement of the nineteenth century, founded by Ram Mohun Roy. It was monotheistic and rationalist and absorbed Christian and deist influences. |
| Chamar | a ritually impure, leather-making caste-cluster of north India; Chamars had widely taken to labouring in agriculture by 1750. |
| Chishti | an order of Islamic Sufi (q.v.) mystics. |

| | |
|---|---|
| Chitpavan Brahmin | a brahmin caste of the west coast (Konkan) which migrated into the Deccan and became powerful in the Maratha states. |
| Coorg | a tribal group of Mysore which had created its own dynasty of rajas of Coorg. |
| *diwan* | the financial minister of a Mughal province or Indian state. *Diwani*: the financial control of a province; taken by the British in Bengal in 1765. |
| *dubash* | an Indian manager or factotum, for, e.g., a European administrator or merchant. From '*do bhasha*', one who spoke two languages; particularly in Madras. |
| Gond | a tribal group of central-south India. |
| Gujar | a semi-nomadic, pastoralist Hindu grouping found in north-central India; sometimes agriculturalists by 1850. |
| *guru* | a Hindu spiritual guide. |
| Jain | a member of an Indian religion, originating in or before the sixth century B.C., common among merchants of Gujarat and the north and some agriculturalists in Kanara and Mysore. Stressed attainment of perfection through humbling of earthly desires. |
| Jat | a Hindu agriculturalist caste-cluster of Gujarat, Rajasthan, the Punjab and the North-Western Provinces. Jats rose in revolt against the Mughals in the late seventeenth century. |
| *jotedar* | an under-tenure holder in Bengal, often a substantial magnate who controlled production and bodies of share-croppers. |
| Kallar | a warrior and hunter people of the south; Kallar leaders became rajas in the dry parts of Tamilnadu. |
| *kazi* | the official in Mughal government; a jurisconsul learned in Muslim law; under the British became little more than a registrar. |
| Komati | a Hindu merchant caste of the Andhra Coast; some emigrated to Madras in service of the East India Company. |
| Kotwal | the chief executive officer of a Mughal city; became a sort of police chief under the British. |
| Kunbi | a major agricultural caste-cluster of western India; from them 'Maratha' war leaders were recruited. |
| Kuran (kuranic) | the Muslim sacred book; dictated by God to the Prophet Muhammad. |

| | |
|---|---|
| Lingayat | member of a religious community common among farmers and merchants of Kanara, the Deccan and Mysore. Lingayats comprised several castes and were characterised by a special form of worship of Lord Shiva (q.v.) |
| *madrassa* | a Muslim teaching foundation; specialising in the Kuran, Arabic and Persian. |
| Maratha | a resident of Maharashtra (western Deccan); applied to the more prestigious families of non-Brahmin agriculturalists who provided the war-leaders and rajas of the Maratha movement. |
| Maravar | a warrior pastoralist group of dry south India; created their own kingdoms in the seventeenth and eighteenth centuries. |
| Mewatti | a Rajput herdsman caste-cluster (usually converted to Islam) found in the Delhi region. |
| *mirasidar* | holder of a coparcenary proprietory tenure usually found in the wet areas of Tamilnadu. |
| *mufti* | a leading member of the *ulama* (q.v.) or Muslim learned who advised rulers on matters of religious law. |
| Naqshbandi | an order of Islamic sufi (q.v.) mystics. |
| Navaiyit | a Muslim kin group of south India, prominent in learning and administration throughout the Deccan, Mysore and Madras from about the sixteenth century; the early Nawabs of Arcot were Navaiyats. |
| Nawab | deputy or viceroy of the Mughal emperors; nawabs became semi-independent rulers after their decline. |
| Nayar | the Hindu warrior caste-cluster of Kerala. |
| Parayan | a ritually inferior set of agricultural labouring castes of south India. |
| Parava | a Christian maritime caste of south-east India. |
| *pargana* | the lowest level of Mughal administration. Often coterminous with the highest level of kinship organisation of Hindu warriors and land controllers. |
| Parsi | Zoroastrian merchant people and artisans of Gujarat; prominent traders and intelligentsia of Bombay. |
| *patel* | village headman in western India and the Deccan. |
| Pattidar | a term applied to the major peasant caste of Gujarat, similar to the Kunbis (q.v.) of Maharashtra. |

| Pindari | originally irregular horsemen attached to Maratha armies, became military plunderers in Deccan during early nineteenth century. |
| Poligar | Hindu warrior chief of South India. |
| *raj(a)* | a Hindu kingdom, king. |
| Rajput | the great Hindu warrior caste category of north India; especially dominant in Rajasthan. |
| Ramanandi | a sectarian devotee of the Hindu God Rama; established powerful 'monastic' institutions in north India. |
| Rangar | a nomadic herdsman caste-cluster of the Delhi region. |
| Rohilla | lit. 'dweller in the northern hills'; Afghan warriors who established kingdoms in north and central India in the seventeenth and eighteenth centuries. |
| *ryotwari* | a form of land-revenue administration common in western and southern India, whereby tax was levied on the fields of each individual holder. |
| Saint Thomas Christian | a Christian religious community formed by west-Asian traders and local people of Kerala in the first centuries of the Christian era. |
| Sanskrit | the classical priestly language of the Hindus. |
| Satya Narayanis | a *bhakti* (q.v.) sect of western India; followers of the god Vishnu. |
| Shaivite | devotee of Lord Shiva, the Hindu God of procreation and destruction. |
| Shakta (from *shakti*) | Hindu sect prominent in east and north India, devoted to the worship of the universal female principle of divine power. |
| Shia | lit. the 'faction'; a main division of the Muslim faith deriving from an early succession dispute over the inheritance of the spiritual authority of the Prophet Muhammad. Shias, prominent in Iran and central Asia, provided important Muslim ruling families in Bengal and Awadh. |
| Sikh | member of an Indian religion founded in the fifteenth century, influenced by Hindu *bhakti* sects of the Punjab, centred on the revelations of a line of Gurus as preserved in the sacred book, the Guru Granth Sahib. |
| Sufi | a devotee of hidden or mystical knowledge within the Muslim religion. Since the thirteenth century divided into orders, notably the Naqshbandiya, Chishtiya and Qadiriya; centred on hospices (*khanqas*) and the tombs of |

|  |  |
|---|---|
|  | their teachers, popularly regarded as saints. |
| Sunni | the majority division within Islam, dominant in India, often in conflict with the Shias (q.v.). |
| *talukdar* | a great *rentier* landholder, usually in Awadh. |
| Tamil | the major Dravidian language of south India; hence Tamilnadu, the land of the Tamils. |
| Thug | member of a brotherhood of murderous highway robbers. |
| Telugu | a major Dravidian language of south India and the Deccan; Telugu-speaking warriors created kingdoms in Tamilnadu after 1400. |
| *ulama* (sing. *alim*) | Muslim learned man specialising in the Kuran and Islamic law. |
| *Umara* (sing. *amir*) | the (Mughal) nobility. |
| Urdu | originally a language of the army, combining Persian words with a Hindi base, it became the literary language of Islamised north India after the decline of Persian. |
| Vaishnavite | devotee of Lord Vishnu, God of beneficence and protection of the Hindus. |
| Zamindar | lit. 'landholder'; a superior proprietor who paid land revenue to the government. Often, as in Bengal, a large *rentier* landowner, but sometimes, as in the North-Western Provinces, a peasant owner-occupier. |

# BIBLIOGRAPHICAL ESSAY

## I   INDIA IN THE EIGHTEENTH CENTURY

The classic modern treatment of the decline of Mughal dominance was Jadunath Sarkar, *The Fall of the Mughal Empire*, 4 vols, Calcutta, 1932. Equally important on the economic side were W. H. Moreland, *From Akbar to Aurangzeb*, London, 1923 and *The Agrarian System of Moslem India*, Cambridge, 1929. The post-independence revision of this work by the historians associated with Aligarh Muslim University are notably represented by Irfan Habib, *The Agrarian System of Mughal India, 1556–1707*, London, 1963, the same author's 'Potentialities of capitalistic development in the economy of Mughal India', *Journal of Economic History*, xxix, 1969, M. Athar Ali, *The Mughal Nobility under Aurangzeb*, Bombay, 1968, and Satish Chandra, *Parties and Politics at the Mughal Court 1707–40*, Aligarh, 1959. The work of this whole group of historians is extended and summarised in *The Cambridge Economic History of India*, vol. i, edited by Tapan Raychaudhuri and Irfan Habib, Cambridge, 1982. J. F. Richards extended the Aligarh approach to the Deccan with his *Mughal Administration in Golconda*, Oxford, 1975, while the eighteenth century began to receive more attention with Noman Ahmed Siddiqi, *Land Revenue Administration under the Mughals, 1700–1750*, Bombay, 1970, and Zahir Uddin Malik, *The Reign of Muhammad Shah, 1719–48*, London, 1977. An important new work which traces the emergence of successor states and the fortunes of different social groups in the early eighteenth century is Muzaffar Alam, *Mughal Imperial Decline in North India*, Delhi 1986; the same author has extended his ideas in 'Zamindar Revolts in North India, 1700–40' in R. Thapar (ed.), *Situating Indian History*, Delhi 1986. The military culture of pre-colonial India is treated in D. H. A. Kolff, 'An armed peasantry and its allies', unpub. Ph.D. diss., Leiden Univ., 1983. Two of the key Indian sources are Ghulam Hussain Khan, *Siyar-ul-Mutakharin* (tr.), 2 vols., London, 1832 and C. Seddon and Syed G. H. Khan (tr.), *Mirat-i-Ahmadi*, Baroda, 1928.

The analysis of different 'levels' of successor states to the Mughals was initiated by B. Cohn, 'Political systems in eighteenth-century India: the Banaras region', *Journal of the American Oriental Society*, 82, 3, 1962, and taken up by P. Calkins, 'The formation of a regionally orientated ruling group in Bengal, 1700–1740', *Journal of Asian Studies*, xxix, 3, 1970, and K. Leonard, 'The Hyderabad Political System and its Participants' *JAS*, xxx, 2, 1971. A. L. Srivastava, *The First Two Nawabs of Oudh*, Lucknow, 1933, provided useful background. The first full-length modern work on a successor state was Richard B. Barnett, *North India Between Empires: Awadh the Mughals and the British, 1720–1801*, Berkeley, 1980. Ideologies of Indian rule are treated in J. F. Richards (ed.), *Kingship and Authority in South Asia*, Madison, 1981. More recent work on Awadh is by M. H. Fisher, 'The Imperial Court and the Province: a social and administrative history of pre-British Awadh (1775–1856)', unpub. Ph.D. diss., University of Chicago, 1978, partly published as 'The imperial coronation of 1819. Awadh, The British and the Mughals', *Modern Asian Studies*, xix, 2, 1985, and J. R. I. Cole, 'Imami Shiism from Iran to North India', unpub. Ph.D. diss., University of California, L.A., 1983, both of which deal with the ideological and religious underpinnings of the state. Sunil Chander's forthcoming Cambridge Ph.D. dissertation, 'Hyderabad 1740–1860', throws new light on the Deccan over these years. G. Sardesai, *A New History of the Marathas*, 2 vols., Bombay, 1946–8, provides a clear narrative for western India. The recent work of historians in the Punjab was foreshadowed by J. S. Grewal, *From Guru Nanak to Ranjit Singh*, Amritsar, 1972. A valuable article is M. Alam, 'Sikh Uprisings under Banda Bahadur, 1708–15', *Studies in History*, i, 2, 1979. Much material is also to be found in Hari Ram Gupta, *History of the Sikhs*, 2nd revised edn, New Delhi, 1980.

Western and southern India in the eighteenth century are now looking more comprehensible. The classic works on the Marathas were S. N. Sen, *The Military System of the Marathas*, Calcutta, 1928, and *The Administrative System of the Marathas*, Calcutta, 1923. Recent reinterpretations of the Marathas include G. T. Kulkarni, 'Banking in the eighteenth century. A case study of a Pune banker', *Artha Vijnan*, xv, 2, 1973 and an important article by Stewart Gordon, 'The slow conquest: administrative integration of the Malwa into the Maratha Empire: 1720–1860', *Modern Asian Studies*, xi, i, 1977. The implications of Burton Stein's *Peasant State and Society in Medieval South India*, New Delhi, 1980, and other works by this author reverberate into the eighteenth-century literature, notably in N. Dirks, *The Hollow Crown. Ethnohistory of a Little Kingdom in South India*, Cambridge, 1986, an important work on the small poligar state of Pudukottai. For a general treatment see K. Rajayyan, *History of Madurai, 1736–1801*. Some information on eighteenth-century Kerala can be derived from S. Bayly, 'Hindu kingship and the origin of community. Religion, state and society in Kerala, 1750–1850', *MAS*, xviii, 2, 1984. The notion of state and state-building in eighteenth-century India is however in flux at present. Recent contributions have been by Burton Stein who sees the expansion of 'military fiscalism' to South India in the form of Tipu Sultan's Mysore, 'State formation and economy reconsidered. Part I', *MAS*, xix, 3, 1985 and F. Perlin, 'State formation reconsidered. Part 2', *idem*; see also, Andre Wink, *Land and Sovereignty in India. Agarian Society and Politics under the Eighteenth-century Maratha Swarajya*, Cambridge, 1986, which challenges notions of a centralised Indian state, and Sanjay Subrahmanyam, 'Aspects of State Formation and transformation in South India and South-east Asia, 1500–1650', *Indian Economic and Social History Review*, forthcoming, which provides a critique both of the Aligarh model of North India and the segmentary state model of South India previously developed by Stein.

The bibliography of *The Cambridge Economic History of India*, 1, and of Raychaudhuri's contribution in volume 2, cover many works which touch on the eighteenth-century economy as does B. R. Grover, 'An integrated pattern of commercial life in the rural society of North Indian during the 17th and 18th centuries' in *Proceedings of the 37th Session of the Indian Historical Records Commission*, xxxvii, New Delhi, 1966. Dilbagh Singh, 'Local and land-revenue administration of the State of Jaipur', unpub. Ph.D. diss. Jawaharlal Nehru University, New Delhi, 1975, hopefully to be published soon, contains crucial information on agrarian society in Rajasthan. David Ludden, *Peasant History in South India*, Princeton, 1985 provides a refreshing new synthesis of the economic history of Tamilnadu, the *longue durée*. The present author's *Rulers, Townsmen and Bazaars*, Cambridge, 1983, deals with towns and merchants in North India in the later eighteenth century. Frank Perlin's articles, notably his 'Proto-industrialisation and pre-colonial South Asia', *Past and Present*, 98, 1983, and 'Of white whale and countrymen in the eighteenth-century Maratha Deccan, *Journal of Peasant Studies*, v, ii, 1978, present a model of pre-colonial social and economic change. Much valuable information can be gleaned from contemporary descriptions, notably Francis Buchanan, *A Journey from Madras through the countries of Mysore, Canara and Malabar*, 2 vols., London, 1807, and his north-Indian observations partially published by Montgomery Martin (ed.), *The History, Antiquities ... and Statistics of Eastern India*, 3 vols., London, 1838, and other travel accounts to be found in Grover's article (above). General arguments on the pre-colonial economy are found in J. F. Richards, 'Mughal state finance and the pre-modern world economy', *Comparative Studies in Society and History*, 23, 1981, and Karen Leonard, 'The "great firm" theory of the decline of the Mughal Empire', *CSSH*, 13, 1979.

Culture and religion in the eighteenth century are under-researched. The Muslim revival is best charted: S. A. A. Rizvi, *Shah Wali-allah and his times*, Canberra, 1980; M. Zameeruddn Siddiqi, 'The resurgence of the Chishti Silsilah in the Punjab during the eighteenth century', *Proceedings of the Indian History Congress, 1970*, Delhi, 1971, Part I, and D. Gilmartin, 'Tribe, land and religion in the Punjab', unpub. Ph.D. diss., Univ. California, Berkeley, 1979; F. A. Nizami, 'Madrasahs, scholars and saints' unpub. Ph.D. diss., Oxford, 1983; Francis Robinson, 'The ulama of Firangi Mahal and their adab' in B. Metcalf (ed.), *Moral Conduct and Authority in South Asia. The role of Adab*, Berkeley, 1984, W. Fusfeld, 'The shaping of sufi leadership in Delhi; the Naqshbandiyya Mujaddidiya, 1750–1920', unpub. Ph.D. diss., University of Pennsylvania, 1981. For the South, M.Y. Kokan, *Arabic and Persian in the Carnatic*, Madras, 1976. Popular and syncretic Islam has been treated by Azim Roy, *The Islamic Syncretistic Tradition in Bengal*, Princeton, 1983 and by S. Bayly in her MS 'Saints, goddesses and demons. The religious culture of south India'. Eighteenth-century Hinduism can only be glimpsed from contemporary sources and from brief references in the secondary literature, notably in N. Dirks; see also the relevant sections in A. Appadurai, *Worship and Conflict under Colonial Rule. A South Indian Case*, New York, 1981. Banmali Tandan, 'The architecture of the Nawabs of Avadh between 1722 and 1856 A.D.: A descriptive inventory', unpub. Ph.D. diss., Cambridge, 1978, begins the reassessment of eighteenth-century architecture.

## 2 INDIAN CAPITAL AND THE EMERGENCE OF COLONIAL SOCIETY

The early history of European expansion in maritime India is one of the best-covered areas of Indian history. Notable are: K. N. Chaudhuri, *The Trading World of Asia and the English East India Company 1660–1760*, Cambridge, 1978, Om Prakash, *The Dutch East India Company and the Economy of Bengal, 1630–1720*, Princeton, 1985, Ashin Das Gupta, *Malabar and Asian Trade 1740–1800*, Cambridge, 1967, and the same author's *Indian Merchants and the Decline of Surat*, Wiesbaden, 1979, P. J. Marshall, *East Indian Fortunes. The British in Bengal in the Eighteenth Century*, Oxford, 1976. The western Indian story has been carried into the later eighteenth century by L. Subramanian, 'The West Coast of India: the eighteenth century', unpub. Ph.D. diss., Visva Bharati University, 1985 and much can be learnt about the Coromandel coast from S. Arasaratnam, *Merchants, Companies and Commerce on the Coromandel Coast, 1650–1740*, Delhi, 1986. An overview of trading empires is provided by H. Furber, *Rival Empires of Trade in the Orient*, Minneapolis, 1976.

Surprisingly the sequence and motivation of British expansion is still relatively obscure. V. Harlow, *The Founding of the Second British Empire, 1763–93*, London, 1964, supplies some general context. P. J. Marshall's volume in this series, *Bengal; the British Bridgehead*, Cambridge, 1987, provides a lucid account of the takeover in Bengal. It can be supplemented with material from S. Bhattacharya, *The East India Company and the Economy of Bengal from 1704 to 1740*, London, 1954, and A. M. Khan, *The Transition in Bengal, 1756–1775. A Study of Saiyid Muhammad Reza Khan*, Cambridge, 1969. The impact of the subsidiary alliance system on Awadh is dealt with by Richard Barnett, *North India Between Empires*, but the only analysis (as opposed to description) of this process for Hyderabad is in Sunil Chander's forthcoming Cambridge Ph.D. diss. Expansion in the Madras Presidency is particularly poorly covered. S. Arasaratnam, 'Trade and political domination in South India, 1750–90' *MAS*, xiii, 1, 1979, provides some material on the Andhra Coast as he does the old London thesis of R. Subba Rao partly published in the *Journal of the Andhra Historical Research Society*, 1937–9. The Carnatic fares worse. There is excellent material in J. Gurney, 'The Debts of the Nawab of Arcot', Ph.D. diss., Oxford, 1968, alas unpublished. Otherwise one has a competent narrative in K. Rajayyan, *History of Madurai* and in N. S. Ramaswami, *Political History of the Carnatic under the Nawabs*, New Delhi, 1984. The Indian side provides some printed sources in S. M. H. Nainar, *Sources of the History of the Nawwabs of the Carnatic. Madras University Islamic Series*, 5 vols., 1952–8. No published modern work treats the history of British expansion in western India before 1784 in an analytical fashion, though the situation improves thereafter with P. Nightingale, *Trade and Empire in Western India, 1784–1806*, Cambridge, 1970. Unpublished work includes the dissertations by Subramanian and also B. Swai, 'The British in Malabar, 1792–1806', unpub. Ph.D. diss, University of Sussex, 1974. The general issues of British expansion are debated in P. J. Marshall, 'Economic and political expansion: the case of Oudh', *MAS*, ix, 4, 1975, his 'British Expansion in Indian in the eighteenth century; a historical revision', *History*, 60, 1975, and *Problems of Empire. Britain and India, 1757–1813*, London, 1968. For a view which stresses economic motives even more vigorously, see R. Mukherjee, 'Trade and Empire in Awadh, 1765–1805', *Past and Present*, 94, 1982.

The early settlements of the land revenue are dealt with in several classic Anglo-Indian studies, notably, H. T. Colebrooke, *Remarks on the Husbandry and Internal Commerce of Bengal*, London, 1806, and also in N. K. Sinha, *The Economic History of Bengal from Plassey to the Permanent Settlement*, 2 vols., Calcutta, 1956–62, but new insight on their governing ideologies was provided by R. Guha, *Towards a Rule of Property for Bengal*, The Hague, 1963 and new information on the economic background in Ludden and Ratnalekha Ray, *Change in Bengal Rural Society, circa 1760–1850*, New Delhi, 1979, for Bengal and Tamilnadu respectively. R. E. Frykenberg, *Guntur District, 1788–1848*, Oxford, 1965, set the trend by arguing for the constraining force of local political interests in the making of revenue settlements.

The early history of Calcutta has received treatment in S. N. Mukherjee, *Calcutta. Myths and History*, Calcutta, 1977, A. Tripathi, *Trade and Finance in the Bengal Presidency, 1793–1833*, new edn. New Delhi, 1979, in Pradip Sinha, *Calcutta in Urban History*, Calcutta, 1979, and D. Basu, 'The Banian and the British in Calcutta, 1800–50', *Bengal Past and Present*, xcii, 1, 1973. Good material on the British is found in S. C. Ghosh, *Social Condition of the British Community in Bengal, 1757–1800*, Leiden, 1970. Madras is once again largely unresearched. H. D. Love, *Vestiges of Old Madras, 1640–1740*, 4 vols., London 1913, is a mine of information, as are H. Milford (ed.), *The Madras Tercentenary Volume*, Madras, 1939, and C. S. Srinivasachari, *History of the City of Madras*, Madras, 1939, H. Dodwell. The *Nabobs of Madras*, London, 1926 and Hilton Brown, *Parry's of Madras. A Story of British Enterprise in India*, Madras, 1934, fill in some gaps. Practically the only modern treatments are Susan Neild-Basu, 'The Dubashes of Madras', *MAS*, xviii, 1, 1984, and the same author's, 'Colonial urbanism. The development of Madras City in the eighteenth and nineteenth century', *MAS*, xiii, 2, 1979, and R. E. Frykenberg, 'The silent Settlement in South India, 1793–1836', in Frykenberg (ed.), *Land Tenure and Peasant South Asia*, New Delhi, 1977. But a social history of the origin of Indian Madras is still missing. Bombay fares little better. For the very early period there is S. M. Edwardes, *The Rise of Bombay. A Retrospective*, Bombay, 1902 and on the Anglo-Indian side Nightingale and H. Furber, *Bombay Presidency in the mid-eighteenth century*, London 1965, contains useful information. Otherwise one must glean material from works such as J. Forbes, *Oriental Memoirs*, 3 vols, London, 1813 and the *Asiatic Annual Register*. H. G. Briggs, *The Cities of Gujarashtra*, Bombay, 1844 is also useful for the west coast. Some aspects of British institutions are treated by D. Kopf, *British Orientalism and the Bengal Renaissance*, Berkeley, 1969 and in S. Mukherjee, *Sir William Jones*, Cambridge, 1969 and the introduction to P. J. Marshall (ed.), *The British Discovery of Hinduism in the Eighteenth Century*, Cambridge, 1970. For Whiggish reform in India see, C. Ross (ed.), *Correspondence of Charles, First Marquis Cornwallis*, 3 vols, London, 1859.

### 3 THE CRISIS OF THE INDIAN STATE, 1780–1820

Treatments of British expansion have concentrated on the commercial, particularly private commercial motivations and on the period of Robert Clive and Warren Hastings. A modern treatment of the Cornwallis and Wellesley period is still lacking, and there is little which discusses analytically the structure of the Company state or its ruling ideologies. E. Ingram, *Two Views of British India*, London, 1969, provides a useful selection of Wellesley's earlier Indian letters and an introduction, while the same author deals with the broader context in his *In Defence of British India. Great Britain and the Middle East, 1775–1842*, London, 1984, though from the point of view of grand strategy rather than Indian imperatives; thereafter one must turn to M. Martin (ed.), *The Despatches, Minutes and Correspondence of the Marquess Wellesley, K. G.*, 5 vols, London, 1837 and S. J. Owen (ed.), *A Selection from the Despatches relating to India of the Duke of Wellington*, London, 1880. Iris Butler, *The Eldest Brother, the Marquess Wellesley* is a good, popular biography of Richard Wellesley, while C. H. Philips, *The East India Company, 1784–1834*, Manchester, 1940 and B. B. Misra, *The Central Administration of the East India Company*, Manchester, 1959, deals with some of the administrative changes. For opposition to the Wellesley policy, A. Embree, *Charles Grant and British Rule in India*, London, 1962, should be consulted. The whole period is covered by the narrative of H. H. Dodwell (ed.), *The Cambridge History of India*, v, Cambridge, 1929, and R. C. Majumdar (ed.), *History and Culture of the Indian People*, vols viii and ix, New Delhi, 1959–65. See also, the Countess of Minto, *Lord Minto in India*, London, 1880 and H. T. Prinsep, *History of the Political and Military Transactions ... during the Administration of the Marquess of Hastings*, 2 vols, London, 1925. P. J. Marshall has begun to delineate the changing imperial ideologies of the period in his 1981 inaugural lecture in the Rhodes Chair of Imperial History, London University, 'A free though conquering people. Britain and Asia in the eighteenth century'.

The decline of the subsidiary alliance system in Awadh is recounted in Barnett, C. C. Davies, *Warren Hastings and Oudh*, London, 1939, and Purnendu Basu, *Oudh and the East India Company: 1785–1801*, Lucknow, 1943. Warren Hastings's own diary, though propaganda, in 'The Benares Diary of Warren Hastings, *Camden Miscellany*, xviii, London, 1948, remains the best account of this incident, but can be used in conjunction with K. P. Mishra's valuable socio-economic study, *Banaras in Transition, 1738–95*, New Delhi, 1974. The Rohilla incident still lacks a modern historian so reference must be made to J. Strachey's polemical, *Hastings and the Rohilla War*, Oxford, 1892. Hyderabad is dealt with in Sunil Chander and S. Regani, *Nizam-British Relations, 1724–1857*, Hyderabad, 1963, also in H. G. Briggs, *The Nizam. His History and Relations with the British Government*, London, 1861. The final annexation of Arcot has not been reassessed, so one needs to rely on Wellesley papers, Nainar's documents and Ramaswami. The tangled Tanjore issue can be traced in W. Hickey, *The Tanjore Maratha Principality in South India*, Madras, 1913, and *Copies of papers relating to the restoration of the King of Tanjore*, 2 vols, London, 1783.

Mysore's social organisation during the sultanate would be a good field for detailed research, and Devadas Moodley of S.O.A.S., London, has begun to work in this area. Some basic information can be gleaned from *Mysore and Coorg. A Gazetteer compiled for the Government of India*, 2 vols, Bangalore, 1877, and from the relevant sections of Buchanan's *Journey*. Attempts to conceptualise Mysore's state and society are found in Stein's *MAS*, 1985 article and A. Sen, 'A pre-British economic formation in India of the late eighteenth century', in Barun De (ed.), *Perspectives in Social Sciences*, Calcutta, 1977, i, *Historical Dimensions*. The career of Haidar Ali is treated in a fascinating contemporary account by a French officer, N.M.D.L.T., *History of Ayder Ali Khan Nebab-Bahadur*, London, 1784. The politics of Tipu's reign are covered in Mohibbul Hasan, *History of Tipu Sultan*, Calcutta, 1971 and in W. Kirkpatrick, *Select Letters of Tippoo Sultan*, London, 1811, though the latter is biased by contemporary British propaganda against Tipu. Another lively indigenous account is M.H.A.K. Kirmani, trans. W. Miles, *History of the Reign of Tipu Sultan. Mir Husein Ali Khan Kirmani's 'Neshani Hyduri'*, London, 1844. M. Wilks, *Historical Sketches of the South Of India*, 2 vols, London, 1810, new edn, Mysore 1930–2 completes the 'Black Legend' of Tipu.

The classic Anglo-Indian account of Maratha politics, replete with scheming Brahmins and heroic Englishmen is J. Grant-Duff, *History of the Mahrattas*, 2 vols, London, 1826. S. N. Sen's two volumes provide a much more balanced account, but by a Bengali historian who still thought of the Marathas as a centralised state system prey to processes of 'feudalisation'. Indigenous sources in plenty exist in the form of K. B. Marathe (ed.), *Selections from Satara Rajas' and Peshwas' Diaries*, 12 vols, Bombay 1908–11, J. N. Sarkar (ed.), *Persian Records of Maratha history*, 3 vols, Bombay, 1953, in the letters of Mahadji Scindia, A. V. Vakankar (ed.), *Shri Shindeshahi Itihaschin Sadnanen*, Gwalior, 1930–40 and in R. D. Choksey (ed.), *The Last phase. Selections from the Commissioner's Files, the Peshwa Daftar*, Bombay, 1948. An interesting contemporary British account is H. Broughton, *Letters from a Maratha Camp*, London, 1812. Attempts to rethink the nature of Maratha polity are Wink, Perlin, G. T. Kulkarni and D. P. Divekar, 'The emergence of an indigenous business class in Maharashtra in the eighteenth century', *MAS*, xvi, 2, 1982.

## 4 THE CONSOLIDATION AND FAILURE OF THE EAST INDIA COMPANY'S STATE, 1818–57

The British revenue systems have generated an enormous and largely indigestible literature. The classic treatment is B. H. Baden-Powell, *The Land Systems of British India*, 3 vols, Oxford, 1892. Brief summaries of the present state of knowledge about their effects in different parts of India are to be found in *The Cambridge Economic History of India*, ii, with suggestions for further reading. B. Cohn, 'Structural change in Indian rural society' in R. Frykenberg (ed.), *Land Control and Social Structure in Indian History*, Madison, 1961, added yeast to the dough, as did E. T. Stokes, *The Peasant and the Raj*, Cambridge, 1978, and interesting regional studies of land control have more recently emerged, notably: T. R. Metcalf, *Land, Landlords and the British Raj*, Berkeley, 1976, A. Siddiqi, *Agrarian Change in a Northern Indian State. Uttar Pradesh, 1818–33*, Oxford, 1973, Ratnalekha Ray, *Change in Bengal Rural Society*, R. Kumar, *Western India in the Nineteenth Century*, London 1968, N. Charlesworth, *Peasants and Imperial Rule*, Cambridge, 1984, S. Guha, *The Agrarian Economy of the Bombay Deccan, 1818–1941*, New Delhi, 1985, and D. Ludden, *Peasant History in South India*. Much can still be learned from the early colonial reports, e.g., G. W. Forrest (ed.), *Report of the Territories conquered from the Peshwa*, London, 1884, or M. Wilks, *Report on the Interior Administration, Resources ... of the Government of Mysoor*, Calcutta, 1805.

Cultural change and social control in early colonial India have received some attention, notably in A. Appadurai, *Worship and Conflict*, N. Dirks, *The Hollow Crown*, and Pamela Price, 'Resources and rule in Zamindari South India, 1802–1903: Sivaganga and Ramnad as kingdoms under the Raj', unpub. Ph.D. diss., University of Wisconsin, Madison, 1979. Muslims are, as usual, better covered: Barabara Metcalf, *Muslim Revival in British India*, Princeton, 1983 can be set in context of P. Hardy, *The Muslims of British India*, Cambridge, 1972, and F. Nizami, 'Madrasahs, scholars and saints'. In addition the works of Cole, Fisher and Fusfeld mentioned under Chapter 1 can be consulted. A useful article on the residency system is M. H. Fisher, 'Indirect rule in the British Empire. The foundations of the Residency System', 1764–1858, *MAS*, xviii, 3, 1984. See also, D. A. Washbrook, 'Law, state and agrarian society in colonial India', *MAS*, xv, 3, 1981.

On early colonial economic change, *The Cambridge Economic History of India*, ii, has a full bibliography and succinct treatments; but see also I. Habib, 'On writing colonial history without perceiving colonialism', *MAS*, xix, 3, 1985 for a 'nationalist' counter-blast and F. Broeze, 'Underdevelopment and dependence. Maritime India under the Raj', *MAS*, xviii, 1984.

The Age of Reform and the debates connected with it have received attention from the 1830s onward. The classics here are E. Stokes, *The English Utilitarians in India*, Oxford, 1959, and K. Ballhatchet, *Social Policy and Social*

*Change in Western India, 1817–30*, London, 1961. A revisionist interpretation has been advanced by J. Rosselli, *Lord William Bentinck. The making of
a Liberal Imperialist, 1774–1839*, Berkeley, 1974, and J. Clive's *Thomas
Babington Macaulay. The Shaping of a Historian*, London, 1973, provides
useful material. The whole subject has benefited from the publication of C.
H. Philips (ed.) *The Correspondence of Lord William Cavendish Bentinck*, 2
vols, Oxford, 1977, which makes it possible to perceive some of the limi-
tations of 'reform' imposed by finance as much as by ideology. E. T. Stokes
also considered some of these issues in his later essays notably, 'The rationale
of Indian Empire', paper presented to the S.O.A.S Study Group on policy
and practice under Bentinck and Dalhousie, 1978 and 'Bureaucracy and
Ideology in Britain and India in the nineteenth century', *Transactions of the
Royal Historical Society*, 5 series, xxx, 1980. For the later modernisers, D. J.
Howlett, 'An end to expansion. Influences on British policy in India, *c.* 1830–
1860', unpub. Ph.D. diss., Cambridge, 1981, convincingly links the dilemmas of this period with the evolution of British policy since Wellesley. M.
Yapp gives a magisterial account of India's external policies in his *Strategies of
British India*, 2 vols, Oxford, 1980, while H. T. Lambrick, *Sir Charles Napier
and Sindh*, Oxford, 1952, remains an excellent book on this little-known
region. On Afghan events, see J. A. Norris, *The First Afghan War, 1838–42*,
Cambridge, 1967.

## 5 PEASANT AND BRAHMIN: CONSOLIDATING 'TRADITIONAL' SOCIETY

Ecological change in India is the coming subject, but no overview has yet
appeared; see, however, M. Gadgil, 'Towards an ecological history of India'
and N. Sengupta, 'Irrigation traditional v. modern', *Economic and Political
Weekly*, xx, 45–70, and J. F. Richards, J. Hagen and E. Haynes, 'Changing
land-use in Bihar, Punjab and Haryana, 1850–1970', *MAS*, xix, 3, 1985,
which is the first fruits of a large-scale quantitative study which will deal with
the period after 1870. R. Grove's forthcoming Cambridge Ph.D. dissertation
opens up the official debates on deforestation for a somewhat earlier period, *c.*
1820–60. Material on the tribals' incorporation into 'India' is to be found in
G. Prakash, 'Production and the reproduction of bondage', unpub. Ph.D.
diss., University of Pennsylvania, 1983, and in C. Bates, 'Regional dependence and rural development in central India, 1820–1930', unpub. Ph.D.
diss., Cambridge, 1984. The Bhils are receiving attention from S. Gordon,
'The Bhils and the idea of a criminal tribe in nineteenth-century India', in A.
Yang, *Crime and Criminality in British India*, Arizona, 1985, and B. Chat-
terji of the Nehru Memorial Museum and Library, New Delhi. See also E. S.
Brandstater, 'Human sacrifice and British-Kond relations, 1759–1862', in the
Yang volume. But information on many facets of ecological, social and clima-
tic change can only be gathered from contemporary works and documentary
sources. There is a good deal in the various works of Buchanan, E. Thornton,
*A Gazetteer of the Territories under the Government of the East India Com-*

*pany*, 5 vols, London, 1854, E. Balfour, *Cyclopaedia of India and of eastern and southern Asia*, 6 vols, Madras, 1857 and 'Pharao's' *Gazetteer of Southern India*, Madras, c. 1850.

Social change in 'settled' India is dealt with more fully in the various regional economic histories mentioned above, but the quantitative dimensions of these changes and the evolution of social groups and standards of living remains very unclear. G. Pandey, 'Economic dislocation in nineteenth-century Eastern U.P.', Centre for Studies in Social Science, Calcutta, Occasional Paper, 37, 1, 1983 deals with the social effects of 'deindustrialisation' while A. K. Bagchi, 'Deindustrialisation in Gangetic Bihar, 1809–1901', in B. De (ed.), *Essays in Honour of S. C. Sirkar*, Calcutta, 1976, and M. Vicziani, 'The deindustrialisation of India in the nineteenth century. A methodological critique of A. K. Bagchi', *IESHR*, xvi, 2, 1979, deals with the quantitative evidence. The evolution of professional and commercial communities during this period is dealt with by K. Leonard, *The Kayasths of Hyderabad*, Berkeley, 1979, F. Conlon, *Caste in a Changing World. The Chitrapur Saraswat Brahmins, 1700–1935*, Berkeley, 1977. T. Timberg, *The Marwaris. From Traders to Industrialists*, New Delhi, 1978, C. A. Bayly, *Rulers, Townsmen and Bazaars*, L. I. and S. H. Rudolph, 'A Bureaucratic Lineage in princely India', *JAS*, xxxiv, 3, 1975, and in Nizami, 'Madrasahs, Scholars and Saints', B. Kling, *Partner in Empire. Dwarkanath Tagore and the Age of Enterprise in Eastern India*, Berkeley, 1976.

Works on change in religion and mentalities are heavily concentrated on issues connected with the 'Bengal renaissance': D. Kopf, *British Orientalism and the Bengal Renaissance*, Berkeley, 1969, and the same author's *The Brahmo Samaj and the Shaping of the Modern Indian Mind*, Princeton, 1979, B. Kling, *Dwarkanath Tagore*, A. F. Salahuddin Ahmed, *Social Ideas and Social Change in Bengal, 1818–35*, Leiden, 1965. Ideology is also treated in C. Killingley, 'Vedanta and modernity' in C. H. Philips and M. D. Wainwright (eds.), *Indian Society and the Beginnings of Modernisation, 1830–50*, London, 1979, which also contains an iconoclastic article by B. De, 'The colonial context of the Bengal renaissance' which neatly debunks the whole notion. Some material on the early history of 'reform' in Bombay is to be found in C. H. Heimsath, *Indian Nationalism and Hindu Social Reform*, Princeton, 1964. The best edition of the works of Ram Mohun Roy is by K. Nag and D. Burman, *The English Works of Raja Rammohun Roy*, Calcutta, 1958 and Brojendranath Bannerji and Sajanikanta Das, *Rammohun Granthabali*, Calcutta, 1359, A.D. 1952; see also, D. Tagore, *An Autobiography of Maharishi Debendranath Tagore*, London, 1914, and on literature, Rajnarayan Basu, *Sekal or Ekal*. Bangiya Sahitya Parishad, Calcutta, 1929.

Changes in Hindu organisation and belief less directly influenced by the west are much more poorly treated in the English literature. There is a little material on the Vallabhacharyas and other sects in N. A. Thoothi, *The Vaishnavas of Gujarat*, London, 1935, and the old missionary work by J. N. Farquhar, *Modern Religious Movements in India*, London, 1918, remains useful. R. Suntharalingham, *Politics and National Awakening in South India, 1852–*

*91*, Arizona, 1974, contains references to contemporary changes in Tamil-nadu as do the works by Appadurai, Price and Dirks. There is a good Hindu study for the north Indian heartland in Prabhu Dayal Mital, *Braj ke Dharm Sampradaiyon ka Itihas*, 2 vols, Delhi, 1968, Dr Motichandra's, *Kashi ka Itihas*, Bombay, 1962, and much more in Indian languages.

Here again the recent works on the Muslims are more developed, notably, B. Metcalf, *Islamic Revival in British India*, and the early chapters of C. Troll, *Sir Sayyid Ahmed Khan. A Reinterpretation of Muslim Theology*, Delhi, 1978, and W. Fusfeld, 'The Chishti Silsilah' (see Ch.1 section). Q. Ahmed, *The Wahhabi Movement in India*, Calcutta, 1966, and S. A. A. Rizvi, *Shah Abd al-Aziz. Puritanism, Sectarian Polemics and Jihad*, Canberra, 1982, deal with the 'Muhamadiya' persuasion. See also, S. F. Dale, *Islamic Society on the South Asian Frontier. The Mappilas of Malabar, 1498–1922* (Oxford, 1980).

## 6 REBELLION AND RECONSTRUCTION

There have been several attempts at overviews of Indian resistance in late eighteenth and early nineteenth century: K. K. Datta, *Anti-British Plots and Movements before 1857*, Meerut, 1970, S. B. Chaudhuri, *Civil Disturbances during British Rule in India*, Calcutta, 1955, and notably, R. Guha, *Elementary Aspects of Peasant Insurgency in Colonial India*, New Delhi, 1984, which deals with the symbolic codes of peasant resistance. Rajayyan's *History of Madurai* has much on the Poligar wars, as has his *South Indian Rebellion. The First War of Independence, 1800–01*, Mysore, 1971. N. Kaviraj, *A Peasant Uprising in Bengal, 1783* and A. N. Zilli-Chowdhury, *The Vagrant Peasant. Agrarian Distress and Desertion in Bengal, 1770–1830*, Wiesbaden, 1982, treat Bengal. The only modern account of the Vellore Mutiny is P. Chinnian, *The Vellore Mutiny, 1806*, Madras, 1982.

The standard Anglo-Indian version of 1857 is J. W. Kaye, *History of the Sepoy War in India*, London, 1867 while the best of modern Indian versions are S. N. Sen, *Eighteen Fifty-seven*, New Delhi, 1958 and S. B. Chaudhuri, *Civil Rebellion in the Indian Mutinies*, Calcutta, 1965. See also J. Pemble, *The Raj, the Indian Mutiny and the Kingdom of Awadh*, London 1983. S. A. A. Rizvi and B. Bhargava, *Freedom Movement in Uttar Pradesh*, 5 vols, Lucknow, 1972–6 are an excellent source for contemporary material. The most sophisticated modern accounts are to be found in E. T. Stokes, *The Peasant and the Raj*, Cambridge, 1978, *The Peasant Armed*, Oxford, 1986, and T. R. Metcalf, *The Aftermath of Revolt*, Berkeley, 1973, and *Land, Landlords and the British Raj, 1857–70*, Princeton, 1964. Useful essays by E. I. Brodkin, 'The struggle for succession. Rebels and Loyalists in the Indian Rebellion of 1857, *MAS*, vi, 3, 1972, and 'Proprietary Mutations in Rohilkhand', *JAS*, xxviii, 4, 1969 qualify the notions of 'loyalty and resistance'. Awadh is extremely well treated in R. Mukherjee, *Awadh in Revolt. A Study of Popular Resistance*, New Delhi, 1984, and this along with G. Pandey's 'View of the observable. A positivist 'understanding' of agrarian society and political protest in colonial India', *Journal of Peasant Studies*, vii, 3, 1980, provide a corrective to what these authors regard as an 'economistic' approach to the events of the rebellion. Ideology is also treated in a different way by F. W. Buckler, 'The political theory of the Indian Mutiny of 1857', *Transactions of the Royal Historical Society*, 4 series, v, 1922, B. S. Cohn, 'Representing authority in Victorian India', in T. Ranger and E. J. Hobsbawm (eds.), *The Invention of Tradition*, Cambridge, 1983, and by F. A. Nizami (above). Social background to rural society can be found in R. G. Fox, *Kin, Clan, Raja and Rule*, Berkeley, 1971 and M. C. Pradhan, *The Political System of the Jats of Northern India*, New Delhi, 1974.

The aftermath of 1857 is studied in T. R. Metcalf (above), M. McLaggan, *Clemency Canning*, London, 1962 and in S. Gopal, *British Policy in India, 1858–1905*, Cambridge, 1967. A useful article on this period is F. C. R. Robinson, 'Consultation and Control, the United Provinces Government and its allies, 1860–1906, *MAS*, v, 4, 1971.

# INDEX

Abdul Ali, Maulana, 40

Abdul Rahman, 176

Abdul Aziz, Shah, 40, 165–7, 186

Afghanistan, 92; campaign, 1838–42, 110, 126–8, 179

Afghans, 43, 58, 138; invasions of India, 4, 8, 19; kingdoms, 24, 41; religion, 41, 43; tradesmen, 75

Africa, south, 1, 80, 86, 143; east, 205

agency houses, 71, 119, 154

Agra city, N.W.P, 18, 36, 100, 124, 153, 166, 189

Ahmedabad city, Gujarat, 36, 154, 204; district, 64

Ain-i-Akbari, 18

Ajmer, 41, 168

Ajodhya city, N.W.P, 41, 159

Akalis, 127

Alivardi Khan, nawab, 50

Allahabad city, N.W.P, 160, 166, 182, 189; Maulvi of, 186

Almas Ali Khan, 38, 91, 92

Americans, 83; Civil War, 129, 199; cotton, 145, 199; revolutionary wars, 65

Amritsar city, Punjab, 127

Andhra, 110, 141, see also Deccan, Northern Circars

Anjengo city, Malabar, 62

Anwaruddin Khan, nawab, 58

Arabia, 97, 166; Arabian Sea, 49

Arabs, 35, 45, 62, 83; in India, 96, 106; horses, 143

architecture, 43

Arcot, nawabs of, 15, 16, 20, 31, 58–61, 67, 93, 111, 168, 172–3, 179; nawab's debts, 58–61, 70, 77; economy, 33; palace, 43, 72; religion, 40–1; town, 58, 152

army, of East India Company, 1, 84–6, 117, 179–84; artillery, 86; cavalry, 85–6, 106, 143–4; commissariat, 86; mutinies, 61, 84, 110, 179–84; of British Crown, 200; of Sikhs, 126–7, 134, 143, 183–4; of Marathas, 100, 143

Arya Samaj, 158, 206

Asaf Jah, Nizam-ul-Mulk, 19–20, 45

Asaf-ud-Daulah, 91

Assam, 133, 140; Tea Company, 145

Auckland, Lord, 127

Aurangzeb, Emperor, 7, 14, 17

Austrians, 53

Awadh, 90, 140, 170, 173, 197–8; British penetration, 90–2, 180; economy, 36, 53; nawabs of, 15–16, 19, 53; Queen Mother of, 181, 187; revolt in, 181–2, 191–2

Bahadur Shah, emperor, 180, 187

Bairagis, 159

Balaji Vishwanath, 100

Balfour, E., 143, 165

Ballabgarh, raja of, 187

Balrampur, raja of, 191

Bangalore city, Mysore, 36, 95

banians, 55, 72

bankers, Indian, 10, 12–13, 48–51, 56, 59, 95, 104, 154, 187

Bankura dist, Bengal, 72

Baqir Agha, 40–1

Bara Sayyids, 153

Baramahal Terrs, 107

Baroda state, Gujarat, 154, 183, 197; town, 37

Bassein, 1802 Treaty of, 98

Bayana town, Rajasthan, 33

Beda tribe, 97

Benares, 51, 90, 92, 99, 153, 156, 159, 193; Hindoo (Sanskrit) College, 40, 114; raj of, 24–5, 51

Benfield, Paul, 59

Bengal, 45–55, 108, 145, 153, 175–6, 184; agriculture, 37–8; British seizure, 48–55; famine 1770–1, 33, 51, 65; nawabs of, 15, 17–20, 45–6, 51–5; religion, 40, 159, 167; revenues, 4, 19, 35, 51–5, 64–7, 72; see also land revenue

Bentinck, Lord William, 109, 120–6, 162, 163

Berar, 133, 140; raja of, 98, 101

bhakti, devotion, 41–2, 157–9, 162–3

Bharatpur, raja of, 22, 152

Bhatti tribe, 31, 175, 188

Bhil tribe, 30, 107, 126, 141, 147, 174; Bhil Corps, 107, 183

Bhuinya tribe, 141

Bhumihar Brahmins, 84, 151, 180, 182, 193, 205

# INDEX

# THE NEW CAMBRIDGE HISTORY OF INDIA

## I The Mughals and their Contemporaries

## II Indian States and the Transition to Colonialism

## III The Indian Empire and the Beginnings of Modern Society

## IV The Evolution of Contemporary South Asia